The book is dedicated to family – nurture and nature work together, but nurture is there first and provides the starting point.

My grandad, James 'Jimmy' Gargan, gave me the nature – his enthusiasm to listen to others, laugh and recount stories is the reason I love human psychology.

Dr Ian Gargan, BSc, MSc, MB BCh BAO, MBA, Reg Psychol AFPsSI (PsSI), CPsychol FBPsS (BPS), is the Clinical Director of Imagine Health, a Dublin-based medical and psychology clinic. Ian received his BSc in Applied Psychology from the National University of Ireland, Cork, in 1996 and his MSc in Forensic Psychology from the University of Leicester in 1997. He went on to study medicine at Trinity College Dublin, obtaining his medical degree in 2004. Following the receipt of an MBA from UCD's Michael Smurfit Graduate Business School, Ian established Imagine Health in 2009. He currently lives in Dalkey, Co. Dublin, and has two children, Ruby and Sebastian, with Carrie.

NOTE REGARDING ANONYMITY

Throughout this book I have presented cases as examples and to illustrate the content under discussion. These are real cases, taken from my own practice, both general and forensic. I have anonymised these cases by changing the names involved, omitting telling details and changing any identifying elements. Not one person described in this book is a reflection of one patient but rather a hybrid of many people I have met and worked with. Any of those facets of the individuals' personalities that have been cited in this book have been anonymised and de-identified to a point where individuals are not recognisable. Moreover, the people's stories and any aspects of their personality that appear on these pages have been included with the express permission of the individuals who contributed to the amalgam of each of those descriptions about human psychology. All of the names cited in the book are false names, bearing no relation to the actual identity of the people involved.

CONTENTS

PROLOGUE: DRAWING THE LINE   VII

1. WHY DO PEOPLE CROSS THE LINE?   1

2. THE WORK OF THE FORENSIC PSYCHOLOGIST   19

3. THE ROOTS OF CRIME: PARENTS AND FAMILY   44

4. JUVENILE OFFENDERS AND THE CHILDREN COURT   63

5. THE BOLD NEW WORLD OF CYBERPSYCHOLOGY   93

6. SELF-MEDICATION AND WHERE IT TAKES YOU   111

7. LOSING CONTROL? ANGER AND VIOLENCE   134

8. SEX: IDENTITY, DEVIANCE AND DISORDERED THINKING   157

9. THE PSYCHOPATHIC SPECTRUM   191

10. THE VERY THIN LINE: MENTAL HEALTH CHALLENGES

FOR EVERYONE   210

EPILOGUE: REDRAWING THE LINE   220

THANK YOU   226

PROLOGUE: DRAWING THE LINE

When I was fourteen years old I worked in an amusement park, and one of the people I worked with there was very lazy. He was a little older than me, about sixteen, and as the weeks went by I grew more and more frustrated with his obvious, unembarrassed laziness with regard to his job. One morning I was on the opening crew with this boy, which meant we had to ready the park for the gates to be opened at ten o'clock. I was working methodically through the opening routine, but Lazy was sitting on a bench, smoking a cigarette. I steeled myself and called over to him. 'You shouldn't sit there and not help.' He slowly stubbed out his cigarette with his shoe, stood up, walked over to me and asked me to repeat what I had said.

'You're lazy,' I said. 'Why don't you help me carry out some of the work instead of sitting there doing nothing?'

He didn't flinch, but immediately thumped my face and continued to pummel my nose and jaw until I was fairly bloodied. When he was finished beating me, he got up and continued on with his work. I was upset and stunned by what had happened and I left the amusement park to walk around and compose myself. My bloodied face was a sight: it was completely swollen and my nose was broken, which required surgery later that day. Someone found me walking around groggily, got me to the hospital, and my parents were called. Naturally my parents were also very upset, but the surgery went fine and I was okay.

There were no security cameras in the area, it was many years ago now, and no one had witnessed the event. The police came to our house and I made a statement, but there was little they could do without corroborating evidence, Lazy was never charged. They did, however, go to have a quiet word with him, to try to ensure he never launched such an attack on anyone else. It was a pretty horrible incident, but I got over it. Nonetheless, it was important in that it was the first time I really understood the vulnerability of the human race, how we can be hurt and our lives can be changed by someone else's actions, someone who is willing to cross the line into socially unacceptable, deviant and dangerous behaviours. The fact that I didn't understand his actions that day bothered me. I had annoyed him; he got angry. I felt vulnerable; he felt powerful. It seemed that simple, and that complex. He did something I would never have done, have never done to anyone, yet for him it was the best and easiest option. He did it without pause, without compunction, without regret – and without consequence, as it happened. The line that seemed to exist between us fascinated me precisely because I didn't understand it: what made us so different? Or could I be like him if circumstances were different?

I never forgot that incident, but I didn't carry any bitterness about it either. I disliked the feeling of vulnerability he gave me and the knowledge that I had to accept what had happened. But it also made me realise that I had to be cleverer the next time. I had to learn from it and not make the same mistake again. Perhaps his actions served to make me fearful of the population, more respectful of those who have power and strength superior to mine albeit used in an aggressive fashion. I never lost that respect for others with that power, and I never allow it to be absent when I am assessing or treating criminals. It is an important component of my work and my approach. I look at criminals and at forensic populations with as much medical and psychological concern as I do the general health population.

So do I have the ability to cross the line, as he did? I think that everyone has the ability to cross the line, whether in subtle or extreme ways. The common thread among the people I have worked with who have crossed the line – and often who have been convicted for doing so – is disordered thinking. But it would not be correct to say that the rest of us are possessed of perfectly ordered thinking. The truth is that we could all be placed somewhere on the spectrum of disorders. That might be a sinister thought for some, but at base it underlines our shared humanity, our shared flaws, the fact that any one of us could fall foul of a disorder of the mind that could lead to disordered behaviour. That could lead, in other words, to us crossing the line into socially unacceptable or even criminal behaviour. There is no 'us and them' when it comes to the criminal population – there are just humans who are at different points on the psychological spectrum and who have different ways of dealing with the challenges they face. There is agency and choice, but circumstance, nature and nurture all play a huge role, and those are things we have very little control over, especially as children. My tormentor might have been living in a chaotic household where beatings were normal, which meant to him it was a normal reaction. I didn't think like that, but if I grew up in his house, it's quite possible I'd have the same layers of distorted emotions and thinking as him.

In this book, the 'line' is not just about crossing over into criminality, it is more about the extremes of human behaviour, many of which I've seen at the negative end with the criminogenic population. However, that experience has allowed me to gather insight into general human psychology, which is of course the backdrop for more extreme psychologies. The knowledge that one attains as a psychologist from the thousands of hours of listening to stories is worth much more than any education can provide. The education received at university to qualify for this work is merely a means to enable us to be a *tabula rasa*, an open mind that can listen objectively and gather such information for the greater good. It is too easy for us to point towards the 'bad people', the criminals, the negatives, the people who have dodgy psychology that is so different from ours and that sets them apart from us.

We draw a line between criminals and ourselves, deriving comfort from its presence and using it to justify how we treat criminals. The truth is that a distinct line does not exist – it is much more a matter of grey areas. You may never have broken the law, but have you ever cheated on a partner? Shoplifted? Siphoned off money from your employer? Kept money you saw fall from the pocket of the person walking down the street in front of you? Been in a fist fight? Insulted someone so vehemently you made them cry? Have you ever slapped your child? Spread a rumour or gossip you knew to be false? Kept the extra change the shopkeeper mistakenly gave you? The line isn't a fixed space that you are not capable of crossing, it is far more fluid than that – there are many ways to hurt, to belittle, to cause emotional distress and we are all probably guilty of those behaviours at some time in our lives.

When I was a younger psychologist, at the start of my career, I was fascinated with the criminal but even more fascinated with why someone would choose to engage in a behaviour that would cut them off from the population and lead to grave punishment. Did everyone have a darker side? Was it okay to want to do things that were wrong? But the fundamental of what I wanted to know about the line and criminal behaviour was to gain insight into what motivated others to entrench themselves in violent, sadistic, sexually masochistic or downright manipulative and dangerous behaviours. I have learnt much more since then, both from people I have spoken with and from the stories I have heard and, at times, witnessed, but there is still so much more to hear and write, so that I can continue to understand what lies at the extremes of our psychology, what ingredients constitute the line and is it possible, even healthy, that we traverse both sides of it?

The fact is that the line is constantly shifting, being narrowed or widened as culture allows. All of the behaviour we witness in this age has been witnessed before – none of it is new. We are appalled by acts of terrorism, genocide, random and senseless murder, paedophilia and domestic violence, but these things have always been with us and what is considered 'socially acceptable' is open to reinterpretations by each successive generation. So, for example, paedophilia was once considered acceptable behaviour, condoned and facilitated and indulged in by the aristocratic class. Over time that changed and now it is deemed criminal and punishable by law, but it shows how human psychology can accommodate different beliefs at different times.

We don't yet understand the genetics behind all of our behaviours, but we must continually open our minds to the fact that any behaviour is possible and that our minds will grow and learn to carry out such behaviours, even if only in a virtual way. As you venture through the book you will understand very extreme behaviours through the stories of people I have assessed for the courts or seen within my general practice, and who agreed to be represented in this discussion. Their stories highlight how all of our behaviours are shared, and how we are all capable of crossing the line in some way, whether with intention or by accident, premeditated or not. Negative activities and actions or thoughts that we partake in can cause harm to ourselves, as well as others, with far-reaching effects. Knowing what we are capable of, not being fearful of the darker sides of our personality and embracing the differences is, to my mind, important and should be kept to the forefront of your mind when reading this book. It may even be psychologically helpful to transgress every now and again, to feel like you are a little bit dangerous, a little bit naughty, wanting to turn over that stone, search for what is going on underneath, albeit some of that information may be ugly and uncomfortable to understand.

To finish, I will say that even though it does appear that we all have the potential to cross the line, there also appear to be some very common and consistent traits among those who end up in prison, such as chaotic family backgrounds, disordered thinking, mental health challenges and very poor parenting, as well as a genetic predisposition to engage in behaviours that can be self-destructive as well as damaging to the community at large. The opening chapter of the criminal's story is very often one of impoverishment and social isolation, along with poor role-modelling and substance abuse. The specifics of where that started, how that manifests and what it can cause are addressed in this book. However, there are also those in society who are high functioning, live in a much brighter place and still feel the need to engage in illegal behaviour, whether that need stems from bio-chemistry, genetics or unique episodes in life where they have experienced damaging learning. It may not be as common for this population to be convicted of crimes, but equally anyone can argue that those with a good level of education can often avoid being caught by the law even if they are doing harm to others. That is why my work is so endlessly fascinating – I have never learned all there is to know; I have never heard every story. It has been an adventure and continues to be a learning curve that tests me daily. I hope that this book gives some insight into what I have learned and into what aspects of human psychology contribute to malevolent and to positive behaviour, both of which are very apparent in our society, on both sides of the line. The stories and information described in these pages highlight that darker aspect of human behaviour, which causes individuals, families and groups of people to exist on the shadowy, limited and more punitive side of society's line, but one thing is clear: we always have a choice.

CHAPTER ONE

WHY DO PEOPLE CROSS THE LINE?

B enjamin was a murderer with a great sense of humour. He was being processed by the police, by forensic psychology (through my assessment interview) and through the legal system and the courts, and every step along the way he made people laugh. He was an unusual man, an unusual offender with his wide smile and ready wit. The book of evidence compiled by the police and detailing his crime made for uncomfortable reading, but in person he was charming, witty and full of fun. It was Ben who said to me with a theatrical sigh, 'I can't wait to meet a one-armed psychologist.' I looked at him in surprise, wondering what he meant. Then his face broke into his trademark smile and he said, 'Then he wouldn't be able to say, "On the one hand … but on the other hand".' It was a very amusing remark, and he had perhaps unwittingly hit on one of the key characteristics of a career in forensic psychology: there are always many different factors to consider, but it is essential to bring them all to bear as evidence because often someone's liberty is at stake – and that's no laughing matter.

As a forensic psychologist my job (the detail of which is set out in Chapter 2) is to meet with criminals and assess what they did, what led up to what they did, the consequences of what they did and the likelihood of them doing it again. This means I spend my working life examining the make-up of individual crimes and individual criminals. My contribution is understanding – helping the judge, the jury and the criminal him/herself to understand what happened and, crucially, why. It's the sort of work that provokes huge interest at dinner parties, with a few central questions being put to me again and again by the curious: *have you ever worked with a serial killer? Do you think we should lock them all up and throw away the key? Why do criminals do such awful things?*

While I have worked with murderers, I haven't yet worked with a serial killer, and no, I don't think those who cross the line should be simply punished and neglected. After two decades working with criminals, I believe in seeking to understand and treat the psychological mechanisms behind criminal acts through comprehensive rehabilitation. The Scandinavian model is one I would like to see adopted in Ireland in the future, whereby the prison population is kept to a minimum because the whole focus of the justice system is to help convicted criminals to examine their thinking, take responsibility for their actions and reintegrate into society in a more productive way.

Why is a far more complex question – and answer. The why differs from case to case, person to person. What I have learned, however, is that there is always a why. It is very rare for someone to cross the line just for the hell of it. Some might argue that it does occur in cases of impulsive, unplanned stealing or random acts of violence, but even then I'd guarantee that you'd find a deeper why behind the assertion *Because I could* or *Because I wanted to*. Far more likely is a series of events, throughout the person's life, that have knitted together into the moment of transgression. *Why* goes to the very heart of what I do – in order to figure out the crime and the likelihood of reoffending, it's necessary to know why the person did what they did.

In order to discover why someone did something, be it robbery, bullying, sexual abuse or any other challenging behaviour, it is necessary to study their individual psychology. Psychology research promotes the idea of a fixed number of personality traits possessed by every human being, and that we all fit into one of those types. This sort of 'summing up' is continually being challenged and changed by ongoing research, but it comes up again and again as a popular idea. Referred to as the 'Big 5', these commonly cited human traits along the psychological spectrum are: extroversion, agreeableness, openness, conscientiousness and neuroticism. These can be useful markers for a psychologist to use when discussing behaviour with a client, but it is too simplistic to say that each one of us fits neatly into one of these character niches. In fact, each human psychology is unique and equally interesting. Our personalities are the product of genetics, nature, nurture and environment, education or lack of education, and the myriad experiences that shape us over the course of our lives. Each mix is therefore unique to each person – every one of us has our own individual pattern.

In the past, psychologists were more linear in their thinking, seeking to place individuals into useful categories, such as the 'Big 5', in order to understand and treat their behaviour. In recent times, however, the approach has changed significantly. Many practitioners look to other aspects of personality that represent convergent and divergent thinking. Convergent thinking is a person's ability to correctly answer standard questions; divergent thinking is the ability to synthesise current knowledge into creative and innovative new ideas, in other words to sort through different possible solutions to come up with the best solution. The aspects of personality that represent these modes of thinking are linear, logical problem-solving for convergent types (such as doctors and mathematicians), and artistic and lateral thinking for divergent types (architects, software engineers). Among the criminal population I would generally see more divergent thinking, although it's not a defining characteristic. In addition, modern practitioners also look very closely at environment and prior experiences to build up a much broader profile of the individual psychology of the person they are assessing. The thinking now is that human psychology is grey, not black and white. A sophisticated assessment diagnostician or therapist is unafraid of the grey and doesn't seek to find black or white because they understand that our thoughts and actions do not fall into easily defined labels at either end of the spectrum. In truth, the grey, the space in between is really the most interesting and significant part of what they're trying to understand, diagnose and/or treat.

So how, then, do we study these unique patterns of human behaviour in any consistent and meaningful way?

The basic tool of psychology is to examine generic trends to find patterns. This is essentially what the *Diagnostic and Statistical Manual of Mental Disorders* (DSM) is – a listing of trends that serves as a helpful guideline when assessing behaviour. (Now in its fifth edition, *DSM-V*, the DSM is a diagnostic and classification manual for mental health disorders and presentations.) A good psychologist will refer to the DSM but will then augment that information with knowledge derived from experience, in order to tweak those basic generic trends to allow for individual idiosyncracies. This is not a reductive practice because, by and large, the majority of the human population exists on a known spectrum. There are outliers, of course, such as those who are exceptionally bright – people like Mark Zuckerberg and Professor Stephen Hawking, for example – or those exhibiting extreme autism or extreme mental disorder that prevents them communicating with the world in a linear fashion and means they cannot cope with daily stressors and stimuli, but in the main we all show up somewhere on the basic spectrum of behaviour, which runs from 'normal' behaviour to disordered behaviour. It is not the case that there is an abnormal spectrum and a normal spectrum and the two exist in separate spheres. There is instead a human spectrum that includes disordered thinking and behaviour. No one is immune from these aspects of thinking and behaviour.

Often the difference between a criminal and a non-criminal is the level of the disorder experienced. Psychological disorders can be borderline, intermittent, acute or chronic. You could live your whole life with borderline personality disorder or borderline depressive disorder and never get into trouble with the law, or you could, through circumstance or genetics, be pushed towards the chronic end of the spectrum, which could result in life-changing behaviours, in behaviours that could land you in prison and sitting across the table from a forensic psychologist who will piece together why you ended up at that level on the spectrum. The key thing to understand is that it is a matter of grey areas and blurred boundaries. For example, there is much crossover apparent between the criminal population and the high-functioning 'normal' population in terms of the psychological aspects of introspection, lack of introspection, frustration and detailed self-criticism. These aspects could as easily be apparent in the ambitious and successful CEO of a multinational, in the painter or in the child who wants to write, as in the young man who got high and broke into a house to steal from its owners. The thinking is similar, but it is the playing out of that thinking in behaviour that is different.

While we may be inclined to see anything 'disordered' as a negative thing, something to be aggressively punished when it tips over into unlawful behaviour, in the wider picture of humanity such disordered thinking is necessary for creativity and new ideas. For example, taking our successful CEO again, she may be challenged and frustrated by her own limitations, which can lead to disordered thinking. However, her life circumstances, healthy thinking patterns and sense of self-esteem mean these negative feelings can be converted into positive thinking and actions in seeking to resolve those feelings and the problems that gave rise to them. So in the case of the CEO, the disordered thinking leads to positive, problem-solving behaviour; in the criminogenic personality, the same feelings lead to destructive, problem-creating behaviour.

Psychologists are essentially 'behaviourologists'. The first and most important question we ask in every case is: what is the function of the behaviour? What function does the behaviour serve? People sometimes make the mistake of thinking in terms of psychological/mental disorders and behavioural disorders. In fact, what we deal with are personalities, which are characterised as the product of genotype plus phenotype. Genotype is related to genetics – basically what our parents gave us to create our DNA. Phenotype is the environment into which we are born and in which we are raised. Therefore, it is genes coupled with environment that mould personality. What we commonly find in forensic psychology is that the behaviour is a symptom of the psychological disorder – in other words, it is the manifestation of the inner thought processes. Therefore, the first step of assessment is to find out what function that destructive behaviour is serving in the perpetrator's mind and/or brain.

There can be non-physical functions to our behaviour, for example when someone does something wrong because of low self-esteem, trying to 'plug the hole' inside themselves. In that instance, the mind/self is being served by the behaviour, but that's not something that's measurable. There can also be physical functions, serving the biochemistry of the brain. One of the fascinating aspects of the study of criminal behaviour is studies into the differences in brain activity that can be measured in the criminogenic personality. While brain anatomy isn't markedly different, as you travel along the spectrum of challenging behaviour it is possible to see differences in brain activity. In general, those people who cross the line into criminality tend to be more risk-prone, meaning they need a greater level of risk to achieve arousal and fulfilment. So while the brain of Mr or Mrs Average might experience a release of pleasure chemicals from shopping or sport or music, this won't be the case for the brain of the offender. For them, it takes extremely risky behaviour to stimulate the production of norepinephrine, oxytocin, dopamine and serotonin – our 'happy' chemicals. Interestingly, it is also the case that brain growth is stimulated by love and attachment in our early years, which means the parenting we receive has a massive influence on our brains and their development. What's more, studies on the brains of monks who practised a life of silent reflection and meditation have shown that in their brains the hippocampus grows to a larger size than in the brains of the rest of the population. In other words, the brain responds positively to a positive environment; the corollary, of course, is that the brain's development is hampered by a negative environment.

The real difficulty is that it can be very hard to find the function of any given behaviour. The approach I use in attempting to determine the function is a three-phase interview. The first session establishes a rapport and invites the client to describe their formative challenges. The second session focuses on their developmental family history to date, their forensic history if they have one and the events that led to their committing an offence. In the third session, findings from the first two sessions are merged into a 'bigger picture' profile with the aim of discovering how these aspects have led to the behaviour that they find challenging or what some of the sources of this behaviour might be and what functions it might be serving for that person. It's a delicate and detailed conversation that works from the endpoint – the crime – back to the source of that act in the person's disordered thinking. When working with offenders, the main behaviours I look for are mental health challenges, anger, anxiety, poor communication skills and low confidence. The interview drills down into these behaviours, seeking the source. If someone is angry, for example, and does something criminal out of that anger, the function of that act may be a lashing out against what's perceived as oppressive experiences throughout their childhood. The act takes place now, but the trigger could lie far in the past.

Psychologists differ in their approach to assessing patients, with many preferring a holistic approach that takes all of the personality together, believing that the personality is greater than the sum of its parts. I don't adopt this view. Instead, and no doubt related to my other qualification as a doctor of medicine, I take the approach that categorisation is important. I approach psychology in a scientific manner, with a surgical eye for detail, which means

I prefer to dissect the personality into its component parts. In assessing a client, I compartmentalise each disorder, look at the function of each, then try to pinpoint any common behaviours across all of these disorders. Co-morbidity is very common, which means the existence of dual or multiple disorders in one person. This is why I take a disorder by disorder approach, isolating each source of the behaviour, because the offenders I work with very often present with more than one disorder. So, for example, an offender may have depressive disorder, anger management difficulties and a process disorder, such as alcohol addiction. In working with that person, I will prioritise which of those to focus on first, then go back to try to discover what function that behaviour serves, before moving on to the next challenge and seeking to identify its function. Through experience I have found that this approach gives the client more confidence that each challenge can be overcome through specific treatment that focuses on that challenge. This in turn leads to better engagement with the process and with the treatment, leading to better outcomes.

In terms of diagnosing the source of the behaviour, on crime TV shows you will often hear it pronounced that the offender has a 'personality disorder'. I find the term 'personality disorder' largely unhelpful. It's too generic, plus it doesn't contain any solution to manage the disordered thinking involved. The key for a forensic psychologist is how we define the disorder, how we interpret it in the context of the person's life. That is useful and revealing. The broader term is too wide to encompass an individual life – the work is in breaking it down into its component parts for a greater understanding. For example, extremely ordered thinking can be high on the 'normal' end of the spectrum or on the 'disordered' end. It depends on the person and how they live out that 'personality disorder'. So at one end is the thoroughly organised careerist who is lauded for their hyper-attention to detail and methodical work. At the other end is the person with Obsessive Compulsive Disorder (OCD), whose life is marred and even halted by their high-level 'ordered' thinking. It is the same diagnosis, but only by understanding how that thinking is lived through behaviour can we assess, diagnose and treat that behaviour.

In forensic psychology cases I work with all manner of crimes and criminals, covering the worst of human behaviour. In criminal profiles, it is clear to see how genotype and phenotype work in tandem to create the criminogenic personality. (Criminogenic covers behaviour from flirting with illegality to engaging wholesale in unlawful acts.) In terms of genotype, that takes in the common psychological disorders. In terms of phenotype, this relates to Social Learning Theory and the effect of nurture and environment on our personalities.

The most common psychological disorders I encounter among the offenders I interview are depressive disorder, process disorders, cognitive disorder, oppositional defiance disorder and features of personality disorder, such as narcissism. In terms of gender breakdown, I see a 50/50 split of these disorders among male and female offenders but a very marked difference in terms of manifestation: the behaviour of the male will generally be far more aggressive. As described above, it's very common for more than one disorder to be present, so the forensic psychologist has to follow the thread from behaviour to source, taking into account the evidence of the presence of different disorders.

Depressive disorder is very common and often presents as comorbid with anxiety and substance abuse. It's a case of the initial depressed feelings leading to a state of anxiety about those feelings, which the person then decides to self-medicate against with alcohol or drugs. I have seen this presentation again and again, and in offenders as young as fourteen years old who are residing in juvenile detention centres. Research is still ongoing into this disorder, but it does appear that there is a genetic predisposition to it. The specific DNA sequence involved and where the genes sit that may be responsible for depression have yet to be identified, but retrospective analysis of various cohorts of schizophrenic, bipolar and depressive individuals has found that a family history is in existence in over 40% of those diagnosed with depressive disorder.

Therefore, it does seem that if you have a parent or close relative with a psychological or psychiatric disorder, then the chances of you also experiencing such a challenge is much higher.

The fact that I see depressive disorder in so many of my forensic clients is reflected in the very disturbing statistic that 60% of the prison population in Ireland have mental health problems. It is a positive thing that mental health is now becoming a focus of attention and media promotion, but clearly this is long overdue, as the problem has been allowed to spiral. It is a key factor in the criminogenic personality, it would seem, but sourcing help can be difficult. For example, I dealt with a case where a man was arrested after a tense stand-off with police. He was very drunk and armed with a sawn-off shotgun loaded with three cartridges. He ranted and roared as he discharged two cartridges into the ground. The police asked what he intended to do with the third cartridge. At that point, he became melancholic and emotionally upset and said it was to end his own life. His anger evaporated and he broke down in tears, at which point the police were able to disarm him and lead him away. When I worked with him for his assessment report, it was clear that he was suffering from a depressive disorder, exacerbated by suicidal ideation. Twelve months after that incident, when he had received support and help, he told me that it would never have reached that criminal endpoint if he'd been able to secure that same support and help earlier. That story has always stayed with me because it's a good illustration of how a person can cross the line, even though they never intended to, because of undiagnosed and untreated mental illness.

Cognitive Information Processing (CIP) is a technical term that was coined by two researchers, Eysenck and Keane, whose work examined the building-blocks of the brain with regard to memory and information retrieval. Under this heading fall emotional language, memory, recall and ability to retrieve information. When a person has difficulty with these areas of thinking, he is less able to articulate his emotions and therefore less able to understand them. He will have difficulty understanding, recalling and processing information according to what is expected for his age, education and demographic. CIP pathology can commonly appear in patients with acquired brain injury, usually resulting from an accident. These patients find the loss of memory and thinking ability very difficult to accept. From the point of view of my work, those with difficult memories to process often want to sabotage them, which can be achieved quite effectively through substance use. When I interview a person with CIP pathology, what I commonly see is struggle and frustration with emotional dysregulation, an absolute giving up on oneself, a claustrophobic loneliness.

The CIP heading also includes people with Asperger's and Autistic Spectrum Disorders or Intellectual Challenges. It's a sad fact that the criminal population has a large percentage of people with such disorders because it shows that, as a society, we do not care for, understand or treat intellectual disorders as well as we should.

The other very common presentation among the criminogenic population is process disorders, which includes alcoholism, drug addiction and sex addiction. They are called process disorders because they arrive at a fixed 'endpoint', unable to process emotion, comprehension, others' opinions or semantics. As a result of this the person becomes aloof from their understanding of society, their background, their personality and has no confidence in anything in their life. Such disorders are very often rooted in an inability to name feelings and to understand why relationships keep playing out in the same destructive patterns. As a result of this inability to connect with emotional language or rationalise their behaviours, people with process disorders mute those feelings through excessive use of drugs, alcohol or sex. They are seeking meaning in an external locus of control because they cannot coincide their feelings with an internal locus of control. Their thinking is, therefore, disordered because of this central lack of honest self-awareness, and this leads to dangerous and risk-taking behaviours. Such disorders are a form of hiding from oneself because the truth underlying the behaviour is too difficult to manage.

As with all disorders, it is possible to be high functioning even while suffering from them. I have worked with career men and women who from the outside appear to be living a successful and fulfilling life, only to hear the lonely reality during therapy – that they are using alcohol to get through the day, hiding it from everyone, existing on a dangerous tightrope that depletes them mentally and physically. Alternatively, at the high-functioning end of the spectrum are those who are wealthy and very successful, but who are in fact addicted to power and external validation. Addiction has very negative connotations and people perceive it as weak-minded behaviour, but I have often been struck by the numbers of people living with some form of it – it seems to be a component of being human rather than a weakness afflicting a small percentage of people.

In my work with juvenile offenders, I regularly encounter oppositional defiance disorder (ODD). As categorised by the DSM-V, it is characterised by 'a pattern of angry/irritable mood, argumentative/defiant behaviour, or vindictiveness lasting at least six months'. In the young people who end up being interviewed by me, there is generally a clear anti-authoritarian mindset, accompanied by outbursts of anger when anyone is perceived as 'telling me what to do'. For example, I went to a juvenile detention centre to interview one of its residents, a girl called Lucinda who had been given a 'second chance' by a tolerant judge after her arrest for shoplifting and unruly behaviour, which included verbally abusing and attempting to bite her arresting officer. Lucinda came into the room in a defiant slouch, slamming the door behind her. I stood up and offered my hand, which she stared at with something approaching hatred. Then she looked at me aggressively and said, 'What the f**k do you want?' She ignored my outstretched hand and I ignored her greeting. She slumped into the chair opposite me, eyes on the wall, body tense, ready to fight or flee. I spoke to her gently, calmly, introducing myself and telling her the purpose of my visit. Before I even reached my first question, Lucinda suddenly leapt to her feet, screaming at me to 'leave me the f**k alone and get the f**k out of my face'. She embarked on a tirade against me, the police, the judge, the detention centre staff that was both wide-ranging and very personal – she took issue with my jumper. I sat back and let her have the tantrum, knowing she couldn't keep up that intensity for too long. She eventually sank into the chair, spent, glaring at me through narrowed eyes, telling me she wasn't going to 'do a single f**king thing you ask me to do, so f**k you'. I'm sure there are parents of teenagers thinking this sounds like standard fare, but her level of anger and aggression was disturbing to witness. She wasn't fully in control when she let loose, and I could see how her thinking – which didn't allow for her to assess the actual situation before her – could all too easily lead to very challenging behaviour.

The DSM-V includes all of the above disorders and also the personality disorders of narcissism and self-sabotage, which also present regularly in my forensic work. These are two key elements in the criminogenic personality. A narcissistic and self-destructive nature often culminates in a personality that does not know why they want things, but they nonetheless want them in an extreme way and will go to any lengths to get them. Once they have them, however, be they material objects or relationships, the narcissistic person immediately starts plotting to destruct those very things they wanted so much, just so they can go and search for more. The challenge to get the desired thing and the hardship the pursuit entails give more pleasure than the actual attaining of the relationship or the material object. As with all disorders, narcissism can move in opposite directions, depending on the person. On the one hand, there are self-serving narcissists who see themselves as the fulcrum point of the universe, with every single action and thought designed solely to allow them to enjoy life more. They often build up material wealth and assets, even if causing havoc to other people as they do so. It doesn't matter, though, because they don't recognise or care about the emotions of others or the consequences of their actions on others. On the other hand, there can be narcissists whose self-focus is less positive and more self-deprecating. They often suffer from negative thoughts about themselves, which can lead to depressive disorder and substance abuse and an inability to sustain relationships. Their lives are more often marked by unemployment, a series of short, unsatisfactory relationships and loneliness, which is far from the image that springs to mind when we think of narcissism.

When we ask: why has this person engaged in criminal behaviour?, the unspoken question behind that is: why does this person have a mind that is willing to engage in criminal behaviour? This is the area of Social Learning Theory and psychology as a social science – essentially, the 'nurture' debate. Modern psychology examines how the cultural and environmental contexts in which we live can shape human endeavour and individual thinking processes, which facilitate the resulting behaviour. This area of psychology puts great emphasis on environment and nurture in the make-up of our personalities, which is why it is called social psychology.

The renowned psychologist B.F. Skinner was the first to describe ABC theory: the Antecedent leads to a Behaviour, which ultimately results in a Consequence. The best-known example of this is Pavlov's dog, which was a study conducted by Ivan Pavlov in the 1890s. What it showed was that if you allow a dog to become very hungry and you then show him food but don't allow him to touch it, the dog begins to salivate and desires the food and as a result can be manipulated to engage in certain behaviours in order to obtain the food. So the Antecedent is hunger, the Behaviour is salivation and the activity the dog is forced to engage in ultimately secures the Consequence, which is receiving and eating the food. This sort of conditioning is apparent in criminogenic behaviours, where an impoverished person sees that he doesn't have enough, yet knows what he desires can be obtained through other means, which may not be legal.

The crucial factor in the criminogenic personality is that the immediate environment – home and local community – has made this thinking acceptable, even the norm, with the justified consequence of getting what is needed. Conditioning can happen in childhood, as a result of not knowing any different – this is, for example, how a person can accept racism or particular religious beliefs without questioning them. This is a learned mode of thinking, handed down as 'normal' and 'acceptable'. It is the same with alcoholism or drug addiction – if the child is exposed to this early on, it becomes the norm and there is a greater likelihood of that child repeating these behaviours.

This is not to excuse deviant behaviour: it is to explain it. It is an inescapable truth that when meeting with and talking to offenders, many come from the same areas, those described as 'disadvantaged' by government studies and community activists. It is not that being brought up in those environments condemns every person there to a life of crime, but it is the case that living where socially deviant behaviour is commonplace, where activities constantly skirt the edge of legality, creates an ability to cross lines that others would be reluctant to cross. If you are surrounded by different levels of line-crossing as you grow up, it fosters the belief that it is acceptable to do the same, once the rewards are worth the risk.

I have found that a constant feature of offenders from disadvantaged areas is their complete loyalty to their local community. I often have to cross the city to meet with offenders because they see the journey to my city-centre office as too far, too difficult, way beyond their geographical comfort zone. They limit themselves to tiny horizons because of this very localised viewpoint and identity that they construct for themselves. Their world shrinks to the immediate vicinity of their parents' house, shutting down all and any other opportunities. Of course, if you don't see opportunity, it doesn't exist. And this is a limitation common to the criminogenic personality – the offender does not see any other choice. He sees only one life, one future and is blind to every other suggestion. The bars of a prison window might present a tiny horizon, but this process of not seeing beyond the end of the nose has started long before he embarks on a criminal act. It is a form of conditioning that doesn't allow him to think other than how he has been taught to think. It robs him of any sense of or belief in agency.

The difficulty in trying to treat the thinking behind the offender's behaviour is exactly this strong and pervasive conditioning. Psychology is a long-term process – it takes time to change behaviour. For an offender whose background has narrowed his mind, widening out those thought processes is extremely difficult. The invitation to engage with treatment and try something new can be perceived as very threatening and destabilising. He learned long ago what is socially acceptable in his peer group, and that learning has become an integral part of his cognitive information processing. Without it, who is he? How can he return to his peer group and be a natural part of it again? In the criminal population, the kind of social learning required to change thinking and behaviour is nigh on impossible to gain, unless they fall in love, perhaps, which can have a positive influence because someone cares about them and their life, or find and join a mentor group that normalises new social learning rules. These are very difficult things to achieve when you don't even regard them as possibilities in your life.

It is clear, even from this brief overview, that there are many factors at work to create a criminogenic personality. It is far from a simple matter of there being 'bad people', which is tempting to think when one has been the victim of crime. Human psychology is both very fragile and very complex, which means it can be warped by outside events and experiences. In my work, I hear similar stories over and over again – of impoverished backgrounds, absent or neglectful or abusive parents, lack of education compounding the inability to connect with meaningful language, socially deviant environments, experience of physical or sexual abuse. There are other stories too, of course, but there is a common narrative thread woven through the lives of many offenders. People cross the line because of mental illness, because of addiction, because they were brought up to believe it was either okay or necessary, because of disordered thinking stemming from the broad spectrum of personality disorders. While there are common threads, it is never straightforward. Each offender has his or her own story of exactly how they reached the point of crossing a line and thus changing their life substantially.

From my own experience, I think one of the key factors in behaviour that leads to the line being crossed is the relationships in the person's life. I believe it is vastly underestimated how counter-productive, negatively influenced and very poorly constructed relationships can change people. Such relationships make them feel bad about themselves, make them feel there is a limit to the choices they have, make irrational decisions seem inevitable and change the way they perceive the world around them. Poor peer relationships, marital relationships, sexual relationships and friendships have far-reaching consequences for the individual. We vastly underestimate how positive relationships can make us much better people in very complicated ways.

For a forensic psychologist, the study of human behaviour is both challenging and unendingly interesting. We are further along the path of understanding the brain and mind now, in the twenty-first century, which feeds into our approach as psychologists to understanding and treating challenging behaviours. However, I think that in one hundred years' time, we will look back and consider our current knowledge of the human mind to be quite superficial. The growing body of knowledge derived from the study of genetics, in particular, is presenting whole new areas for study and reflection. I believe that, in future, psychologists will need to become far more knowledgeable of genetic lineage, as well as the switching on and off of certain genes and the effect of that on human thinking and behaviour.

I have been working with offenders for a long time and I've heard thousands of different stories. The key thing I have learned is that we are all human beings on a certain spectrum of order or disorder and we can be very positive and affirmational, but we can also be negative and punitive towards ourselves. How we think and behave results from our environmental and genetic influences, but there are many ways for us to create solutions when that thinking or behaviour needs to change. We can work effectively towards leading a healthier, more contented, more reliable, structured lifestyle, which is ultimately what humans thrive on. People often interpret 'structured' as 'boring', but it is a truth of human psychology that structure is hugely important for our development and happiness. When we live in chaos, disorder and confusion, those states of existence are reflected in our mental state, which in turn gives rise to disordered behaviour. The successful outcomes of forensic psychology – and I have been involved in many, with offenders who may have been deemed 'beyond the pale' – show us that it is possible to change thinking and behaviour for the better. People aren't condemned to cross the line – they always have a choice. The common denominator I have seen, and one that I reflect on continually and at length, is that people, criminal or not, very often underestimate their own value, which in turn makes them underestimate the effect and value of their decisions. It is this lack of value that makes them feel they have no agency and which can lead directly to behaviour that steps them over the line. In my work, which can be tough and appalling and dispiriting at times, it is this that makes me continue on with great optimism and enthusiasm: humans can always be better humans.

CHAPTER TWO

THE WORK OF THE FORENSIC PSYCHOLOGIST

T he words 'forensic psychologist' or 'criminal psychologist' immediately excite interest, but most people couldn't describe what such a psychologist actually does in their working day. We are familiar with the 'please lie on the couch' general psychologist, but the work of the forensic psychologist often seems to be shrouded in mystery and sinister hidden knowledge of the darkest sides of human personality.

Popular culture has given us a particular image of the forensic psychologist, especially through the America TV drama *Criminal Minds*. In that, the psychologists are presented as highly skilled people-readers, with an ability to see into the criminal's mind and divine his/her next move. Even the name given to the group – 'Mind Hunters' – is quite macho and suggests hunting down prey in an aggressive manner. Similarly, on *CSI*, the profiler examines the crime scene and from it puts together a personality profile of the perpetrator, which usually leads to their being identified and arrested. This sort of characterisation suggests that the forensic psychologist is possessed of very special skills and an ability to know the mind of others in an almost God-like way. As one critic said of *Criminal Minds*, 'it confuses critical thinking with supernatural abilities' – that's a very good assessment of the popular portrayal of the forensic psychologist.

While our work is challenging and interesting and generates huge insights into human beings and the human condition, it is also far more methodical and repetitive than TV series suggest. Unfortunately, it isn't all about startling insights that lead to high-profile criminals being averted and apprehended. In fact, it's barely about that at all. It's a scientific process that works to serve the good of the community by correctly assessing criminal behaviour and identifying the best treatment or sentence to deal with that behaviour. The key element in forensic psychology is the crossover with the law and the courts: that is what defines what we do and how we do it. At base, it can be defined as the assessment and treatment of psychological matters that have a relationship with the legal context. It is psychology that facilitates and examines human personality and behaviour in relation to the law and legal matters. This means that my working day will involve criminals, the courts and the police and legal authorities and I have to be the link in the chain between them all.

My days vary enormously, and they aren't all forensic psychology either, as I also see general patients, but a 'typical' day will feature a call from a solicitor who has a client they need assessed. The call comes through my office and, once costs have been agreed and approved, the solicitor sends over the book of evidence, which contains the list of charges being brought against the person, details of interviews with the police, observations by the police, the perpetrator's statement, notes of any forensic evidence taken from the crime scene or from searches conducted at the perpetrator's house and any exhibits or lists of anything being used in evidence. I'll be given the trial date, which can be only weeks away at times. I study the book of evidence, interview the offender, then write a report for the court. The report will contain a treatment recommendation, but this is unlikely to be carried out. (In eighteen years of writing reports, only 1% of my recommendations have been implemented.) I may be called into court to testify, which can be both interesting and nerve-wracking – and at times it can be downright horrible if I face an aggressive prosecutor/defender. Finally, as part of my own professional development, I also have regular therapy and psychological supervision to help me cope with the cases I'm hearing about and critically assess my role and contribution in each case. That, in a nutshell, is a 'typical' day.

I recently dealt with a parental capacity case that was interesting for a number of reasons – and that serves well to illustrate the various facets of my daily work. Parental capacity means that the ability of the parents to provide safe and nurturing care has been called into question, and a psychological assessment is required to recommend if the baby should be removed from its parents and placed in care. The call came through asking me to assess this particular couple, and I immediately set about reading all of the available reports. As I prepared to interview both parents, I familiarised myself with their whole story, which is the norm. But there was one part of their story that didn't fit the norm at all and that greatly complicated matters for me. I read that the father was accused of murdering their first child. At this point he stood accused, but there was no conviction, and that case was yet to come to court. By law, this meant I could not factor the pending trial or the possibility of his criminal conviction into my report on their parental capacity.

As I read the account of the death of Andreas and Mariana's first child, I knew it was going to be very difficult to have this information and yet be unable to allude to it in the report or in any testimony I might be called to give. Their baby was just a few months old at the time of its death. Andreas and Mariana had separated but shared custody of the baby. While in Andreas's care, the baby had died and the medical reports on the death all stated that the death could not have been accidental. Three different medical experts all submitted the same opinion.

Since then, the couple had reconciled and Mariana had given birth to their second child. Given that a case was pending against Andreas regarding their first child, the social workers dealing with the couple had stipulated that Andreas must live apart from Mariana and the baby and must only see his child in the presence of a social worker. The reports I read pointed only to Andreas posing a potential threat; Mariana was not regarded as a threat to her new baby. However, reading between the lines of the various reports, I knew I would have to probe and assess if Mariana had the ability to keep her baby safe from Andreas. As it stood, Andreas and Mariana declared themselves to be in love, but if they insisted on living together, the baby would likely be taken into care.

The interview forms the basis of the psychological profile and subsequent report. It is one thing to read a report describing certain actions and allegations, but it is another thing entirely to sit in front of a person accused of a crime. What I usually find is that the person doesn't seem to fit the crime – I read a report of someone who sounds frenzied or indifferent or angry or reckless, then I walk into a standard interview room and meet a very normal, often meek person who is trying to be helpful in order to help their own case. It can be hard to put the person before me into the scene described by the book of evidence. That is probably an important and helpful thing, though. It is easier to have empathy and sympathy and compassion if one has not witnessed at first-hand what the offender has done.

In every interview, the key consideration for me is to build rapport quickly, so that I get as much information as possible from the offender. In this regard, the first ten minutes are crucial because I must establish a positive framework for our discussion if the person is to talk honestly to me. I've often had people remark that it must be hard to sit in a room with an offender and hear them tell their side of the story, but I've never felt like that. To my mind, I am their last chance to have their voice heard, to explain themselves and to seek justice, and everyone deserves that chance. I take that responsibility very seriously and see it as one of the cornerstones of a democratic and just society. For that reason, I ask each person I interview to push themselves to be more honest than they've ever been before in their life. If I can elicit a totally honest account of themselves and of their crime, it gives the court a very clear picture of the events and what led up to the events. And that clarity is in the offender's favour.

The interview room will usually be in a prison or in my own clinic in the city centre. The prison interview rooms are generally as you'd expect them to be: small, cement-block rooms with grey walls, a utilitarian table, which in some prisons has a glass partition, two chairs, two doors – one from the prison side and one from the visitor side, both with a glass window for guards to check through – and a panic button. Thankfully, I've never had to press the button, but I did come close on one occasion. That was in a prison interview, where I was due to meet a man who had been accused of assault. His solicitor briefed me: he assaulted another man in a pub brawl, he has anger management issues, we need to ascertain where this anger stems from, any contributory factors from his past. That was all very clear. Then she alluded to another incident that had happened between the first incident – which I was assessing – and his arrest, but, she said, that other incident wasn't of any concern to me. I studied the book of evidence, which described his drunken assault on another man, and then I went to interview him.

In that particular prison, there was no Perspex between us, it was just a small room where we faced each other across a table. Victor was brought into the room by a guard, who then went off to bring other prisoners to their visitors. He closed and locked the door behind him as he left, leaving me and Victor alone together in the small space. I proceeded as normal, discussing his crime and his background. He told me he was perpetually angry, that the red mist could descend at any minute and had done so recently as well. I asked him about that – the incident the solicitor had mentioned but dismissed. He began to tell me how he was arguing with his wife, his anger was rising, she got between him and the door, told him not to leave – and that was it, the trigger. He pushed her hard, to the floor, then hit her repeatedly with a sledgehammer until she was very still and no longer arguing with him. I sat there, listening, astounded but not allowing it to show. The man had murdered his own wife in cold blood and no one had given me any kind of warning. *Anger management issues?* This was a whole other level of violence and I felt a jagged anger streak through me as I realised the solicitor had put me in a risky situation. I continued to talk calmly, but I was mentally going through how I would get out of this room quickly, should I need to. Victor was almost in tears talking about his wife, but what if that changed and the red mist descended again? That was the most nervous I've ever been in an interview. I was poised for flight for the next fifty minutes, wanting to get out through the door and beyond it. It was not the right condition for a good interview, as I was distracted and on edge. But I got through it, and Victor didn't lose his temper. It was a very uncomfortable feeling, however, and I let the solicitor know – very plainly – that she must never put me or any other psychologist in such a situation again.

The interview surroundings were open and more comfortable when I went to meet with Mariana and Andreas. It was in a social-work room in one of the centres around the country that allows for parents and children to be interviewed by and interact with social workers taking care of their case. I chose to meet with Mariana first, and I brought two junior colleagues with me. Both psychologists as well, one of them came in to interview Mariana with me, while the other went to talk to Andreas and administer assessment scales to add to his profile. Establishing rapport isn't a given, but I have developed some methods that work well to put the interviewee at ease. I always introduce myself by my first name and then explain that I am a doctor and the reason for my visit. I ask the person how they are, how their day has been, if they are nervous about today's discussion. I ask some basic questions about their lives and show an interest in their general livelihood. This sort of approach lets them know that I am not defining them solely by the actions that have led to our conversation. I am letting them know that I'm not judging them and that I see them as a whole person. I allow time to pass in general chatting before I broach the subject of why they are sitting before me and what happened. I use my hands to gesticulate as I'm talking, keeping them open. I dress quite casually, nothing too 'authoritarian' or intimidating. I never shy away from them or seem frightened. I am comfortable with getting close when talking to them. This approach quickly reassures the person that I'm an objective assessor, with no particular axe to grind, and that I'm there to help them have their story heard.

When my colleague and I entered the interview room, Mariana was sitting quietly, waiting for us. She was a young woman of twenty-one, with a chaotic family background. She hadn't known her birth father, but had enjoyed a good relationship with her step-father, until he split up with her mother and they never saw him again. After that, they'd moved around regularly, and Mariana had spent time in residential care. She was just seventeen when she'd first met Andreas, who was twenty years older than her. As we talked about her background and her new baby, Mariana visibly relaxed. I could tell by the movements of her hands that she would have liked to light up a cigarette, but of course this is no longer permitted. When I started out in forensic psychology, smoking was permitted in areas of the court and prison buildings and interviewees could request a cigarette break at any time. It has actually been a help to have the anti-smoking laws enacted. Before, when we'd reach a difficult part of the session the person would often use a cigarette as a way of breaking the session by getting up and going outside to smoke. Outside and away from my gaze, they could think over the question. As a result, I lost their spontaneous, impulsive answer, which meant certain details could be hidden from me. Now, every interviewee has to stay the course. I am allowed to interview for two hours, then we must take a break. But in a few focused hours, with no breaks or interruptions, I usually have everything I need to compose a report.

During the interview, what the forensic psychologist is doing is called formulation, or profile building – a skill that is particularly difficult to learn. Formulation is the ability to gather and then interpret the beginning, middle and end of the person's story. It is a process of linking the different parts of their story to connect behaviour back to their thinking, while at the same time finding out why they think as they do. Formulation provides a context to a person's personality that explains and elucidates their behaviour. The reason it is difficult to learn is that it requires huge presence of mind in order to listen very intently and hear every detail, even the tiniest, most unimportant seeming detail. A forensic psychologist can never underestimate the smaller details because they might hold important clues. Although it's taught in college, in reality one learns to formulate through experience, through wide reading and reflection and in-depth study into particular personalities. At this stage, I'm inclined to think formulation is a natural skill, rather than a taught one, although I do feel that my years of medical history taking have contributed hugely to my ability to formulate. By building up a profile in this way, it allows for insight into and understanding of the person and the act, which is essential for the court to properly assess the crime.

After two hours with Mariana, I felt I had a good handle on her thinking and behaviour. She seemed to be, as the social workers had described, a good and committed mother. She felt love towards her baby and a desire to protect it. She was clearly very taken with Andreas, however, and displayed an inability to understand that the outcome of the pending criminal court case could be a custodial sentence for Andreas. She talked of them continuing to live together, even if the judge ruled that their baby's death was deliberate. She struck me as a vulnerable person whose thinking was largely ruled by Andreas. She admitted that he was an intense person and that she was used to receiving threatening text messages from him. When we talked about her baby who died, there was a lack of connection to that event or the grief it must have triggered. There was clearly a risk that she would break the terms of any agreement designed to protect the new baby from Andreas.

I felt a great deal of empathy for Mariana, whose scattered life had left her with very few skills to develop a healthy psychology or robust coping techniques. Empathy is a key trait in a forensic psychologist. It is essential to listen patiently and intently to everything that is being said. The ability to listen intently is a particular skill, so that it's a respectful and positive experience for the interviewee. So often, people can go through life feeling as if no one has ever heard them. The job of the forensic psychologist is to listen, record and interpret. In order to do that properly, we must have empathy, sympathy as well as a strong ability to collect data objectively and cut through to the heart of the matter. It is necessary to listen with a wide open mind – not to decide in advance that you know what the story of this person will be. Research in medical journals has shown that medics often make a diagnosis from just a few key facts, then go in search of information to back up that diagnosis. Not considering all the facts before making a diagnosis can fulfil a self-believed diagnosis, which can often be wrong. In the same vein, forensic psychologists must be very careful to engage fully with each interviewee and their unique story. Boredom is the enemy of the psychologist because it leads to lazy thinking. Our critical-thinking faculties must be turned up to High for every encounter.

After our two hours with Mariana, we then went to interview Andreas. In his early forties, Andreas was unemployed and displayed elements of a passive-aggressive personality. He was possessive in his relationships and his history showed a marked tendency to go out with young women, many years his junior. As we discussed his life and background, certain events he described suggested that he could easily become overwhelmed by his emotions, which would lead to aggressive behaviour. He was also very traditional in his thinking, expecting Mariana to mind the baby, do the housework and prepare a dinner for him every night. We talked about his past and slowly came round to the night of his baby's death, which Andreas described.

On the day of the death, Mariana had posted a note on a social networking site announcing that she had started a relationship with a new man. Andreas read this post while minding their baby. According to Andreas, what happened next was a simple accident. The baby managed to get hold of some items next to the changing table and put them into its mouth, which resulted in choking. Andreas called the emergency services, and an operator talked him through how to dislodge an object from an infant's mouth. Andreas didn't understand the instructions and instead took the baby to the sink and poured water into its mouth. The baby died of asphyxiation. Andreas maintained that the baby had pushed the items into its own mouth; every report argued that this wouldn't have been possible for such a small baby to accomplish.

In spite of the problems in his story, I did feel that Andreas's remorse was genuine as he talked about the baby and the events of that day. However, I also felt that he was impulsive and could be irrational, which together could lead to devastating consequences. His need for dominance meant that he could lose control when things went against him – such as Mariana leaving him for another man. It seemed quite possible that the baby's death was the result of a jealous rage.

It is the concept of building a profile that seems to grab the public's imagination when it comes to forensic psychology. As noted earlier, this is the premise of *Criminal Minds* – that awe-inspiring ability to divine a person's inner thoughts and motivations. But it's not a supernatural ability, as was also pointed out, it is a skill derived from thousands of hours of reading, interviewing and writing reports. Our work creates a unique intimacy with the human personality, and this is what allows us to interpret what the interviewee says into useful information on their psychology. When I was in college, in my callow youth, this was my party trick: to listen to someone for five minutes, then build a psychological profile of them – to the laughter and teasing of everyone gathered around to hear. It was just a game, but it was informed by the principles of formulation nonetheless. If you gave me five minutes and quickly answered the following questions, I'd be able to compile quite a bit of information about you:

Where are you from? When were you born? Are your parents together? Do you have any siblings? Did you enjoy your childhood? First childhood memories? Where did you go to school? How were your friends at school? Ever bullied? Secondary school? Enjoyed school? What subjects did you enjoy? What did you want to be when you grew up? Have you fulfilled ambitions? What ambitions have you fulfilled? What was the most enjoyable part of your life? When did you first have sex? Your first relationship? What do you think about relationships? What are your career goals and ambitions for the future? Family? Who do you like to engage with? What is your vital interest outside of work? What are the personality traits you enjoy in others? What are your stronger personality traits? What challenges do you find in yourself? Challenges in others? What do you think your limitations/strengths are?

There is another tool available to us with regard to formulation and personality profiling, and that is the various scales we use. The scales can be retrospectively filled in or can be conducted and filled in during the one-to-one session, either by me or a junior psychologist colleague. The format is a series of questions to which the answers scale from 'Never' to 'Always', with all the variations in between. Alternatively the answers can be constructed as Yes, No or Known, Unknown. There are many different tests and I would use, for example, the Wechsler Adult Intelligence Scale, the Risk Rating for Sex Offences Recidivism, Parental capacity–Parent stress Relationship Inventory, Parent–child Relationship Inventory, the Parenting Stress Index, the Gudjonsson Suggestibility Scales, the Violence Recidivism Scale and the Hare Psychopathy Checklist. They provide another angle on the person's psychology, which can question or corroborate the formulation built up during the interview. Andreas had completed the Wechsler scale with my colleague, and that told us that he exhibited a significant compromise to learning, especially in relation to comprehension, processing speed and cognitive processing and memory. The scales can provide another dimension to the experiential history but can also contradict it, giving a platform to return to the interview process and ask further questions of the client.

While it's very helpful to have the extra insight provided by the scales when interviewing and profiling, it is necessary to be careful in choosing which to use because the scale you use must be fully validated. In the UK, there is a clear demarcation of acceptable tools from those that are not acceptable, but this demarcation doesn't exist in Ireland. Here, such tests are considered a backup to the experiential history that we compile, but not a necessity for every assessment report. Essentially, they validate what the assessment has already concluded.

Once the interviews had been completed, it was time to compile the report on the parental capacity of Andreas and Mariana. The fact that I couldn't mention Andreas's pending trial made it very difficult to justify my findings in full. Normally, I would have formulated that Andreas posed a risk because of his forensic history, but in this instance I couldn't give that forensic history because the court hadn't yet made a ruling on the matter. I had to be careful because if I were to be cross-examined in court, I could not refer to a potential future conviction. Andreas's barrister would obviously argue that, without a relevant forensic history, my findings were wide open to question and criticism. A previous conviction has a significant impact on subsequent convictions and sentences, but while a conviction was a possibility for Andreas, it was in no way an admissible argument at this time. So if such an argument were put to me in court, I would be left defenceless by virtue of being unable to give a full account of the information in my possession. It was, therefore, a very tricky report to compose, but the well-being of the baby was obviously my greatest concern – and not putting Andreas in any situation that could trigger his emotional aggression.

As with formulation, learning to write reports is a long process and the psychologist improves and develops that skill over the course of his career. I had an excellent teacher in this – not at college, but in my first job as forensic psychologist. I spent the early years of my career in Australia, where my supervisor was a tough, meticulous woman. My first three years under Alessia's supervision were a very steep learning curve, but I was lucky that she was a gifted trainer and supervisor. Reports are always subject to supervision, but in Alessia I had a supervisor who was a stickler for protocol, a good articulator and very clear-eyed with regard to providing entirely objective descriptions and conclusions. Her report-writing mantra was the rule we lived by: get the background; understand the development of the background; give depth of insight into the person's life; describe how they think and behave; describe what they did; describe their attitude towards the victim; describe the nature of the offence; describe the act they committed in detail; describe what the motivation was and what function it served; assess how likely the person is to offend again. Looking back, those first reports I wrote were quite basic and simple in nature, but that was not necessarily a bad thing as it meant they were easy to follow and digest.

By the time I wrote Andreas's report, I was very experienced at formulating and articulating within the report format. My conclusion was that Andreas did pose a risk to his baby, but given the absence of a forensic history, I couched that conclusion in very careful terms, making sure it didn't sound as if I wanted to find something to point to increased risk. I gave pros and cons along the lines of: while this increases risk, this doesn't – in other words, I ensured it was fair and even-handed, giving both sides of the argument. I did add, however, that in a forthcoming matter before the courts, a conviction would seriously escalate his risk of harming the baby. In this way, it covered all of the angles of Andreas's story and ensured the safety of his child, which was of paramount importance.

Reports are only ever straightforward if there is a grave psychiatric illness that is clearly present. The more difficult and entrenched the illness and the more overt and obvious it has been prior to the offending act, the more straightforward the report. This happens in only a tiny percentage of cases however. The average report is complicated and always in its own unique way. The key to every report, though, is nuance, which means the reader must be able to see and interpret both, or a number of, sides of how this particular personality presents. In other words, the forensic psychologist does not state that he has definite knowledge of what this person is or will be or will do. Yes, the person's presentation must be extremely clear, but it cannot be given as a 100% accurate conclusion. The reason for this is that behaviour is rarely simple – there can be many overlapping experiences contributing to a person's actions before and during the crime. It is not the role of the forensic psychologist to judge those actions or to assign guilt or innocence – that is for the jury and the presiding judge to do. The role of the forensic psychologist is to assist the jury and the judge by not only clearly stating the facts of the case and of the accused, but also by leaving enough space for them to make up their own minds, given the full breadth of evidence before them.

The report can be commissioned by different sources and for different reasons. In criminal law cases, two reasons for my reports are, first, for sentencing after a guilty plea, when the judge is weighing up the likelihood of reoffending and the report sets this out for him/her, and, second, as part of discovery for a trial. For example, if I am asked to prepare a report on the credibility of a witness, that will be prepared for inclusion in the trial itself. When the purpose is sentencing or suggestibility or fitness to plead, the report is generally commissioned by the lawyer/solicitor. When the purpose is an investigation of parental capacity, the report is usually requested by the health services. Regardless of its purpose, the report follows a template. It gives the offender's presentation, focusing exclusively on the assessment and the offender's point of view of the crime (the victim is always kept out of the report as they are protected, not under scrutiny and their, as well as other's, future care is paramount); it lists my qualifications and declaration to the effect that there is no bias towards the person who commissioned the report. In other words, the report is objective and client-centred.

Report-writing is a skill that develops as a result of experience, which has certainly been the case for me. Over the years my reports have become longer, far richer in description and more mindful of what the court wants and needs to know. Solicitors and barristers are looking for particular information, so while I enjoy and want to discuss the formulation and the logic behind the summations that I provide about the person's presentation, development and personality, I believe that much of it is lost on the courts and on the HSE and other authorities that commission such reports. The reason I deliver such detail and depth of presentation is because I am aware that some day, under the Freedom of Information Act, a criminal or a child in a credibility case or a child in a parental capacity case will ask for the report in order to review it and perhaps to appeal their case or look for compensation for time they believe they shouldn't have been placed in care. I see this as a key part of my responsibility, which is why I prepare reports so thoroughly and so carefully.

A feature of every report is the recommended treatment for the individual, which I also write very carefully and with much thought, even though I know it will likely be ignored. In Andreas's case, the treatment I recommended for him was cognitive behavioural therapy (CBT), to improve his empathy, perspective and emotional language, occupational therapy and work within the community to nurture a sense of purpose and participation. I hoped he would receive treatment with the community, via social workers, but the implementation of such treatment is patchy in Ireland due to the lack of accessibility to services or money to pay for them, and I knew there was a good chance he would receive little help.

I am not a psychiatrist, so even though I hold medical qualifications and have trained in psychiatric care, I do not recommend medication for disorders. I have other treatment options at my disposal, however. The main treatments that I have found to be effective are music therapy, art therapy, vocational training, returning to employment and getting involved in a community group. A report would typically contain eight to ten recommendations covering various aspects and the focus of those recommendations is usually to build self-esteem. While art and music therapy might sound a bit dubious, they do work because they encourage participation in an external activity. The same goes for sport, which I feel is hugely underestimated as a component of wellbeing. Twenty minutes of exercise with the heart rate at more than 20% above normal resting rate is as effective as a mild antidepressant. These 'doing' therapies can have a very good effect. As I feel that peer support and partner support is very important to the success of therapy, I often recommend group support alongside one-to-one therapy. I generally recommend that treatment should last from twelve to twenty-four months, depending on the risk rating attributed to the person, and that it be monitored by the person's GP as well as through ongoing psychiatric assessment and review.

For the forensic psychologist, CBT is a key treatment because research has proven that it is an effective tool in tackling and changing challenging behaviour. My own experience of administering CBT to individuals has also convinced me that it is effective and very worthwhile because it generates change in a short period of time. CBT works on the premise that a mood causes a behaviour. If you can identify the trigger for particular moods and the behaviours those moods lead to, you can give insight into those triggers and options for ways to handle the resulting moods, in other words alternative behaviours from the problematic behaviours. Combining this with a 'wellness toolbox' – behaviours and lifestyle choices to enhance mood and behaviour – can have a marked and real effect on the individual. The wellness behaviours could be as simple as calling up a friend, enjoying time with your family, watching a movie, going for a walk. CBT encourages the person to continually check in with their own feelings and to understand their mood at particular times of the day, with a view to managing those moods through behaviour modification. It gives control for behaviour into the person's own hands, helping them to understand that they have choice and agency and are responsible for all of their behaviours. The other things CBT achieves are to teach the person the perspective of others, thereby increasing their empathy, to improve their problem-solving ability and also to give them coping mechanisms for their personal 'triggers'. For example, I have used CBT with paedophiles to teach them to recognise the triggers that suggest their behaviour is slipping towards offending. If, for instance, they find themselves altering their commute home in order to go by a school, that is a trigger and they can immediately identify it as such and seek help to avoid offending. CBT promotes the important notion that you are in charge of your own behaviour and that you have choice with regard to your behaviour. That can be a powerful idea for those who have fallen or who are in danger of falling prey to their own minds.

As noted with regard to Andreas, the treatment option is rarely taken up by the offender. In my eighteen years as a forensic psychologist, during which time I've written almost a thousand detailed reports, I estimate only 1% of the treatment recommendations have been carried out. There are two problems here: the justice system; and the priorities of the offender and his/ her family. With regard to the justice system, it is a problem of under-resourcing and under-staffing. There are only two or three forensic psychologists working in Ireland today, for example, and reviews of the prison service and sentencing, etc., often point to the lack of psychological support on offer. From my point of view, implementation of treatment recommendations would be the greatest change that could be made to make my work more effective. However, there is no compulsion on the offender to follow up on the recommendations or to participate in treatment. The ideal scenario would be if there were resources in place for a judicial review of the case once the recommendations had been put in place, say twelve to eighteen months after treatment commencing, at which point the court could either revoke the sentence or commit the person to prison if they have failed to comply with the recommendations. If the threat of the law still exists and the person is within the community but must comply with detailed recommendations, then they are far more likely to be rehabilitated than if they simply serve a few years in prison and are released. The norm at the moment is that offenders usually go out and reoffend or are permitted a suspended sentence without having to adhere to any of the recommendations of the court.

The second problem lies with the offender and his/her family. They are so focused on the court case and the sentencing, they completely lose sight of what the report is and what it can offer. The report is important to them only insofar as it is useful in court. Once the court has made its decision, the report is forgotten about. Rarely will anyone say, 'Brilliant, I got my suspended sentence, now I really want to adhere to those recommendations Ian wrote about'. Sadly, that doesn't happen. As a result, offenders and their families don't push to receive the treatment outlined in the report, not understanding that it could have a big effect on the life of the offender. On those rare occasions when an offender does engage with the treatment, it proves the fact that treatment cuts recidivism rates. Treatment and intervention do work: they just rarely get a chance to make a difference, which is a great shame.

I'm sure that sometimes there are people who do follow the treatment recommended and do change their lives but that I simply don't hear about it. This is because it's relatively rare for me to hear the end of my clients' stories. One of the downsides of my work is that it's very piecemeal, and although I request follow-up information from solicitors, I don't ever receive it because they are too busy to remember and make the call. So it is often the case that I get to hear the beginning and middle but not the end of the story.

It is frustrating to know that treatment would cut recidivism rates and promote the general well-being of society, but to be unable to implement it effectively. The system in Ireland has a long way to go to improve implementation rates and there would have to be many changes to facilitate it, such as psychological and vocational training, group work, such as group CBT, and structured follow-up within the community post-release. Countries such as Canada,

New Zealand, Australia and Britain are showing how these models can be put in place successfully. In those jurisdictions, there are mechanisms within the community that follow government agencies' recommendations and psychologists' and psychiatrists' recommendations. In Ireland, by contrast, the community agencies aren't even in existence for those foundations to be laid, nor are there enough psychologists in the justice system to feed into those agencies if they did exist.

Regardless of the shortcomings of the system, as experts involved in and contributing to it, we have to plough on and do the best work we can. I take great care over each and every report I write, which I hope is apparent when it comes to court appearances and making the report easily understandable for the judge and jury. In the case of Andreas I wasn't called to court, but I have been called to testify in many other child protection cases.

The Irish court system is particular to this jurisdiction and comprises, in a hierarchy from bottom to top, the District Court, the Circuit Court, the High Court, the Central Criminal Court, the Four Courts and the High Court of Justice. Each town and each county will have its own District Court and, if it is large enough, its own Circuit Court as well. At District Court level, you only require a solicitor, who will speak on your behalf to the judge. At Circuit Court level, a barrister is normally used in addition to the solicitor. The solicitor instructs the barrister as to what evidence s/he wants, which might include commissioning a report by a forensic psychologist. If approached to compile a report, it will then be the barrister and solicitor who instruct me to attend court and who will take me through the report in the courtroom. Psychological evidence can carry a lot of weight in court, which makes it a valuable addition to the barrister's arsenal. In my own case, my unusual qualifications of being both a medical doctor and a psychological expert lend a lot of credibility to my report and my testimony. Next to qualifications, how I give evidence is the key to the success and credibility of my testimony.

Before I get to testify, I have to be sworn in, which I'm happy to do. I'm not a religious man, but I follow this tradition and hold the Bible. I give my name and describe my qualifications to the judge if s/he is not familiar with me already or if they want to hear them. Then the barrister who commissioned my report gets up to question me first and take me through the report. I have learned that it's very important to answer the questions – and then stop talking. The court is always under time pressure, so it's essential to be straightforward and succinct when giving evidence. I might expand on certain points or simply reiterate them, with the aim of giving the jury and the judge the clearest possible description of the offender and the crime. Every line of my report is numbered, so I can tell the judge to go straight to line number X, to facilitate quick and clear dissemination of the information.

Rarely is an opposing expert brought in to counter my report for a sentencing hearing, so the entire focus of both teams is what I have written and concluded. This means that when the opposition barrister rises to question me, s/he is going to drill down into the minute details of the report and give me a thorough going-over. They pick apart the points I've made, dissecting the evidence and my interpretation of it. I might be cross-examined by one or two barristers, depending on the case, and of course at all times the judge can interject and pose questions – although the judge tends to withhold questions until the cross-examination is completed. All of this can go on for a long time – anything from ninety minutes to eight hours. The questioning can go round and round in circles, which is tiring and frustrating, but I have to remain calm and composed and on point. I have learned from difficult experiences, when I have been hounded and brought to ground by a barrister, that I must stick to my opinion and never waiver or make a jump of logic. It's also essential not to let tiredness get the better of me and make me sloppy in my answers because then the prosecution brings even more pressure to bear on me. My aim is to be articulate and clear-thinking; their aim is to find a chink in my reasoning or make the judge think that at some juncture in the report I've made a leap of logic without any good scientific backing to do so. It can be visceral and can get very nasty in some cases, especially in the circuit and higher courts where the barristers are extremely capable, sharp and vehemently helping their client. They are very comfortable in that setting and with the role of interrogator, with the result that they can quickly put the expert witness well beyond his/her comfort zone. It's a very mentally demanding experience as you have to keep up with them at every turn and twist.

I have become proficient at testifying over the years, but that was not always the case. I learned a hard lesson in one instance, when I was taken apart by the opposing barrister during my expert testimony. That was a credibility case, where I had assessed the credibility of a child witness to a crime. It was one of my first such cases, and I was not as capable then of articulating succinctly and convincingly the amount of research that informed the report. It is a danger that you get so used to your own work, you don't realise you have to explain the rationale behind some of your opinions. You have to 'sell' the report to the court. It isn't sufficient for the court to know you're an expert: you must be able to articulate fluently how your research contributed to the opinion you formed and the conclusions you arrived at. If you can't do this or if you make the mistake of thinking that stating it makes it so, you'll be slammed by opposition barristers and maybe even by the judge. That is what happened to me in that particular case, and it was a lesson very hard learned.

What I have learned is that when I am more myself in court, more familiar and comfortable, I present better testimony than when I've studied intensely. Too much study makes me stiff and tense, which can lead to unscientific language and thinking. I become locked in myself and it always ends badly and I lose the court's attention and belief. But when I'm comfortable in my own skin, using my own language – which for me is scientific and medical language – then my evidence is much more effective. I have always found judges and juries to be very good listeners and well able to grasp the nuances of my evidence. I work hard to ensure they can understand me clearly and easily, to provide insight about the offender's life, and they meet me halfway by focusing and listening to the evidence presented.

In Andreas's case regarding parental capacity, the outcome was that the child has remained in supervised care. After listening to all of the evidence, the judge concluded that the child's best interests were served by continuing with the foster care and visitation arrangement already in place. With regard to the case about the death of his first child, Andreas has not yet stood trial for that. The justice process can be glacially slow as a case is built and evidence is secured, and that particular case is proving to require lengthy preparation.

As the forensic psychologist, I have to manage my own expectations and those of the people I'm reporting on. If I had followed my alternative career path and gone on to work as an orthopaedic surgeon, the rewards would have been clear and obvious: the patient doesn't die and gets better and has a better quality of life, thanks to medical intervention. In my profession, it's rarely so clear-cut. The idea of a successful outcome is both relative and unique to each case. Sometimes, a suspended sentence is a good outcome, or a shorter-than-anticipated custodial sentence – it's all relative to the events and the evidence. What I do tend to find is that human nature is skewed towards greediness. At first, my client and their family are hugely grateful that I'm involved and they give me all the information I require. They are helpful and hopeful in equal measure. But the more they get, the more they want. So, for example, if a family feared they weren't going to get their child back to live with them and I've worked really hard to come up with mechanisms and recommendations so that the child can return over periods of time, they will complain that it's not quicker, that it doesn't suit their expectations more exactly. No matter how sympathetically generous I am in the report, there is a tendency to keep on demanding and keep on taking. This is probably down to their not recognising a successful outcome because it doesn't match their idea of a successful outcome for them. It means what I do is largely a thankless task, which in turn means the work must be its own reward, the feeling that I've contributed positively in some way.

One of the shortcomings of the Irish justice system is that experts are rarely asked to work together to create a comprehensive and complementary report to present to the court. The various reports are usually presented in segments and autonomously. This can lead to confusion among the judge, jury and legal teams, which is never helpful in the court setting. I would hope to see this change in the future, with a greater sense of cohesion promoted with regard to compiling expert testimony for the benefit of the court.

When the Andreas/Mariana parental capacity case was completed, I discussed it during my bimonthly psychological supervision session. This is a key part of our personal and professional development, and every psychologist must engage in supervision to discuss their cases, to ensure they are coping with the material they have to view/hear and that their personal life isn't affecting their professional life. These sessions allow me to maintain a robust approach to my own psychological work and are invaluable. When I described the difficulty of writing the report with regard to Andreas and his pending court case, it was very helpful to hear the opinion of my supervisor, who agreed with the approach I had taken in the report. When you have a query in your mind about a report or a case, getting this perspective and agreement allows you to draw a line under that case and move on, knowing that you did all you could in the circumstances.

I have had many supervisors over the course of my career, and in different countries, so I've had a chance to learn the difference it can make. A good supervisor makes you feel unburdened, so you don't bring home with you any of the difficult things you've heard/ seen. It can make you feel validated and also reminds you that the work you are doing is appropriate and worthwhile. A helpful, realistic, clear and honest discussion replenishes your energy for your work, bolstering your enthusiasm for the next case load. By comparison, a poor supervisor has the opposite effect, sapping the energy and self-belief and making the work much harder. Truly poor supervision, where the supervisor fails to recognise or tackle bad problem-solving or working approaches, can lead to bad practice and ultimately to a dangerous situation because the psychologist is working under false beliefs. Thankfully, I've never had this degree of poor supervision, although the levels have certainly varied from supervisor to supervisor.

All of the above should have delivered quite a comprehensive picture of the working life of the forensic psychologist. It is an unendingly interesting and challenging job, but I would be lying if I said it wasn't also difficult and demanding. This work exacts a price on the practitioner and the best way to handle that is to admit that fact and ensure you take steps to protect yourself. I have found that doing this work 24/7 simply isn't possible – it's too harrowing and it depletes me mentally and physically. Accordingly, I'm very careful to diversify my working day and week, taking on general patients as well as criminal offenders. I recently interviewed a psychologist to join my practice and during the interview she said she could do forensic work about two days a week but needed to switch to other areas for the other three days. I understood her point entirely and applauded her ability to be so honest with herself and to accommodate her own needs within her work. If you did this work without a break, it would haunt you. It would be an unhealthy state of affairs that couldn't last for long anyway.

I'm often asked why I do this work – many people find it difficult to imagine doing it themselves and wonder how I stay in such a demanding job. To my mind, I'm performing a public service by doing my job well and conscientiously. I hope I am helping to keep society safer and to promote healthy perspectives and great understanding, which is always my goal. I remain respectful of everyone I encounter in my work, and I remain hopeful that each and every person can be a better person and overcome their own disordered thinking patterns. This is why I keep doing this work – because I possess a utopian (even naive!)

idealism about human beings. This idealism stems, I think, from my own psychology, which I strive to keep healthy and balanced, and from my experiences. I have had a very lucky and happy life, which I appreciate hugely and want to share with others. In order to do the work of a forensic psychologist, you must have belief in humanity, optimism, a desire to make a change and help people and a scientist's eye for problems and problem-solving. When you have those elements in your personality, this work is fascinating and gratifying, which I'm very happy to say it is for me.

CHAPTER THREE

THE ROOTS OF CRIME: PARENTS AND FAMILY

'I n essence, X has been a victim of child physical and sexual abuse, but had very little knowledge of how to process that information or be aware of how unhealthy and inappropriate it was throughout his/her childhood. As such, he/she is a prototypical example of what can occur from such an unhealthy childhood development and which has now contributed to a plethora of psychiatric presentations which are integral to his/her personality and have contributed to his/her ongoing offending behaviour for many years.'

This is an extract from a report I wrote about a young offender I assessed. It touches on the key presentations of childhood marked by a lack of love and care: inability to process information correctly and the presence of one or more psychological or psychiatric disorders as a result. This is the consequence of poor parenting and an unpredictable home life, a childhood scenario that very often ends up in my office on the back of a crime committed as an adult.

It would be misleading to describe a 'typical offender' because each crime and perpetrator is unique, but it is fair to say that there are typical background circumstances that constitute a criminogenic environment. While it is true that the majority of offenders I interview are in the low socioeconomic status bracket, usually living in disadvantaged areas, I have learned that it is not the area they are from that predisposes them to crime so much as the parenting they receive and their family circumstances. These factors are absolutely crucial to brain development and psychological development. For a baby born into a chaotic and inconsistent household, it will prove very difficult to grow into a productive, caring, empathetic, hardworking adult. That may sound like a controversial statement, but after eighteen years of interviewing offenders of all types, I am certain that environment, or nurture, is the single biggest determining factor in their lives.

There is a 'nature' element, of course, but it can be ameliorated or worsened by environment. For example, mental health challenges such as depression, alcoholism, bipolar disorder, schizophrenia, with features such as poor anger management and melancholy, all appear to have a preponderance genetically. We don't yet know exactly what genes they are or which are turned on to cause this, but they do seem to have a family history. Any one of us can be born with these genes and will have to deal with those genetic inheritances during the course of our lives. However, if we are born into a stable, loving environment, to parents who exhibit warmth, healthy physical contact, high levels of care, problem-solving ability and ethical behaviour, we are far more likely to develop the mental tools we need to understand and mind our psychological and physical health. If we are born to parents who exhibit challenging or aggressive behaviour, the development of those mental tools is hampered, with often far-reaching consequences.

I have mentioned before how the backgrounds of the offenders I interview can be depressingly similar, and this is true. The templates I've developed for my reports are based on the key things experience has taught me about the criminogenic environment. So if I am faced with an offender from a low socioeconomic background, I can almost recite the likely family circumstances in which he/she has grown up. I would expect to find one or both parents unemployed, an absent parent, poor attitude towards education, little motivation to engage their children in community activities, high prevalence of illness, increased use of substances such as alcohol and drugs, poor sense of social community, no interest in using community services or resources, such as hospitals, libraries and clubs. This household won't have consistent boundaries for children regarding what is right and wrong, stemming from a lack of understanding on the parent's part that he/she must be a leader for their child. When offenders describe their relationship with their parent/s, it's often clear that the parent behaves as a buddy or friend rather than as a parent. The bottom-line problem is that the parent doesn't know how to behave as a parent or as a social citizen – a lack of understanding that probably lies with the grandparents and is very likely, unless there is successful intervention, to be passed on to subsequent generations.

The first ten years of a person's life are crucial to their psychological development. This is when who we are is laid down, layer upon layer. If a child experiences adverse conditions, that is layered into their psychological make-up. As it becomes part of the foundations of the person, it makes it harder to tackle and undo in adulthood. From a psychologist's point of view, up to the age of ten (and beyond, of course) children require strong leadership, strong attachment and firm boundaries with clear expectations regarding behaviour. The presence of these elements leads the child to develop an emotional vocabulary and empathy for others. They should absolutely not witness volatile or violent behaviour, or physical, emotional or sexual violence.

That key concept here is 'witnessing'. What you see as a child, what is role-modelled for you, has a huge effect on your thinking and behaviour. It's the 'monkey see, monkey do' dilemma – if children witness something that they are unable to process properly, they will accept it as the norm and quickly become resigned to it as the way life is lived. This is why victims of child abuse so often don't report what is happening to them, or even accept their abuser's explanation that what is happening is 'normal'. It is this resignation that is likely to lead to self-deprecating behaviour and mental health challenges, with comorbidities such as behavioural challenges. When I was working in Australia at the start of my career, my first assignment – the very first interview I conducted, in fact – was with a man I shall call Alastair. When laid out from A to Z, his story was a chain of events that was always heading in one direction, illustrating the disordered thinking that arises from childhood neglect, abuse and 'witnessing'.

Alistair's family life was chronically disordered. His mother was an alcoholic, unavailable to her children emotionally because of her addiction. His father came and went from the family home at unpredictable intervals, but when he was there he was very violent, meting out daily beatings to his wife and his six children. All the males in the family had a forensic history, with law-breaking seen as a normal way of life. Alistair left school at thirteen and was periodically employed as a labourer. He smoked cannabis and drifted, detached from everyone and everything. During the interview it struck me how all of Alistair's past was written on his body – his constantly shifting eyes that refused ever to meet mine, his lean, rangy, tense body, the scars on his face and arms, the sense that he was there but not there, disconnected from his physical surroundings, unable to engage with me and not sensing his place in the world as valid or important or even present.

The crime he was going to be tried for was rape and murder. When I asked him about what had happened, he spoke freely, describing the incident in detail. This is one of the interesting things I have noted about offenders over the years – they want to tell their story in full and, even though I advise them that anything they specify can be left out of the report, they never ask me to omit anything from the official record. It's as if, once they begin to talk the truth, they have to get it all out and have it detailed properly. Alistair was no different.

It happened at a bar, where Alistair was drinking to excess. He noticed a woman, approached her, was rebuffed. He brooded sullenly, then decided to approach her again. This time, she made it clear she wasn't interested, and her friend laughed. Alistair felt humiliated by this 'bitch' who wanted to make him look stupid in front of the others in the bar. He decided to 'show her who was boss'. He hid outside the bar. The woman came out, alone. He jumped out, surprising her, and they fought as he tried to drag her away. He was stronger and extremely determined, so he succeeded in dragging her to a secluded spot. There, he raped her multiple times, strangled her and, while she was still breathing, stabbed her repeatedly. He described the act of raping her so matter-of-factly, it prompted me to ask him if he had done that before. He shrugged and said he had raped a number of women, although this was the first one he had knowingly killed – he admitted he was usually 'shit-faced' when he carried out rapes, so his memory was completely unreliable as to what had occurred.

In his answers and his thinking, Alistair exhibited a plethora of psychological disorders – attachment disorder, conduct disorder, oppositional defiant disorder, manifesting as aggression against women and misogyny. All of this could be traced back to his childhood and the things he had been forced to witness and try to process. He had resigned himself to being beaten, that violence was the norm, which meant perpetrating violence was second nature to him. It transpired that the whole evening – the drinking, the anger – had been preceded by an argument with his mother. He had felt slighted and unfairly treated by his mother, and he then took out those negative feelings on a substitute woman. He did what he had seen his father do so often – and then pushed it right into murder. Alistair displayed no remorse or guilt, no empathy for his victim or her family, only a cursory understanding that what he had done was wrong. His thinking had become so disordered through the effects of his chaotic upbringing, it had made him capable of cold-blooded murder.

Alistair occupies an extreme end of the spectrum, but the consequences of early experiences are very often apparent in the stories offenders tell me about themselves and their crimes. The key to intervening in this unhealthy psychological development is to catch it early, which is why teachers and social workers are trained to look for the signs that a child has been a witness to violent incidents. There are many possible symptoms, but they include: difficulty sleeping; physical complaints, like headaches, that seem to have no physical basis (somatic maladies); withdrawal from friends and social engagement; aggressive behaviour; acting out/reconstructing violent scenes during play; hypervigilance – constantly worrying and fearful; separation anxiety; regression to baby talk or babyish behaviour; indifference; and concentration problems, which inevitably affect schoolwork. My own work is protected by the fact that I haven't seen the crime being committed, which insulates me against heightened emotional reactions to the offenders I meet. For a young child who is forced to witness violence of any kind, there is no buffer. At a sensitive and susceptible stage in their development, they must contend with the visceral reality of violence and its aftermath and try to put some sense on what they have seen. It's impossible for the growing brain and mind to do this in such a way as to protect the child from it. They are too young, too inexperienced, too raw to be able to keep themselves safe, either physically or mentally. As a result, negative behaviour and emotions become integrated with the child's development, perhaps even their DNA.

In our early lives, good parenting fulfils our primary needs – food, love and sleep – and consistently supports us, allowing for calm and insight to develop. As a result we become sure of ourselves, assertive, confident and equipped with emotional resilience and resolve. We have strong coping mechanisms and are capable of loving others and moving forwards in our lives. Poor parenting, by contrast, makes a child afraid of their own ability, leads to a lack of belief in their assertions and fails to promote education, which affects the child's future life and prospects. In this situation, the parents don't provide the all-important buffer between the child and the world. A good parent allows their child to develop and mature at their own pace, hiding from them the nastiness in the world until they are ready to learn of it. A poor parent puts their child in the position of having to confront the nastiness alone and without any perspective to help make sense of it. This affects the child's identity formation, which in turn affects their understanding of the differences between what is possible or plausible, acceptable or defiant and thoughtful or narcissistic. The lack of learning can have many different repercussions.

The result of poor parenting and a chaotic, unreliable home environment is a lack of attachment. Anyone who remembers the news footage of the babies and toddlers in the cots in Romanian orphanages, exposed to the world after the fall of Ceau escu's regime in 1989, knows what a heart-breaking sight it was. Rows of children, many of whom were clearly distressed, often banging their heads against the cot bars, most of whom looked vacant, as if their souls and minds had retreated from the awful reality of their half-existence. These unfortunate children had received no love, no warm physical contact, no stimulation; they were neglected to an extreme extent. They quickly received help once their plight made headlines around the world, but one of the outcomes was that a psychological research team began to investigate the effects of their treatment on their brains. That work has shown conclusively that brain development is affected by care and environment. This means that the brain responds positively to careful nurturing but is hampered in its growth by adverse conditions. In the case of the abandoned orphans, their early experiences shrank the volume of grey and white matter in their brains and also caused lower-quality brain activity, according to electroencephalography (EEG) measurements, which assess the distribution of neuron activity across the brain. The researchers concluded that children 'who develop a secure attachment actually show enhanced brain activity at age eight' (Nathan Fox, University of Maryland).

Brain growth is, therefore, stimulated by love and attachment. The case of the Romanian children underlines the huge importance of attachment, or bonding, to babies and children. Attachment is developed from initial skin-to-skin contact between baby and mother. As the frequency and proximity increases, oxytocin and other chemicals are secreted in the mother's and the child's bodies, which facilitate a positive relationship as well as compassionate attachment. Over time the attachment becomes strong and assertive – the child knows they are loved and the mother knows that she loves the child. This attachment teaches the child that their love will always be reciprocated, that it is constant and that they can turn to their mother for any need, be it physical or emotional. As the child grows, this primary attachment, and those they foster with other family members, gives them emotional resilience, insight and intelligence. The care bond is the emotional spine of the child's psychological development.

That is the beauty of the attachment mechanism that nature bestows on us. When that becomes interrupted, warped or broken, it leads to ambivalent or avoidant attachment, which is the basis of attachment disorder. Where the attachment to the mother is uncertain, intermittent or absent, the child will avoid seeking help or compassion from others or from its mother, and often won't feel anything for the mother or primary care-giver at all. This leads to emotional disorders, personality disorders and, more often than not, a vulnerability and sense of isolation in that person, which in turn leads them to experience a degree of solitude throughout their life. Their relationships invariably become destructive because they don't have any confidence in their ability to talk and communicate with others. Attachment disorder affects the child's ability to reach developmental milestones, which has negative effects on personal and psychological maturity. Attachment is the primary disorder, but it can give rise to many other types of disorder as the child/adolescent/adult struggles to deal with the consequences, including depression, distorted identity and understanding of the interactive world around them, even contributing to schizophrenia, bipolar disorder and anorexia. From my own work, I think that attachment disorder more often leads to difficulties in coping with emotional stimuli and environmental stimuli later in life, which then manifest as psychological disorders.

The reason why so many offenders present with attachment disorder is because that lack of attachment led to disordered thinking and psychological difficulties, which in turn led to negative coping mechanisms, such as addiction or aggressive behaviour, and that led them to cross the line into criminality due to their desperation for a substance, a feeling or a sense of self. What I have found is that the majority of criminals had a mother who was a single parent who struggled financially, often working a number of jobs to keep the family afloat. The worst cases are those where the mother was entirely absent or, through substance abuse, consistently rejected the offender. The very worst cases are those where there is ambiguous or ambivalent attachment, whereby the mother shows some love, then withdraws it, goes missing and comes back again, or acts erratically and with volatile behaviour. This last type of mothering seems to me to cause the most damage.

An offender who always springs to my mind when considering attachment disorder is a young man called James. He was unusual among my clients because he came from a middle-class family, where both parents worked and provided a stable, reliable home environment. That alone made him stand out, and I was curious to hear how he had come to be facing, and pleading guilty to, a charge of assault and false imprisonment. His legal team were facing an uphill battle because of the violent nature of his offence and because it was not his first offence – the first offence being child sexual abuse. A custodial sentence was inevitable in his case, but they felt that he was unforthcoming about his past and that it might prove to hold mitigating, or at least explanatory, factors. It was in this hope that they asked me to interview him and prepare a report for the court.

I met James in a high-security prison. He was in his forties and seemed indifferent to my presence and to the suggestion that my report could help his case. He told me he was one of four siblings, one of whom, his younger brother, had died at the age of six. I asked about his relationship with his parents, and his face clouded over and he told me that he hated them. He said this in a tone of angry resentment and it was clear the feeling ran deep. I asked about his brother and he told me that he was two years younger than him, so James was just eight when he died, and that he had died of rare form of cancer. His short life was punctuated by hospital visits, tests, medicine, which ate up all of the time, resources and emotions of their parents. After he succumbed to his illness, James's parents were distraught with grief. They were religious people, but that seemed to give them no comfort. In this atmosphere of choking emotions, James, the remaining son, became the focus of his mother's grief. She had been a good care-giver up until now, but after her son's death she began to call James 'useless' and told him that God should have left her younger son and taken James instead. As James put it, 'she wished I was dead'. His parents began to discipline him more and more severely, taking to locking him alone in the garage as a punishment, often for days at a time and without food.

James began drinking alcohol at the age of ten. He progressed to drugs, then from the age of fourteen he became sexually promiscuous – usually with women in their thirties and forties who could buy him alcohol. Between the ages of fifteen and seventeen his parents twice committed him to a psychiatric hospital in an effort to address his addiction. After school he did some vocational training, was married at twenty-four and became a father to four children. Ten years into the marriage, he raped his daughter. He explained this act as the fault of alcohol – insisting that he wouldn't have done such a thing otherwise. He had served ten years in prison for child abuse. He no longer had any contact with his ex-wife or children, nor did he see his parents or siblings. He had become disconnected from everyone who had once mattered. Just like Alistair, he seemed incapable of feeling remorse or understanding fully the consequences of his actions. He was resigned to living as he did, detached from any emotions about his life and how it was affecting others.

The story so far already pointed clearly to attachment disorder, process disorder and post-traumatic stress disorder. The abuse he had suffered at the hands of his parents – physical, mental and emotional – had created a well of anger inside him that could overwhelm him at any time. Given the abuse of his daughter and other incidents, it seemed he often served this anger through violent sexual acts against females. His emotional language was poor – this is something we learn from our parents, but he had not – with a very limited understanding of the perspective and emotions of others. When I asked him what he thought the effect of the abuse would be on his daughter's life, he shrugged and muttered he supposed it would be bad. It was a striking underestimation of the consequences of his actions. I felt he was emotionally numbed, which was consistent with dissociative process disorder, which is marked by dissociated thinking, an uncaring, narcissistic disregard for the effects of one's actions on others, on the environment or on oneself and a self-serving, parasitic nature devoid of feelings of responsibility – the hallmarks of a psychopath. His alcohol and drug consumption was an effort at self-medication, but allied with his impulsivity and poor anger management, it was a dangerous cocktail. True to the criteria of attachment disorder, he showed signs of compromised cognitive processing and lack of attainment of developmental milestones.

At this point, divorced from his past and drifting, James had met a woman and struck up an intermittent sexual relationship. On the night of the current offence for which I was assessing him, the two were drinking heavily. They left the pub and he drove them to her house, where she realised she couldn't find her keys. They argued bitterly about her forgetfulness, then climbed back into the car, had sex, which he claimed was consensual, and fell asleep. Sometime later the woman awoke and, realising they were half-dressed in a car in a now bright street, she shook him awake. As she did so, she said, 'Come on, X, wake up.' The name she used was not James. It was the name of her former boyfriend. This slip enraged James and he started to strangle her because, he said, 'I had to let her know how angry I was.' The woman struggled to get free, finally breaking his grip on her. At this point he began to calm down, so she asked him to drive her to the home of a friend and he did so. At the house she showered while James waited in the sitting room, now feeling remorseful. When she was ready he drove her to the police station, where she made a complaint against him, backed up by the distinct bruising on her neck. James was arrested then released on bail pending sentencing. I asked why he was now in jail if he had been granted bail and he looked very uncomfortable. He admitted he had committed another offence in the meantime but refused to say anything about the latest crime

The script James was now living out had been written in his childhood, when he was powerless to change it. The revoking of attachment by his mother, the verbal abuse and then the physical abuse and confinement without food had all combined to wreck his well-being and his psychological health. Unable to cope and with no one to turn to, he had taken refuge in substance abuse, which had compounded all of his problems. By now, in his forties, he was a serial offender who exhibited psychopathic disorder with features such as disinhibition, impulsivity, narcissism and ego-centrism, all of which were warping his ability to process information and emotions. It was a case that has stayed with me because it shows the very far-reaching consequences of ambivalent or avoidant attachment – the ability of parents to write a destructive narrative for their children that leads them to cross the line, in James's case again and again.

When cases of potential child neglect or abuse come to the attention of the authorities, the State provides a powerful intervention tool in the form of care orders. If granted, these allow a child to be taken out of the care of its parents and placed in foster or residential care. In my work I participate in very many parental capacity cases, called in to assess by HSE social workers working with the Child and Family Agency (CFA). These are generally intricate cases that require a great deal of investigation and reflection on my part because there can be serious consequences to my decision. It's taken seven years to prepare the parental capacity template I now use because I have continually updated it according to new research and according to what I have learned over years in court, discovering what exactly the courts need from me. The template is now comprehensive and tailored for purpose, supported by various psychological scales to assess particular facets of the person's psychology. It is a very intricate assessment, weighing the cost of remaining in an unhealthy environment, which may create attachment disorder, versus a stable 'care' environment without biological ties to the primary care-givers. This is, essentially, a hedging game, but if you use the majority of the scientific and developmental facts at your disposal, the hedge becomes smaller. There is always a risk I may be wrong in my assessment, but generally these are not mysterious cases and therefore quite easy to solve.

Parents' capacity to be consistent care-givers can be adversely affected by substance use and abuse, anger management, immaturity, lack of education, lack of assertiveness and poor confidence, difficulty in understanding the role of a parent and lack of family or community support. A parent who is mired in their own psychological problems, especially if accompanied by substance abuse, is obviously not ready to be a committed parent. There are levels of capacity, but usually those who are incapable stand out clearly in their behaviour and actions. A forensic history, for example, where the parent/s have prior convictions is a big warning sign for future asocial behaviour and must be taken very seriously in parental capacity cases. Often, though, I find parents who want to be good parents but simply lack the skills and know-how to carry out this wish. Upon investigation, this will commonly relate back to how they were brought up – likely a less-than-optimum environment that failed to teach them how to be a good care-giver. But once they have the will to learn, they can change this state of affairs and become good parents and raise their children themselves. It's a question of identifying the right supports for them.

I dealt with a case recently that was of the more intricate variety and could have gone either way. The health authorities requested a report on a young couple with a seven-month-old baby that had been in foster care since its birth. The mother, Sophie, had supervised access to the baby, but the father, Oliver, had been denied access by the social workers involved because of a previous forensic history and because he had exhibited aggressive behaviour towards the social authorities during visits. This behaviour led to concerns for the safety of Sophie and the baby. The concern was that one or both parents might cause deliberate or accidental injury to the baby, which was why I was called in to assess the couple and write a report on my findings.

When I interviewed them, I found two people who had faced challenges in their lives – such as poor education, poverty and unhealthy experiences from their own parents – but who had been in a committed relationship for some time. They had a good support network, including grandparents, and exhibited a solid understanding of what being a good parent involved. I found Oliver to be a decent man, although he sometimes struggled to express his emotions, but he nonetheless had good communication skills and an avid interest in his child's well-being and future happiness. Although denied access, he kept fully up-to-date on the child's progress through Sophie and was clearly focused on his child. This gave me two conflicting perspectives to contend with: the forensic history and aggressive behaviour Oliver had engaged in with social workers; and the people I had sat and talked with, who seemed stable and capable of being good parents. My own conclusion was that the risk of causing any future harm to the baby was moderate to low – especially if ample supports could be put in place to help the couple, such as home help, parenting support, parenting classes, vocational training and employment. But I would have to go into court and argue this case, which meant more evidence was required than the interview alone.

This was a case in which the psychological scales proved essential. I administered a raft of different tests to give me – and the court – a full psychological profile of Sophie and Oliver that would back up my own experiential interviews for assessment. They completed the Psychopathy Checklist, the Rapid Risk Assessment for Sexual Offence Recidivism, the Risk Matrix, the Parenting Stress Index, the Parent–Child Relationship Inventory and the Wechsler Adult Intelligence Scale. The profile I was able to build from this multi-test approach was very important in corroborating my findings. As a result, I was able to confidently recommend that Sophie presented a low risk and Oliver a moderate risk of harming their baby. This comprehensive risk assessment allowed the couple to start supervised access with their baby, with a time frame in place for increased access, leading to unsupervised access and, finally, the return of their baby into their care.

I feel great satisfaction when there is clear evidence to support an approach such as this because it is always a difficult decision to remove a child from its biological parents. When I have to recommend a care order be implemented, I don't necessarily feel good about 'saving' that child. The problem is that I rarely come across cases where the parents are completely indifferent. Instead, I am usually dealing with people who really do want to have their child and be good parents, but there are reasons working against their ability to do that. However, the desire to parent is there – that's exactly why I'm called in, because they are requesting care of their child. So to then go to court to argue against them and convince the court they cannot care adequately for their child does not feel good, even when the accurate assessment states that to be the logical finding. It's very complicated.

In terms of intervention and working to protect children in dysfunctional families, I think it's very important to reach out to them at a young age. There are key developmental milestones between the ages of four and ten years, which is therefore a crucial window of opportunity to prevent or undo the damage of attachment disorder. I have found that once the child reaches teenagehood, it is very difficult to reverse the mental and behavioural crystallisation of family dynamics and the entrenched behaviour. This is a controversial point of view, I'm aware, but my experience has convinced me that intervention must take place between the ages of four and ten to be properly effective. This poses a challenge to the State to put in place the agencies and supports necessary to facilitate early intervention in this manner. The Irish care system has often been criticised, sometimes for very serious failings, but thankfully it's not the case that every child who goes through that system finds it to be a bad experience. Yes, there have been cases where children have been failed by the system, but equally there are plenty of children who are very grateful for the intervention and care they have received. I have seen both sides of this over the years. All of the child protection social work teams I have had the privilege to work with are diligent, intellectually strong and committed to the State's care of children – amazing people.

I worked with a company called Fresh Start for five years, which provided care for children who were protected under State care orders. These children needed to be in residential care because their behaviour was so challenging it required specialist skills and a high level of psychological support. The children were mainly aged between twelve and sixteen. Seamus was one of the children in my care. He exhibited a wide range of psychological disorders, requiring intensive support and counselling. Funding was always a challenge in these sectors, and no doubt still is. We were continually fighting a rearguard action against the agencies who sought to implement cuts and tougher budgets. The children in our care desperately needed that care, and to cut it would have, I knew, dire consequences. This proved to be true. I requested full-time care for Seamus, outlining the extensive support his case demanded. The HSE could not afford it. I ended up in and out of court, arguing the case, pushing for this damaged child to be given the chance to change his life. Before the case had reached its verdict, the reason for it was taken away: Seamus was found dead. He had been murdered, having fallen in with the wrong people. Without help, he was defenceless – it's something that has always stayed with me, this disappointment in my country's ability to take care of these children, the shame of not doing more and the guilt of not preventing fatal harm to him and others.

That was an extreme case, with an extreme outcome. But I have been involved in many cases that have had good outcomes. I always strive very hard for the welfare of young clients like Seamus, mindful of how high the price can be if the State fails them. There is the example of Sarah-Jane, a fifteen-year-old girl I worked with for a number of years. Sarah-Jane was subjected to physical and emotional neglect from both parents and sexual abuse. She was reluctant to talk too much about what had happened at home, but it seemed that she had also witnessed many episodes of her parents sexually, physically and verbally abusing each other. It seemed she had formed an attachment to her mother, but when this was discussed further, it became apparent that this wasn't a healthy attachment, but rather one borne out of guilt on her mother's side and a desire to keep Sarah-Jane dependent on her as a way of coping with that guilt. Her mother's guilt meant she wanted to 'make it up' to her child, not bring up the child. The unhealthy emotional agenda became a deleterious emotional attachment.

The level of neglect Sarah-Jane experienced was severe and it led to her self-harming, exhibiting aggressive behaviour, poor performance in school and withdrawal from her peers. She presented as tough and independent, but the cuts she had made on her own body spoke a different story. Intervention for Sarah-Jane began at the age of fifteen and continued until she was eighteen. I began to work with her soon after and we developed a good rapport. I found her to be deeply distrustful of other's affection for her and to have poor problem-solving ability. She often sought to use physical and verbal intimidation to get what she wanted, becoming challenging and aggressive if she was having difficulty understanding what was being communicated to her. It was a slow process, but step by step we built up a good relationship and she began to talk more freely about her childhood and her emotions. The key to helping Sarah-Jane was consistency – I and her wider care team had to prove that we would consistently be there for her before she would trust us.

Sarah-Jane received a cross-platform care programme with a short-, medium- and long-term plan. She was placed in residential care and after a time developed healthy relationships with the staff members there, with a noticeable change in behaviour as a result. Her self-harming reduced dramatically, her aggressive behaviour became infrequent and she began to think about returning to school and moving on with her life. She formed a secure attachment to her care environment, which had a sustained and dramatic effect on her psychological well-being. This was a case where the various supports came together and worked effectively to protect and counsel a child who was in danger from her parents – and, as a result, from herself. She had caused dangerous harm to herself, but through intervention and support she developed the understanding, self-sympathy and communication skills to name and process difficult emotions. It was a very positive outcome, and Sarah-Jane continues to thrive now that she is away from her parents' home. She is an emblem of hope and the power of intervention to make a true and radical difference in the life of a young person at risk.

The psychological world of the person who crosses the line into criminality is one of disordered thinking and challenging behaviour. When we are victims of crime, we see the behaviour, which is the manifestation of the inner turmoil. That emotional distress is what I normally get to see, demonstrated during my communication with the offenders. The sad fact is that this turmoil has often been forced upon them by the people who were meant to love them and protect them. When parents fail their children, they fail the whole of society by creating an individual who isn't equipped to live a fulfilled life, which could contribute to their healthy development in society. This is not to excuse criminal behaviour – there has to be personal agency and responsibility – but it is important for us, as a social community, to understand this and to seek to put in place supports and interventions to protect children. The role of the family and parents cannot be underestimated with regard to psychological well-being and successful living. It is an important message to get out there, so that people don't shy away from speaking the truth about it. Often a collective sigh is heaved when someone like me says anything remotely like 'it's the parents' fault'. People bristle, feel resentful and often seek to find an alternative reason. But my years of experience have shown me, categorically, that the source of much of the pain in the world – inner and then outer – is poor parenting and poor family circumstances leading to developmental, educational and emotional malnourishment. We have to learn to deal with that, to solve the problems and to place children squarely at the front of community care in order to cultivate positive and progressive psychology.

CHAPTER FOUR

JUVENILE OFFENDERS AND THE CHILDREN COURT

T he 'teenage delinquent' has a long history in popular culture and the popular imagination. Novels like *The Outsiders* (1967) and *Rumblefish* (1975) shocked their audiences with graphic portrayals of teenage gangs, the way they spoke, thought, dressed and behaved. Thus the modern teenager was born and became easy to label: rebellious, lustful, selfish, disengaged, focused only on their peer group, lazy, feckless, monosyllabic. These negative portrayals became the stock character of 'teenager', reinforced in films, books, music and newspaper reports. While the sullen teenager is certainly one aspect, there is also so much excitement and newness in this phase. These are the years of our 'firsts' – first kiss, first cigarette, first alcoholic drink, first time to leave home, first sex. For many young people, though, it can also be a time of first trouble with the law, maybe first arrest, possibly first detention. It's an easy time to lose one's way and step off the path and into the wilderness, not least because during this time we are trying to define who we are, who we will be, what we want from our lives and what we shall do with our lives. These are the big existential questions, and we face them in a particularly volatile and vulnerable moment in our lives, when there are so many demands on our minds, brains and bodies. In terms of my work with juvenile offenders, I'm very aware that how a young offender interacts with those assigned to help him/her can have a huge impact on the rest of their life. It's an onerous responsibility and brings with it the prospect of succeeding gloriously or failing miserably.

What I have found through my work is that the two greatest factors influencing a teenager's life and choices are their parents and their peer group. Where family circumstances are settled and reliable, with loving, stable relationships and good role-modelling, the child of that family is highly likely to meet their developmental milestones and progress through their teenage years without ever crossing the line into criminality. A healthy developmental process is marked by several key milestones. So between six and nine months of age, the baby learns that its behaviour has consequences, and may also learn to recognise the word 'no' at this time. By seven months of age, the baby can reliably detect facial expressions of anger. Increasing physical development, cognitive abilities, social skills and receptive language skills as they grow leads to improved abilities to respond to verbal directions. By the age of two, children are generally able to follow simple instructions. Between the ages of two and three, non-compliance with simple instructions is high, but compliance levels subsequently increase with age. In the preschool years, anger and aggression are common to all children, but their coping mechanisms become more sophisticated over time. By the age of five, children are expected to comply with adult requests the majority of the time. Between the ages of seven and ten, children have learned to identify verbalisation of feelings as the most appropriate means of self-expression, followed by facial expressions. By this stage, children have come to understand that the ability to maintain emotional control is important to their social functioning and happiness. Typically in developing children, aggressive behaviours follow a declining trend with age during childhood and adolescence. While boys exhibit more aggressive behaviour than girls, and from very early on, by late adolescence the rates of aggression in males and females are indistinguishable.

Parents teach their children empathy and remorse, two key traits in the disinhibition of negative behaviours. From the ages of ten to twelve our self-awareness and emotions become far more regulated. We become insightful, talking about how we feel, how others may affect us, but gaining more empathy for others also and how the feelings of others may be affected by our actions. Years twelve to sixteen are marked by puberty and adolescence primarily, but also by an increasing awareness of independence and life choices. If a child struggles in secondary school, this can be a very difficult time. There can be many reasons for poor performance at school, such as a chaotic family environment, attention disorder or learning disability. If this is not addressed and remedied, it can quickly lead to aggressive or deviant conduct, truancy and withdrawal. If this occurs, the damage is done by age fifteen or sixteen, by which time the child may be engaging in high-risk behaviours, such as fighting, stealing and joyriding and arson.

We cannot place the blame for such behaviour entirely at the feet of the adolescent or young offender. Our primary environment is provided for us by our parents. While we are small, immature, inexperienced and vulnerable, we are completely reliant on our parents for our welfare, safety and nurturing. When these needs are absent in the home, it disrupts the developmental trajectory and creates psychological and emotional difficulties in the child. Of course, immaturity makes it extremely difficult to process and manage these difficulties, and the child often chooses inappropriate and harmful coping mechanisms instead, such as aggression, self-harming, substance abuse, bullying, shoplifting or membership of a gang, all of which are impulsive behaviours, devoid of inhibition. Once the young person has set off on this road of blind self-medication, it invariably leads to even more negative thoughts, experiences, emotions and behaviours. Typically, if they have been failed by their parents, they will find a peer group that will give them validation and affirmation. If this group is engaged in inappropriate or criminal behaviours, the child is immediately at risk of escalating their behaviour to this level. If the child has followed this unhealthy developmental trajectory, there is a distinct possibility that they will cross the line and end up in an interview room with me.

Over the course of two years, I worked with a young teenager called Harry. His story illustrates well how a child can end up as a juvenile offender. I first met Harry when he was fourteen, at which time he was residing in a children's detention centre. A child can only be detained in such a centre by a court-issued Detention Order, and that is considered the solution of last resort. The court will exhaust all community-based options before agreeing to detain a child. If a child has been so detained, it means they have been persistently engaging in antisocial behaviour. So after reading the reports on Harry and considering where he was, I went to our first interview fully expecting to meet a tough, sullen, non-communicative kid with plenty of attitude.

Harry had received his Detention Order on foot of a charge of joyriding and driving without licence or insurance. The traffic police are very strict regarding such offences, building up a list of charges against the offender that would typically include dangerous driving, reckless endangerment and damage to property. As a result, he had received a twenty-four-month residential order (and typically would serve twelve to sixteen months of that sentence), the conditions of which included psychological therapy once a week. At the time, I was working two days a week at the secure detention centre, which is how I got to know and work with Harry. When he walked into our first session, he was very different from what I had expected. He was a boy of just fourteen years, but sported a shaved head and a strong jawline. He was slim and fairly crackling with energy, unable to sit still, always moving and shifting about. I liked him immediately – he was a talker, with a great sense of humour and an engaging, charming way about him. We established a rapport very quickly, chatting and laughing about this and that, him telling me tall tales like a professional storyteller.

He was very easy to like – he was just so full of life and vigour. I was used to monosyllabic answers, long silences, no eye contact and a lot of 'f**k yous', so Harry was like a breath of fresh air.

We started to talk about his background, and it quickly became clear that he filled all the criteria for a damaged and difficult childhood. His life wasn't entirely devoid of love and care, but it was enough to have caused him emotional turmoil. His mother had walked out early on, leaving him with his father, who was a drug addict prone to aggressive and violent outbursts. When it became obvious that this one-parent situation was harmful to Harry, he was taken in and raised by his grandparents, who cared for him as best they could. The lack of a maternal attachment can cause serious psychological disorders, as we saw in Chapter 3. The same held true for Harry, who was haunted by his mother's absence and her act of rejection in leaving him. The time spent in his father's sole care had left him on edge, finding it difficult to concentrate, and he had of course witnessed substance abuse and violent behaviour, which he had struggled to process. When his schoolwork fell below par, he responded by not trying at all. Given that his social workers had noted attention deficit and hyperactivity, his poor school performance could well have indicated a learning disability, but this possibility had never been explored. By the age of thirteen, he was cutting school regularly and eventually he got caught up in a group of older adolescents who didn't go to school at all and instead hung around, drinking, taking drugs and drifting.

Harry had far more energy than his aging grandparents, so he was well able to ignore their pleas and lectures and go his own way. Still only thirteen years of age, he was now roaming the streets at night, drinking and open to trouble. His peer group took to stealing cars and joyriding, and Harry threw himself into this exciting new pastime with his customary high energy. It is a common factor in adolescents with a history of viewing and experiencing socially deviant behaviour that they require greater risks to achieve arousal, which can lead to recklessly high-risk behaviour. Harry was now in this category, spinning out of control, apathetic, drunk more often than not because he was self-medicating against his emotional pain and disengaged from all social norms and from his family. For their part, Harry's grandparents were distressed and fearful about his new friends and behaviours. They contacted social workers, asking for help, but as so often in the cash-strapped community services sector, help was not available. As Harry now had a reputation as a troublemaker, it wouldn't be possible to find a foster home placement for him, and there were no residential care places available. There was nowhere else for him to go, so the social workers got on with helping those they could, and Harry's grandparents watched as their grandson disappeared from their grasp.

Harry described all of this to me in his own way, frequently blaming everyone else in his life for all he had done. He seemed to lack an understanding of his own actions, and he certainly wasn't taking responsibility for them – it was someone else's problem. Yet I was fascinated to hear how he spoke about his father. He didn't blame his father for anything. In spite of the years of physical abuse and neglect he had suffered at this man's hands, Harry's face lit up whenever he was mentioned. He described him as 'a legend' and told me that he loved seeing him. I asked how often that was, and he told me he got to see his father about twice a year, for just one hour each time. This was the father's own choice, it being all the time he felt he could spare to spend with Harry. It seemed very little on which to build a relationship, but Harry insisted that his father liked him and they were great friends. This worried me because by putting his father on a pedestal, there was a risk that Harry was also putting his behaviour on a pedestal, which would mean he saw substance abuse and violent aggression as acceptable. A child will copy what it sees, even if what it has seen caused it harm. To witness criminal behaviour is one of the worst things that can happen in a young child's life, often predisposing that child to repeating that behaviour. I feared that Harry might fall under that sort of disordered thinking, especially as he seemed unable to think objectively about his father's role in his life.

Harry's case was quite typical in terms of his emotional and psychological trajectory, the abuse and neglect he had suffered, the effect of this on his cognitive processing and the emotional effects his childhood had produced. It is common for children with this sort of background to present with depressive disorder and anxiety, and I felt Harry was no different. He also exhibited poor emotional language and control, which resulted in deep feelings of anger that he often gave vent to through aggressive behaviour. The fact was that Harry's difficult childhood experiences had given rise to a level of mental health illness that was affecting all of his behaviour and thinking. This is an extremely common presentation amongst juvenile offenders. The most common juvenile disorders I see and work with are depressive disorder, oppositional defiance disorder and conduct disorder, attention deficit hyperactivity disorder featuring aggression, non-compliance, impulsivity and disinhibition. These will typically be accompanied by deflecting of/inability to accept responsibility for one's actions, emotionally labile (i.e. mood swings), quick to temper, resentful, spiteful or vindictive. These are the damaging outcomes of an interrupted or disrupted psychological and emotional development.

The umbrella term 'antisocial behaviour' covers oppositional defiance disorder, conduct disorder, aggression, impulsive behaviours and attention problems. When antisocial behaviours constitute legal violations, they become delinquent behaviours. It is not required to provide an extensive study of each of the above here, but it is useful to give a brief overview of these common disorders that afflict young offenders – and often cause them to become serial offenders right into adulthood.

Antisocial behaviour means any behaviour that violates basic norms, rights and rules. Impulsive behaviours are uncontrolled outbursts, such as interrupting others, having difficulty waiting in turn or being unable to sit in a chair for the duration of school – or sometimes even dinner. Aggression is behaviour deliberately aimed at harming people, such as hitting other children. It is unacceptable and will be punished by adults, but the child must be taught to understand why it is wrong and what other coping mechanisms are available. We have already noted that aggressive behaviour declines with age, but it is also the case that in adolescence non-physical forms of aggression can take its place and can be just as damaging. So, for example, teenagers often engage in verbal threats, demeaning language and name calling, malicious gossiping and threatening to withdraw friendships. To this must now be added cyberbullying and threatening behaviour via social media. People are more aware of attention problems now, but it's still very possible for them to go unnoticed and undiagnosed. The best-known attention problem is probably attention deficit hyperactivity disorder (ADHD), but even a simple attention problem such as not following through on instructions can be very disruptive.

Conduct disorder (CO) is characterised as a repetitive and persistent pattern of behaviour in which the basic rights of others or the major age-appropriate social norms are violated. There are four groups of behaviours under this heading: aggressive conduct, nonaggressive conduct that causes damage to property, deceitfulness or theft, and serious violations, e.g. sex crimes. The symptoms of CD are aggression towards people and animals, bullying, threatening and intimidating others, initiating physical fights, use of a weapon, physical cruelty to people or animals, forcing another into sexual activity, destruction of property, arson, theft and lying. I would encounter these sorts of behaviours regularly among young offenders – indeed, some of them are the reason for arrest and detention.

Finally, oppositional defiance disorder (ODD) is defined as a recurrent pattern of negative, defiant, disobedient and hostile behaviour towards authority figures and is very common in juvenile delinquents. A range of oppositional behaviour may be identified, from passive to active forms of resistance. If a child ignores a parental direction, that is classified as passive non-compliance. If the child directly refuses a parental command, that is mildly active non-compliance. If they angrily reject parental instructions or prohibitions, that is a form of severe non-compliance or defiance. Most children who meet the criteria for child-onset CD also meet the criteria for ODD, which are non-conformity with societal expectations, aggressive language against authority figures, anti-authoritarianism and irreverence to rule and regulations, including comorbidities with deficits in verbal intelligence and executive functioning. Both CD and ODD are associated with an increased risk for later process disorders with substance abuse and antisocial personality disorders, as well as anxiety disorders, eating disorders, schizophreniform disorder and mania. Offenders can be classified in many different ways, but one of the categorisations is that of early starter, which means the first offence occurs in childhood, pre-adolescence. For these offenders, the early starter pathway often leads to serial offending, commonly across their lifespan. This is because the early start precludes involvement with healthy peer groups, which reject them, and participation in schools and normative learning environments also quickly become closed to them. By comparison, those whose first offence occurs in the adolescent years, who are termed late starters, are more likely to experience offending as a temporary hiatus in their life. The reason for this is that the typical early starter has significant difficulties with regard to violence, mental health and substance use, stemming from the high levels of stress they have experienced in childhood, while the late starter's behaviour may just be rooted in negative peer leadership.

Of course, the course of adolescence is further exacerbated by sexual development and now by social media as well. The adolescent can be at the mercy of their hormones, curious, full of emotional conflict, wanting to experiment but afraid to – it can be a confusing and anxious time for them. It takes much support and empathy to develop a healthy sexual identity, but this can be corrupted and fragmented by unwanted sexual activity, sexual bullying, fears around one's orientation or having witnessed sexual or physical abuse as a child. The psychological self is fragile, and children and adolescents who aren't treated with care can be damaged, sometimes irreparably. Today's teenagers also have to contend with the global phenomenon of social media, which can have positive and negative effects on their lives. There are many obstacles for them to navigate and if they are, like Harry, without effective parental input, love and guidance, it becomes tremendously difficult to get through those uncharted waters without capsizing.

As we have seen, when the circumstances conspire to produce mental ill health, deep anger and a feeling of helplessness, the young person is primed for criminal behaviour. One of the key traits I have noticed in young offenders is an inability to see any future for themselves. 'What are you going to be when you grow up?' is a question children are forever being asked by curious adults, but it does serve the purpose of making them envisage a future, of seeing themselves as a person with a future – even if they have to give up on the superhero dream at some point. But for the young offenders I interview, there is a striking similarity in their complete lack of interest in creating a future. They don't think that way, and if I suggest it, they don't feel it's something they can do. Their future notions are vague and ill-fitting, like they've borrowed someone else's ideas just to be able to provide an answer to the question. They don't think of their offending in terms of what it's taking away from them – such as reputation, employment, foreign visas, for example – because they don't have any ownership of those things, of those futures. They look ahead and see more of the same, an unending horizon of law-breaking and punishment and not caring either way. This has a deadening effect that heightens their emotional withdrawal and their lack of a sense of purpose – factors that allow a person to cross the line.

Harry's offences were relatively typical of the juvenile offender – truancy, fighting, substance abuse, stealing, joyriding. These are the 'gateway' offences, and the offender either realises that and decides to change course, or they fail to realise it, or fail to care, and they continue on to become an adult offender. For those of us tasked with working with them and treating them, this is a crucial time, when they are still young enough to make significant changes and not have an adult criminal record in their name. There are numerous treatment options available, but for Harry I recommended one-to-one weekly sessions, with specific CBT interventions. The CBT sessions would focus on anger management, as that had been identified as one of Harry's key behavioural problems. He was doing well in the one-to-one sessions with me, being open to discussion and new ideas about why he did the things he had done. He was now comfortable enough with me to talk about his family, his feelings and his crimes, which was a good step forward. My hope was that CBT would break through his myopic view of how to cope with the world. When he was confronted or talked to in a way he didn't like, he would go on the attack, lashing out with punches and kicks. I asked him if he felt this was the best response, and he told me it was, that if someone disrespected him he was obliged to hurt them in return. It was a black-and-white matter for him, and my suggestions that he could try talking, staying calm, dealing with it differently, made him incredulous – in his mind, there wasn't a single other option than hitting out, and he was right to do it.

The CBT did seem to be helping to an extent. I showed Harry breathing exercises to control his reactions and helped him to see the triggers he should be aware of that would announce an angry outburst was likely, so he could deflect it. We did role-playing, acting out scenarios and the possible ways of handling them. I then decided to expand this into a group CBT session, something I had seen work very well during my time in Australia. The first session went very well, with all the boys listening and seeming interested in the process and the hoped-for outcomes. The second session did not go well. I posed a simple question – what makes you angry? – and one boy said he got angry when people didn't take him seriously. Harry burst out laughing. The boy shot him a sullen look and demanded to know what the f**k he was laughing at. There was a split second of silence, and then it happened. Harry leapt across to where the boy was sitting, knocked him back onto the floor and pummelled his face with his fists. I was so shocked, it took a few moments to react, then I hit the alarm and a number of care workers rushed in and helped me to drag Harry off the boy. After all the time I'd spent with Harry, it was hard to make sense of seeing him like that – breath ragged, face twisted in rage, fists clenched, ready to beat up the world. His victim was in a bad way, bleeding and bruised, with a broken nose and suspected broken jaw. It was a horrible scene to witness. It was also a very difficult moment, seeing all the hard work we'd done washed away in a tide of violent anger. But that feeling didn't last long. I knew I had to start again, that Harry was open to treatment and that it was his only chance of learning to control his behaviour so incidents like this one didn't happen again. I had to continue to hope that he would change his thinking, then he could change his ways.

It can always happen that there is a 'one step forwards, two steps back' dimension to treatment, especially with juvenile offenders who can be emotionally labile, immature and who put up a lot of 'front' to hide their feelings and experiences. It is one of the key traits of a forensic psychologist that they exhibit great optimism and hope and trust in their work, and that applies to me too. An incident such as that with Harry does have an effect, of course, but I've seen enough such incidents to know that it's not definitive – it doesn't spell the end of the line for that person. Even though I had seen Harry at his worst, he was still a funny, talkative, energetic and likeable young man and I felt he could be brought around to viewing his life and his behaviour from a different, more helpful angle. He could overcome the difficult start to his life and go on to be a happier and healthier person. This was my hope for Harry. I moved on to other work from that detention centre soon after, leaving Harry behind in the capable hands of the other care workers in the centre. I hoped to one day hear news of him, but it would be a number of years before I heard his name again.

The hope I had that Harry might turn things around and change his life isn't a hope that always exists when it comes to the psychopathic offender, which makes such offenders very difficult to work with in any meaningful way. Psychopathy will be examined in detail in Chapter 9, but it is relevant here because of a boy whose case has always stayed with me. Conor was a juvenile offender who scored high on the psychopathic scale, a result that was borne out by my experience working with him over the course of six months.

I met Conor when, like Harry, he was resident in a secure detention centre. He was thirteen years old and was remanded in detention because he had absconded from school and had committed acts of arson. This was his latest antisocial behaviour, but from the age of about five he had been engaged in serious bullying behaviour. This is why Conor's case has stayed with me, because he was a very disturbed person, sometimes sinister and difficult to be around, and yet he was so young. He was skinny and looked like the quintessential nerdy victim of the beefy bully, and yet he remains the worst bully I have worked with, deeply manipulative and with absolutely no sense of remorse. His psychopathic personality tendencies emerged early on. He tormented his infant classmates with threats about breaking into their homes at night and killing them or hurting their mothers. When parents began to complain about night-time bed-wetting and children too terrified to sleep without the lights on, the resultant fuss didn't bother Conor at all. He seemed to enjoy it and came up with new threats to whisper into their ears. He had also enjoyed torturing animals, doing things like tying them to railway lines, then watching as the train approached and the animal struggled wildly to get free, before being crushed to death. This is regarded as a serious warning signal for future criminal behaviour and psychopathy as it takes a huge amount of detachment and lack of empathy to commit such acts.

Interviewing Conor was always very difficult as he was clever, insightful and manipulative in equal measure. I would ask questions, and he would counter with deeply personal questions, designed to make me uncomfortable and sabotage the attempt at conversation. I did learn that he came from an impoverished background and a broken family: his father was violent towards

his wife, eventually walking out on her and their two sons when
Conor was six years old and cutting himself off from them entirely.
His mother did her best, but the combination of poverty and a
difficult, troublesome child finally defeated her, and her two boys
were taken into care. Conor's brother went to a foster home,
but with his record, no one was willing to take on Conor. He
had been apprehended for arson, which indicated an escalation
in his antisocial behaviour. He started small, but the thrill was
intoxicating and he began to set bigger and bigger fires, with no
regard whatsoever for the consequences. The more panic a fire
caused, the more he enjoyed it. This is a characteristic of the
psychopathic character and the reason why arson appeals to them
so much: it involves premeditation, planning and delivers joy
and satisfaction in witnessing the shock and upset it causes. His
behaviour was dangerous, worrying and escalating: that was why
he had ended up living in a secure residential unit.

At the residential unit, Conor quickly set himself apart from
the other boys through his behaviour. He orchestrated a sustained
bullying campaign, watching carefully to see who the lonely boys
were, the vulnerable ones, those who didn't receive visitors. Once
he had identified their Achilles heel, he would start his subtle
remarks – for example, he would ask a boy if he had received any
visits that day and when told no, Conor would say something like,
'No one likes you, do they? You've really got no one who cares
about you at all, do you?' It was insidious, designed to get under
their skin and speak to their fears and worries. These boys were
already fragile, so this devious whispering could really bother
them, making them feel even worse about their situation. There
were a number of occasions when Conor's whispering resulted in
him receiving a beating from someone he'd pushed too far, but
he seemed entirely unconcerned when this happened. In fact, he
seemed to gain some level of satisfaction from the beating, from
being able to have such a demonstrable effect on his target. Each
time a new boy entered the unit, Conor would be first to befriend
him. He would put himself across as kind and trustworthy, helping

out the newbie, but the pattern was always the same: once he had their trust, he would crush them with a deliberately horrible act, such as stealing prized possessions from them, destroying a letter from home or putting insects in their food. As a result of his constant baiting of the other boys, the staff often had to confine him to a room of his own, for his own protection.

I did my work as well as I could with Conor, but it was a difficult task. Contrary to the beliefs I had held until now, I felt there was something unpleasant about him, that it permeated his whole personality and was somehow at the base of it. I suppose I mean that it seemed like his nature, which is a difficult thing to accept in such a young person – it seems wrong, somehow, to think of a child being intrinsically 'bad', but that's how Conor came across. This struck me afresh one day when his mother came to the unit to visit him. When Conor entered the room, it was as if she held herself smaller and tighter – for all the world like she was scared of him and flinching before an attack. Conor's behaviour around her was also very interesting. He held her in a long and grippingly tight hug, but it looked more like an assertion of control over her person than a loving gesture. In my mind's eye I saw an image of a tree caught in the chokehold of ivy. That was how Conor hugged his mother, and that was how she endured it.

In sessions with Conor, I tried to focus on his arson attacks because they seemed to hold the key to his thinking. Setting fires is an act of power by a powerless person, by someone who is deeply affected by the feeling of having no control of their life, that they are drowning in chaos. The fire is an externalising of those feelings into the environment; this is in contrast to those who self-harm, which serves the same function but the feelings are internalised and the act carried out against the self. The act of self-harm is a release and it hurts no one else. Arson, on the other hand, is premeditated and malevolent, the act of someone whose hatred is directed outwards. Conor had tortured animals for the same reason – directing the hatred outwards onto a defenceless victim. These actions suggested a level of psychopathy, so I administered the Psychopath Scale with Conor. As I had feared and suspected, he scored high for psychopathy. The personality characteristics of psychopathy are an absence of empathy, guilt and anxiety, shallow emotions and an inability to form and sustain lasting relationships. The defining features in children are callous, unemotional traits: lack of guilt and empathy and callous use of others for one's own gain. Conor's behaviour meshed with the criteria and pushed his behaviour into a more dangerous category.

I decided to treat Conor with CBT and active listening, as well as emotional focused therapy (EFT), focusing on teaching him empathy for others, introducing a new narrative that would allow him to understand the emotions of others, as well as his own. Promoting the value of emotions and rewarding him for rating generosity and empathy highly in turn would reduce his desire to cause harm. For a while I thought it was achieving some good, but that was only because Conor was so clever at manipulation. He would appear to be listening intently, his answers would suggest these new ideas were taking hold, he said all the right things and behaved like his moral compass had been switched on at last, but slowly I realised that this was all a game to him. There was no change, he didn't care in the slightest about the emotions of others and he continued his bullying tactics within the unit. It's a very difficult thing, as a psychologist, to realise that someone might be beyond help, but with Conor I felt his thinking and behaviour were already entrenched. He received huge stimulation and pleasure from upsetting others, from prodding the other boys into extreme reactions, and this seemed to be his only source of pleasure. All other options presented to him came nowhere near the high delivered by his tormenting behaviour. I eventually came to realise that the only reason he participated in our sessions was because he enjoyed the level of attention it gave him. Otherwise, it meant nothing to him. This detachment made him hard to care for and to invest concentration into because I was essentially trying to administer treatment to a person who didn't care and who I really didn't like at all.

In my work with an offender like Harry, there is always something likeable about them, something human to ground the therapy and make me feel that there is good reason for optimism and a way to move forwards. With Conor, there was an emptiness that was chilling. I prepared my assessment for the court and in it concluded that Conor posed a high risk of reoffending. I told the court that he had to stay on at the secure unit because the escalating nature of his behaviour suggested he would move on from damaging property and animals to damaging people. He couldn't be let out into society, but required ongoing and extensive treatment in an effort to quell and control his psychopathic urges. I later found out that he had been released for a time, but during his release he set a huge fire in a commercial building, almost killing the ten people who were inside the building at the time – a fact that didn't remotely deter his actions. For this crime he received a twenty-year prison sentence, which he is still serving.

Conor was like a dark spot, sucking all the light out of people's lives, whereas Harry was a bright spark, which is why he also made such an impression on me. But I have worked with very many juvenile offenders over the course of my career, in Ireland, England and Australia. Once they have been apprehended for criminal behaviour – once they have crossed the line – in Ireland, if they are under eighteen, they fall under the remit of the Children Court, which must review their case and decide on the best course of action. The age of criminal responsibility has been raised to twelve (from seven, which corresponded with the Catholic Church's 'age of reason'), so the Children Court is involved in all manner of cases involving very young children and juveniles. The psychological assessment is an important part of the testimony on the child's behalf, but there are other reasons for conducting interviews with children and with young offenders, primarily to assess credibility and to assess suggestibility.

Over the past five to ten years I've noticed a big increase in the number of credibility cases I'm asked to work on. When I'm asked to assess a child's credibility, it means I must assess the credibility of the narrative supplied by a witness or victim in order to ascertain if it can be used in evidence to prosecute the perpetrator. It's normally the case that I'm asked in by the prosecution, but on occasion I've been invited to assess by the defence, in order to nullify the witness testimony submitted, i.e. discredit the child's testimony. In order to assess credibility, I watch the recordings of the police interviews with the child and then I interview the child in person. I examine whether the questioning by the police was appropriate or whether it was leading the witness, which is always a possibility with a young and frightened witness who may also be the victim of the crime being prosecuted. Credibility can be rated as high or low. A high level of credibility means the evidence can be submitted to the court. A low level indicates that the witness may be lying, misremembering, is highly suggestible or was coerced to deliver an inaccurate story or account of events. The factors that contribute to a rating of high or low are memory control, accuracy of recall, ability to explain the facts, age-appropriate language, comprehension of the questions posed, specificity of the narrative, whether the memory is of an episode or an understanding of the meaning (which may be highly subjective).

There are a few reasons why I'm seeing more of this type of work. The 2012 referendum of children's representation in court advocated for the child's voice to be heard during the judicial process, which means their evidence is now thoroughly heard and can be used as a cornerstone on which to build a case against the defendant. As a result of this, the court demands that such witnesses are given adequate assessment and that the credibility of their evidence also be assessed. The child's voice may be represented by social workers, solicitors or guardian-ad-litems, among others. It's probably also the case that lawyers have seen how helpful and useful assessment and credibility investigation have been in recent cases, and therefore are convinced of its efficacy and seek it out as a tool to help their cases. It is extremely interesting work for me and makes an important contribution to the course of justice.

The credibility assessment can aid the course of justice and ensure a child's true testimony is given full weighting as evidence. This is crucial in seeking justice for the child, correct sentencing and appropriate treatment thereafter for the both abuser and child. I was asked to assess the credibility of a ten-year-old girl called Matilda, who had alleged serious sexual abuse against her mother's boyfriend and two of his friends. The defence had questioned the child's credibility as a witness, requesting her statement to be withdrawn from evidence. This was when I was called to assess her ability to bear witness to the allegations made. Those allegations were deeply disturbing: this young girl, who came from a chaotic home where her mother's boyfriend lived intermittently, was regularly brought to a house where her mother's boyfriend and his two friends would force her to administer oral sex and facilitate their masturbation. She alleged that each man took turns to take her into a bedroom or into the bathroom for this purpose. When I spoke to her, it soon became clear that she was telling the truth and was a credible witness. This stemmed from the fact that she described the alleged activities with a sexual knowledge beyond appropriate for her years, her retelling of the story was completely consistent over the course of three separate interviews with the police and with me, she was able to mimic the sexual acts accurately and in a manner that was completely inappropriate for the knowledge to be expected of a child of that age, she had a good recall of times and dates and an excellent memory for specifics and facts not relevant to the actual offending, such as colour of bedroom, the swings in the back garden, the structure and layout of the house. In addition, she exhibited appropriate distress and emotion as she provided her statement to the police. I was able to recommend that her witness statements be deemed admissible, and her abusers were convicted of sexual crimes against her and sentenced accordingly.

The bars to credibility are factors such as compromised information processing due to low level of education, vulnerability to exploitation by others, a desire to appease the interviewer, being

very affirmative in all answers, not wanting to be overly assertive or
to upset the interviewer and a high level of suggestibility. This last
factor – suggestibility – is another key area of work in my practice.
There are generally two strands to it: assessing the suggestibility
of a witness, and assessing the suggestibility of an offender and its
role in the offence.

In terms of the suggestibility of a witness, this relates to how
the witness was interviewed by the police, the types of questions
put to him/her and his/her ability to answer those questions
objectively. If a person is suggestible, asking them leading
questions that prompt them to answer in a particular way can
lead to non-objective or even dishonest answers, even though
the person him/herself might not realise that this is happening.
It's a tricky area – on the one hand, there is the police, who are
trying to do their work and ascertain the truth and bring a case
to court, while on the other stands a witness, or even perpetrator,
who could prejudice their own case because of their suggestibility
during the interview. Naturally, solicitors and barristers are always
concerned if a client seems to fall under this category because it
can go against the presentation of an accurate argument, which
could in turn pervert the course of justice. There has been a lot
of research conducted into this extreme aspect of suggestibility,
for example with Gareth Pearce, the barrister for the Birmingham
Six, who were the victims of false confessions and a miscarriage of
justice in the aftermath of the Birmingham bombing in 1975. The
police are now well trained to question objectively, but the process
remains complex relative to witnesses' learning abilities, emotional
fragility and other developmental aspects of their personality.

I worked on a suggestibility query on behalf of a young man
called Shane that was typical of this sort of case. Shane was
accused of murder, but was pleading guilty of assault only because
he claimed that, while he was present during the events that led
to the death of the victim, he had not participated. The assault
had taken place on New Year's Eve, when people were drinking,
partying and having fun. Shane left the house where the party was

on in order to return home, and an older male friend walked with him. On their way, the other man's sister ran frantically towards them, screaming that she had been attacked and pointing in the direction in which her alleged attacker had fled. Shane and his friend set off in pursuit, running into the darkness in search of the man. They caught up with the man, and Shane admitted that he punched him once in the face. At this point, his memory went blank. The next thing he could remember was hearing the wailing sirens of approaching police cars, at which point he ran back to the party house, lost himself among the guests and forgot about what had happened. The next day he found out that the alleged attacker had died of injuries sustained in the assault on him by Shane's friend, and Shane went to the police station and presented himself for questioning.

By the time Shane was sitting across from me, he still could not recall the central events of that night, but he had been shown CCTV of the vicious attack that killed the man and had admitted that he was present, had assaulted the man and had run away from the scene. However, he also still maintained that he threw only one punch and took no further part in the assault, which he believed made him innocent of the charge of murder. Shane and I talked about the night in question, then I broadened out the discussion to get a better sense of his personality. He had no forensic history and was employed in a warehouse, where he was consistent in his timekeeping and work routine, but it quickly became apparent that he had no interest in anything beyond work and home. He lived with his grandmother, who cared for him well, but over the past few years his tendency to introversion had become chronic, leading to lack of motivation, low mood, social withdrawal and isolation. He exhibited guilt, remorse and empathy with the victim and his family, his mood shifting constantly during our discussion from tearful apology to terse defence of his actions that night. Taken altogether, his presentation suggested mild to moderate depressive disorder. This personality type is susceptible to exploitation by peers and role models, with a tendency to go along with the crowd unthinkingly. I recorded in my report: *appears to be susceptible to compliance and leadership by others whether they are in authority or a negative role model ... poor understanding of social cues and suggestibility presents this person as a vulnerable individual.*

In order to further my assessment, I administered the Gudjonsson Suggestibility Scales (GSS 2), which are the gold standard of assessing suggestibility. As predicted, Shane scored high on the scale, with a rating of 12, which put him at a greater level of suggestibility than 60–65% of the population. This indicated a relatively high level of vulnerability to suggestion. I then examined footage and a transcript of the police interview with Shane, applying what I had learned of his personality. There were clear occasions when his answers were the result of his desire to say what he felt they wanted to hear, even if it went against himself. There were examples of questions that were not open-ended, which meant they invited a particular answer, which Shane was too willing to give. For example, saying *Were you delighted to take a crack at this guy?* is very different from asking *How did you feel after you hit him?* when dealing with a suggestible person. It can no doubt be irritating for hard-pressed detectives to have to consider the nuances of question-making when trying to solve a crime, but in the interests of justice, it is essential to take care during interviews, in case the subject is psychologically primed or predisposed to follow a prompted line of thinking.

Suggestibility of an offender is a factor that often arises in juvenile cases because teenagers are usually loyal to their peer group, lacking in self-confidence and self-assurance and vulnerable to group-think. These attributes are common among the non-offending teenage population as well, but it is the nature and attitude of the peer group that determines whether this behaviour becomes problematic or not. Among juvenile offenders, I have seen a common pattern: with limited cognitive information skills, low self-esteem, social awkwardness and poor peer experiences comes a willingness to go along with the suggestions of others in order to be popular and connected. This can be the case whether the juvenile is within a peer group or before the legal authorities – they are eager to do the right thing by everyone else and slow to assert their own opinions.

There are two cases I worked on that amply illustrate the phenomenon and effects of suggestibility among juveniles. The first concerned a nineteen-year-old man called Daniel and was a simple enough case of naivety and not trusting one's own instincts – simple, but with significant ramifications. He came to my office for the assessment interview accompanied by his girlfriend. He had been in the relationship for eighteen months and they seemed devoted to one another. He had a steady job and good prospects – life was going well for them and they hoped to get married in the future. For his girlfriend's birthday, Daniel surprised her with concert tickets for a gig in Dublin and an overnight stay in a hotel. A friend from their town, who Daniel knew through work, heard about the trip and asked Daniel if he would collect a package for him and bring it back from Dublin – nothing big, 'a work thing', but it was important and urgent. As Daniel described this conversation, his eyes kept shifting uneasily, and I got the impression that, while he said he had no suspicions about this man, he did, in fact, have reason to wonder if this was all above board. When I asked why he had agreed to such a vague question he replied, 'I felt I couldn't say no.' My feeling was that his instincts had been urging him to refuse, but his compliant nature had been unable to do so.

As they packed their bags the morning of their departure, Daniel's phone buzzed and a man he didn't know told him to come down to the lobby for the package. He told his girlfriend – who was oblivious to everything – that he was going to settle the bill. In the lobby, the man came up to him and handed him a plastic supermarket bag with something in it the size of a brick. That moment presented Daniel with a choice, but once again he acquiesced and went along with it, playing the role of the good friend even though he wasn't obliged to do so. He accepted the bag and went upstairs and put it in his case, then they left the hotel and hailed a taxi to the train station. As they were putting their bags in the boot of the taxi, police cars surrounded the vehicle. The officers went through the bags and pulled out the plastic bag. To the utter shock of Daniel's girlfriend, it contained three kilos of cocaine – an amount that would fetch around €200,000 on the street. That sort of volume carried with it a mandatory sentence of ten years in prison, and Daniel wept as he told me this and berated himself for being so stupid. The 'friend' who'd put him in this position couldn't be linked in any way to the crime, so he wasn't facing any arrest or charges. In Daniel, he had chosen the right person – the right personality – to obediently take the rap for him. There was very little I could do, but I emphasised in my report that Daniel's risk of reoffending was very low and that it was more in the nature of a mistake than a crime because he was highly suggestible. Daniel was convicted and received a ten-year sentence, four of which were suspended with parole. It was a stark illustration of how a moment of non-thinking compliance can change a whole life.

That sort of case is always difficult because I can't help feeling truly sorry for the person so harshly punished. It was the same with Peter, another young man who seemed to sleepwalk his way into a serious crime. He was referred to me while awaiting trial for the charge of Accessory to Murder. In this case, my report would form part of the defence argument. The lead barrister explained in a phone call that the victim had died of a bullet wound to the head and that Peter stood alongside two other accused. The question on which the case would revolve was: was it a premeditated and planned murder, because this negates the possibility of accident or manslaughter and therefore carries a greater sentence upon conviction. The barrister went on to say that Peter was a gentle person, a bit removed from the world, and he felt there was a chance that his behaviour had been sheep-like, rather than an aggressor who willingly participated in a killing. I understood his line of thinking – if Peter was suggestible, it would also affect the answers he gave in the police interview, which would question the reliability and validity of his testimony and could affect his trial prospects.

I prepared for meeting Peter by first going through the case notes and then watching the footage of the police interviews. The tape showed a well-conducted interview, during which Peter became very upset and the police were empathetic and careful with him. There was no swearing or intimidating language and they gave him time to tell his story. However, there were some questions that were suggestible in their phrasing, such as, 'You did kill him, didn't you?' If a person is easily manipulated, they will instantly answer 'yes' to a question phrased like this. In the video, Peter is shown to respond to this question by at first not understanding it and then, when it is put to him again, totally agreeing as he perceives, wrongly, that this is what the police 'want' to hear. I also noticed that there was persistent questioning about Peter luring the victim to his death. Peter's reactions and crying showed a high level of guilt, remorse and stress throughout the interview, which can lead a person to admit to things they did not do because they feel so terrible about what happened and so angry at themselves for being involved. It was notable that Peter replied 'yes' to luring, but when then asked, 'so it was premeditated?', he vehemently refused that this was the case. His answers were inconsistent – again suggesting that he was trying to say whatever he felt the police wanted him to say – and also confused. Confusion plus willingness to answer with inconsistencies points to suggestibility.

I met Peter in person at my office. He was a smiling, friendly young man of nineteen, with an air of warmth and likeability. He came from a loving family, with no forensic history of any kind. Peter didn't drink alcohol, but instead liked to relax by smoking cannabis. He had a girlfriend, but was unemployed. I asked about his friends, and Peter talked about the young men who were his co-accused. He described one of them as 'a kind of leader ... you know, he talks, we jump'. This man had come into possession of a shotgun, which he had stowed in a field. The three would go to the field and shoot at trees and rabbits, 'just for fun'. But then the man had got into some trouble regarding a drug debt. He didn't have the money to settle it, so he hit on the idea of frightening the dealer into leaving him alone – they would arrange to meet the dealer, warn him off and back up their warning by waving the gun about threateningly. That would do the trick.

On the appointed evening, they drove to the field and collected the gun. Then Peter was deputed to make the call and set up the meeting, which he did without argument. The dealer met them in a quiet spot, and while Peter and the third friend stayed in the van, their 'leader' got out to confront the dealer. When he pulled out the gun and pointed it in the dealer's face, the man laughed. As Peter and his friend watched, their 'leader' pulled the trigger and shot the dealer at point-blank range, right between the eyes. The dealer was decapitated by the shrapnel. In shock, the shooter raced back to the van and they took off, driving away from the scene as fast as they could. They didn't think to take the dealer's phone; they left it on him. They drove to the field, disposed of the gun and went their separate ways. Peter didn't think for a moment about phone records. Just as he hadn't foreseen how the gun plan might go, he didn't for one second foresee the crime being traced to him. He seemed incapable of plotting out likely consequences, which is very common in people prone to following the suggestions of others.

I asked about his family, and while Peter maintained that all was well, there were other things he hadn't mentioned before. It transpired that his father had died a few years earlier, leaving Peter with a complicated grief to deal with. It was complicated because a few months before his death, Peter's sisters, now in their twenties, had alleged that their father had subjected them to sexual abuse as children. As a result of these allegations their mother had asked their father to leave the home, so for the three months before his death from a sudden stroke, he was separated from them and the situation was highly tense and acrimonious. Peter was certain he had never been abused by his father, but there was nonetheless an unhealthy history of sibling rivalry and infighting between him and his brother and sisters. It appeared that the cannabis use was a form of self-medication in the aftermath of these difficult events.

I formulated that he was suffering from a depressive disorder, often exacerbated by excessive cannabis use. He also admitted, as we talked more, that he had been subject to physical abuse by his father, which further set him up for depressive disorders and comorbidities like anxiety. These childhood experiences had left him with low confidence and a desire to please, in order to avoid getting hurt.

As with Shane, I administered the Gudjonsson Scales with Peter. The results were conclusive: he scored a very high rate of 18 (a full six points higher than Shane), putting him at a very high level of psychological vulnerability to suggestibility. His risk was 80–85% higher than the average population. Furthermore, I also administered the Gudjonsson Compliance Scale, which uses the mean score of 9, for normal subjects, as its baseline. Peter scored 20 on this scale, which indicated a pathological need to comply with whatever was asked of him. His own personality militated against Peter behaving sensibly before, during and after the events of the dealer's murder, and also against his ability to handle the police interview with honesty and accuracy. Accordingly, my report emphasised his depressive disorder, his inability to process information correctly and his inability to think for himself in stressful situations. The findings via Gudjonsson were stark and formed the backbone of my assessment, showing how he was highly susceptible to suggestion and that this had affected how he gave his statements to the police and the content of them, and why he had gone along with the criminal behaviour.

I was called to give evidence in the case, and the judge was convinced by my findings. He ruled that Peter's statement would not be admissible as evidence. The case proceeded without the statements, and the final verdict was that Peter was guilty of being an accomplice, because he had placed the call to the dealer to arrange the meet. After giving evidence I was obliged to leave the court, as the case was being held in camera, out of the public eye. A few weeks later, I received another call from Peter's barrister. He told me that the shooter had been sentenced to twenty years, the other man to twelve to fifteen, but that Peter had received a much shorter sentence of four and a half years, with the possibility of parole after two years. It was a fair outcome, I believed, and reflected his actual responsibility with regard to the crime.

Peter's case had been heard in the Central Criminal Court on account of the seriousness of the crime, but children and juveniles under the age of eighteen are often heard in the Children Court, formerly the Juvenile Court. The Children Court deals with the majority of juvenile offences, although more serious crimes, such as manslaughter, must be heard in the Central Criminal Court. The Children Court is held in camera, with no persons extraneous to the case allowed in the courtroom and no reporting allowed of the cases heard there. As noted above, the Children Court has a range of treatment options at its disposal, with detention being the solution of last resort.

I have been called to give evidence in the Children Court, and it's a very different atmosphere from the other courts. It is more informal, with greater empathy exhibited by barristers and judges. An example of a case in which I gave evidence illustrates the differences. I gave testimony on behalf of a thirteen-year-old child concerning the necessity of providing him with foster care instead of a period of detention. The child had a deplorable family background and history of abuse, which I described in detail and also demonstrated the scars on his arms from cigarette burns, administered by his father. The judge listened carefully to my evidence, then asked to speak to me and the child in private. In that private session he was strict, but fair. He warned the child about prison, but then gave him 'another chance' by agreeing to the foster care proposal. It was a good example of how the Children Court is sympathetic and always striving to help society and the individuals brought before it. In that case, the judge's trust in my assessment was upheld: the boy went on to live very happily with a foster family and hasn't been in trouble since.

The Children Court is a good example of progressive thinking with regard to juvenile offending and care. The system has its flaws and its lack of resources, but all those involved make huge efforts to help the offenders placed in their care and try to prevent reoffending and encourage a positive change in behaviour and outlook. I have worked on a number of cases – such as that of Sarah-Jane, whose story was recounted in Chapter 3 – where the intervention of the court was very effective. In Sarah-Jane's case, she received a detention order and went on to enjoy and greatly benefit from her time in the detention centre, which crucially put her beyond the influence of her family. I believe that intervention changed her life, helping her to stop self-harming and form a vision of a future she wanted to live. In other cases, while the level of help and intervention is the same, the outcome is not so good. While the detention centres offer educational courses alongside psychological support, many of those who reside there between the ages of sixteen and eighteen go on to become serial offenders, especially with relation to drunk and disorderly violations and traffic violations. Research shows that if the offender receives vocational training by the age of twenty-three/twenty-four, attains a qualification, has a partner and a family, then at a later age their recidivism rates drop precipitously. It's just unfortunate for all concerned that it often takes until then for the opportunity to stop offending to be finally grasped by the young person.

And what of Harry? We hadn't crossed paths in about nine years, when one day I got a call to ask me to include Harry in the work I was doing for the Residential Institutional Redress Board investigation about conditions in certain children's detention centres. If the allegations put forward by the former inmates proved true, they would be entitled to compensation from the board. I hadn't been aware that Harry had gone on to reoffend and become resident in St Patrick's Young People's Institution, but that is what had happened, and now he wished to add his account to the others that described substandard care and inadequate conditions in that institution. I asked the solicitor who had called where I could reach Harry to set up a meeting. The very disappointing reply was: he's in a medium security adult prison.

I met with Harry at the prison, where he was serving a sentence for assault. When he saw me, his face broke into the wide smile I remembered so well, and he shook my hand vigorously and then hugged me. He told me his grandmother had died, but he never once mentioned his father. I didn't broach the subject. He regaled me with stories about the conditions at St Patrick's, alleging solitary confinement and uncaring behaviour by the staff. He railed against the staff, his psychologist, the police, his girlfriend – and then he went on to blame his victim, the man he assaulted, who, he said, 'totally deserved it' because he didn't hand over his shop takings quickly enough. I realised why Harry was a serial offender – he could see no future other than this life because he had never once taken responsibility for this life. It was everyone else's fault, and that's a position that doesn't allow for any forward movement – it's a thinking trap, and he was completely stuck in it.

I subsequently explained Harry's case to the Redress Board and he received a compensation payment, but unfortunately nothing that happened was capable of turning Harry from the life he was living. I asked after him intermittently, and I know that he is now homeless. His life has gone from bad to worse, even though I know he is capable of being a better person. All that life and energy and warmth has been soured and lost, which is a great shame. But stories like Harry's only serve to make me redouble my efforts. These young people are worth fighting for, even if they can't see that themselves. I think of Harry and I think of Seamus, the young offender who ended up dead, and I remember them by pouring my energy into the juvenile cases that come my way. Our children and young people – and our juvenile offenders – deserve our care and attention, our help and our support. For every person we deter from a criminal lifestyle, there are generations who will benefit, within their own families and within the State.

CHAPTER FIVE

THE BOLD NEW WORLD OF CYBERPSYCHOLOGY

The internet is celebrating only its fortieth birthday, but it has been an astonishing four decades of exponential growth and progress. For those born since the millennium, it is hard to grasp the idea of a world without computers, mobile phones and social media. The past is most certainly a foreign country and the millennials have no desire to ever travel there because it sounds monumentally boring. In just forty years the internet has changed our world, giving us brand new vocabulary – lurkers, trolling, tweeting, vlogging, HCI, URL – and brand new challenges and opportunities. The world watched on with fascination as social media became the engine of the Arab Spring and as Wikileaks, Anonymous and terrorism online impacted on our political and social structures. This is the age of human and machine, and it requires a new way of thinking about ourselves and the world we create and inhabit – both online and offline.

Cyberpsychology is a relatively new branch of psychology that seeks to explore, understand and treat the psychological challenges posed by the advent of the computer. Within that, forensic cyberpsychology is becoming increasingly popular as a module at third-level, with more and more undergraduates gravitating towards this end of the forensic spectrum. As a discipline it covers a wide range of issues, including processes of the law, eyewitness memory, policing and the courts and, of course, criminological psychology as it manifests via online behaviour. Cyberpsychology examines how we behave online and why we behave in these ways.

So, how do we behave online? A large part of internet usage is very straightforward: shopping, making friends, uploading photos, blogging – in other words, connecting with other people for mutual enjoyment and convenience. One of the greatest benefits of the internet is that it allows likeminded people to find each other, connect and share their interests. In psychological terms, this can be very helpful because it can mitigate loneliness or alienation and make a person feel connected to a wider world, even if they haven't left the house. At this end of the spectrum, it can have very positive effects on users. At the other end of the spectrum, one of the greatest perils of the internet is that it allows likeminded people to find each other. When we hear of the cannibal who found a willing meal online, we shudder, but that's the flip side of the coin – the vast landscape of the internet can accommodate any kind of thinking and, crucially, normalise it for the user. That can have a very dangerous and potent effect on users.

One thing is certain: our cognitive processes and our behaviour are evolving with the computer – as it develops and evolves, so do we. Neuroplasticity, neurolinguistic processing (NLP) and the pain/pleasure principles, among other facets of psychology, are shaping and being shaped by how we interact via the web. There are simple experiments you can carry out to test this thesis. For example, leave your phone at home for a day and note down your thoughts and feelings through the day – you might be very surprised by what you read. Or unlock your phone and hand it to someone next to you – how does that feel? Our devices are fast becoming an extension of ourselves, which can produce stress reactions when we are parted from them or they are open to the manipulation of others. It's a fascinating development that needs to be closely monitored and studied.

It is often said that people present their best selves online, curating the images and captions about their lives to make things seem that little bit more interesting and colourful. That is no crime, of course, but the problem it creates is that our online selves can be a fragile construct. Accordingly, if they are attacked by trolls or by negative comments or by indifference and no 'Likes', those online selves are in danger of being dangerously undermined and possibly toppled. Mary Aiken, director of the Cyberpsychology Research Centre at the Royal College of Surgeons Ireland, describes the 'cloak of anonymity' that veils the identities and intentions of users, and this is a very apt description. Aided by anonymity, people can be freed to be their best selves or their worst selves, indulging in behaviours they might be highly unlikely to engage in offline. The internet can provide a buffer zone between real life and the online world, allowing people to convince themselves that what the 'online me' does has no real effect and, furthermore, the 'offline, real me' is not responsible for it. This line of thinking can have a detrimental effect on the mental health and the decisions of users. If you follow the line of thought it leads to confusion: who is to say what is real and what is presented? This very question has always been pertinent to social psychology and all human development: who are we, what do we want to be and how do we govern our environment to support our needs and desires? So it's not a new question, but it's given a very new dimension through the virtual world of constant connectivity.

Divorced from the offline sense of morals, ethics, right behaviour and conscience, users can become engaged in disruptive and hurtful behaviour. Think about your own behaviour online – if you had to carry with you a banner displaying all of the things you had typed online, would you feel comfortable with that or very uncomfortable? There are all kinds of lines that can be crossed online, the worst are illegal, but there are many that are legal but nonetheless have a hugely detrimental effect on the online community, on individuals and on people's real lives. The internet is not a huge video game where everything resets to normal after 'Game Over' – the things we do online can have very real impacts on the mental health of other users. The information we present has longevity, and effects and consequences we wish for, but also other sequelae not envisaged.

In my own work, it is this legal bad behaviour and its effects that I deal with most often. We could call it minor cybercrime, and it comes to my attention via my general practice with the non-criminal population. I would expect the whole area of cybercrime to become a much larger percentage of my work into the future, but for now the most common effects I work with are on interpersonal relationships. I see people who have been adversely affected by extramarital affairs that were born online, and also those struggling with restraint and self-discipline in the face of the unending vistas of images and knowledge that the internet offers. My patients often attribute difficulties with peers, poor social interactions, deviant behaviour and marriage breakdown to social media. Another associated problem with 24/7 connectivity is the constant visibility of the partner or spouse online, which can change the dynamics of the relationship. Examples of these problems would include a partner reading an affectionate text from their lover to another person, discovering what sexual preferences their partner may have through seeing how they viewed preferred pornography or learning about what a partner or friend says online to another person, perhaps even about their own relationship. It can be one large event – like the cheating text – or just subtle exercises over time. In my forensic clinic, I have also observed the new phenomenon of boasting about criminal activity via social media, which gives younger users a thrill, even though it could lead to them being caught and convicted. Before, peer groups gave affirmation to the young offender; now his online, faceless followers often fulfil that role. A common example of this that I encounter regularly is filming a car-jacking via mobile phone, then recording the high-speed journey before the car is burnt out, all of which is recorded and uploaded for feedback and comments – in other words, for affirmation.

The major cybercrimes occur in areas such as pornography, human trafficking, illegal hacking, sexual offences and blackmail.

In my own clinic I haven't dealt with many of these larger issues, but I regularly deal with porn addiction in young men or with the effects of sensitive material on the employees of some of the large US tech and engineering firms. Here, my role is to counsel those who have to view traumatic imagery as part of their work to combat and contain searches and viewings of such material. They have the unenviable task of viewing flagged content in order to ascertain if it is possible – subject to legal policies – to provide for paradigms facilitating general rules to remove such material from the internet. They are also helping to develop algorithms that will 'automatically' remove this deviant material at source. However, as the algorithms are written, the nature of the imagery becomes even more complex. The work they are doing is very important, but it does subject them to material such as child pornography and images of gruesome violence and of animal abuse. They are doing it in order to shield others from such content, but their viewing of it can create personal psychological challenges. The common challenges I see as a result of this work are worries about their own sexual lives having been subjected to traumatic sexual imagery, fear of being somehow infected by what they have seen and falling prey to such thinking themselves, nightmares, stress symptoms and cynicism. While cynicism might sound benign, its tentacles can wrap around the healthiest mind and make it question the validity of its values and belief systems. It destabilises the 'normal' thinking processes, introducing huge uncertainty and fear. The more a person is exposed to this material, the more he/she believes that it exists everywhere, which is a thought that is very difficult to live with. This effect on thinking is called universality and it is an insidious affliction. I help these employees to detach from their work and feel empowered by what they are doing and achieving, which is protecting the wider population from being subjected to such traumatic material and also preventing socially dangerous propaganda.

This work has taught me a lot about the ways in which humans respond to the vast freedoms of the internet and the deep net (or dark web). I have worked with paedophiles, for example, in my forensic clinic, but I have had to study and learn anew about how they use the internet to facilitate their fantasies. Online sex offenders have different motives for their online behaviour: curiosity or impulsive searching; accessing pornographic imagery to satisfy their sexual fantasies; creating and distributing imagery for financial gain; or using the internet to facilitate contact sex offences. As such, they fall into three categories of offending. The first category are Discoverers, who have no previous evidence of sexual interest in minors but are now interested in and stimulated by images online. The second are Predisposed, meaning they have previously had fantasies about minors and are now using online images to fuel those fantasies. Finally, the Sexually Compulsive use images online to act out their fantasies about minors and looking at such images may heighten arousal and lower inhibitions prior to committing an assault. This is borne out by a polygraph study conducted with child abusers, 86% of whom admitted that they compulsively used porn as a precursor to contact offending. So the way in which the internet is used with regard to sex offences can vary enormously, but all such behaviour must be monitored and discouraged because it is often the case that a user can graduate from non-contact curiosity to contact offences.

The profile of the online sex offender is very interesting because it upturns some of the ideas people might hold about this group of criminals. They are 99% male, disproportionately Caucasian and likely to be paedophilic or hebephilic (preference for young adolescents around eleven to fourteen years old). They have a higher IQ and education level than contact offenders, have less forensic history than contact offenders and are composed of 64% professionals and 17% college graduates. The fact that we know so much about sex offenders and their movements online is down to the work of the global tech firms and also specialist law enforcement agencies. While the personal price for staff viewing this material can be high, their work is making a difference. For example, a US study published in *The Journal of Child Abuse &*

Neglect analysed search traffic levels for common keywords used by people searching for Child Sexual Exploitation Material (CSEM) between January 2011 and August 2014 and found that searches for this material dropped by 67% following the introduction of blocks by Google and Microsoft.

While some teams are focused on sexual offenders, others do the same work with regard to websites offering violent images for view. This overlaps with the psychology of terrorist organisations, many of which are very proficient at using the internet to recruit followers and to spread fear. They regularly upload videos that show acts of violence against humans, including beheading and limb removal. This content is similarly traumatising and can have an adverse effect on the people I work with who must view it as part of their working day. The common effects I see among this group are anxiety, depression, symptoms of post-traumatic stress disorder and increased alcohol consumption. Again, their work is important, but it exacts a toll on their mental well-being. But when you consider that studies have shown a direct correlation between viewing violent imagery and committing violent acts, it is imperative that the agencies continue their work to block this sort of imagery. That means, of course, that staff teams must be subjected to it, which is an unfortunate outcome. However, they do receive psychological support from a variety of experts to help them cope with the mental trauma that can occur as a result of their work. In my own work with such groups, we discuss the noble cause of which they are an essential part and the fact that these images do not represent our values and in no way change our values. I also encourage them to develop a 'wellness toolbox' by prioritising their own well-being through good eating, exercise, getting enough rest and continually talking through their experiences and asking for the help they need to cope with what they are seeing.

As the internet has spread in popularity and usage, so too have grown the psychological theories pertaining to online behaviour and effects on users. It is a burgeoning area, with old theories being adapted to fit the new conditions and new theories being investigated and put forward. In seeking to understand how and why people behave as they do online, there is a series of interesting theories to choose from.

The Equalisation Hypothesis (EH) is a prominent and pertinent theory. It hypothesises that individuals who hold less power in society should have increased power in the online environment, which can be a very positive effect. The reason for this is the loss of face-to-face interaction and with it the host of visual cues – such as gender, age, ethnicity, clothing – on which we base assumptions and judgements. This is the internet as 'the leveller', dismissing the normal social hierarchies that can affect, and perhaps more correctly infect, our interactions. This is put forward as one of the positives of how we interact online, with great potential to push mutual understanding forwards into a more tolerant future. That is the hopeful view; there will be alternative views of equalisation that will pour cold water on this ambition because most people who want to contribute to the 'good' of society can overcome their fears to do it publicly and visibly. Take away that visibility, however, and it appears that equalisation is more useful to facilitate malevolent behaviour.

When stories emerge of online bullying or scams or about the dark web, people often shake their heads and wonder how others can do such things. The truth is, it is far easier to break rules and laws via online behaviour than it would be in real life. Many users feel there is a freedom and a permissiveness about the internet that protects them from actual wrongdoing. From my own cases, I believe one of the key features of regular use of the internet and social networking is a loss of self-control and an increase in the level of gratification we require instantaneously and on a daily basis. As the online world opens up to us and our insatiable curiosity, our ability to regulate our emotions and impulses is reduced. Self-control and delaying gratification are important skills, which have a large effect on brain activity and development. When I listen to clients talk about their need to be online, their fear of accessing material they shouldn't because of morbid curiosity, their sense of not being fully in control of the reins, I'm often reminded of the 1960 study conducted by Mischel et al. It was an experiment conducted with preschool children, who were given the option of eating a marshmallow immediately or waiting fifteen minutes to receive two marshmallows. When compared to those who ate the marshmallow immediately, the children who were able to delay gratification went on to higher education achievement and increased ability to cope with stress as adults. This is a psychological effect of internet usage that could have much wider ramifications in the future if we have whole generations of people who cannot exercise self-control or delay gratification, or who choose not to because they are, perhaps, bored, finding real life to be insufficiently stimulating.

As all of the above suggests, the world of the internet encourages and facilitates disinhibited behaviour. The frontal lobes of our brains are the seat of disinhibition, regulating our behaviour and enabling us to decide our own moral code, which is derived from society, school, parents, peers and the media. This is not an impermeable site, however, and many different things can invade the frontal lobe and adversely affect disinhibition, such as alcohol and drugs. To these must be added, I think, regular internet usage. It creates a separate world, one where people can convince themselves that the rules are different and often don't even relate to them. In psychological terms, this is called neutralising. According to this theory, while offenders and users might not subscribe directly to deviant norms, they develop ways of rationalising their behaviour in order to reduce feelings of guilt. Neutralising statements would include things like, 'No one actually got hurt', 'It's not my responsibility' and 'Everybody else is doing it'. In this way, we liquidate our moral selves, allowing us to engage in a much wider spectrum of actions. For the online offender, this can be taken to extremes, into cognitive distortion, whereby wildly adjusted thinking becomes the means by which wrong and illegal actions can be justified. As Mary Aiken describes

it: 'Technology amplifies a criminals' underlying disposition …
Someone with sadistic tendencies becomes even more sadistic
online, under the cloak of anonymity and in a forum where they
can meet likeminded people easily' (*The Irish Times*, 4 May 2015).

Labelling theory provides insight into hacking, which is a
criminal offence if it involves access to a device without the owner's
knowledge or consent. (This is listed as an offence, but in reality it
is so far a rarely prosecuted crime.) This relates to how individuals
label themselves and others and the behaviours resulting from
that labelling. In the real world, this can manifest in the young
man who has been labelled deviant by peers or society and goes
on to act out that label. 'Give a dog a bad name' as it were. Online,
teenagers, in particular, can identify with the anti-establishment
stance and underworld-type culture of hacking and then seek
to label themselves as part of that group. They want to become
what they admire, and hacking provides a direct route to those
they see as 'cool' and to approval from those same peers. Again,
they commonly fail to see that what they are doing is wrong or
potentially harmful, seeing only the immediate gain of mastering
difficult, elite skills, such as coding, effecting influence and search
engine optimisation, and being elevated by their peers as a result.

This thinking relates to groupthink – a much investigated
psychological phenomenon that has had new life breathed into it
by the global group of the internet. There is an interesting theory
that is relevant here, which bears the daunting moniker of Social
Identity Model of Deindividuation Effects, or SIDE for short. This
examines how group dynamics are affected by anonymity and the
depth of the individual's identification with the group. It has shown
that when complete anonymity exists within a group, then group
salience is enhanced because members' identification within the
group grows stronger – in other words, they start thinking socially
rather than individually. However, where an individual can identify
group members while him/herself remaining anonymous to the
group, in that scenario the anonymous individual will not behave
in a manner advantageous to the group. You have probably seen

this as at work in comment threads, where some users post their real name and profile, while others use false profiles. The comments by those who are anonymous are often far more provocative and controversial than those posted by the people whose identities are known. Often, the thread will degenerate into delighted attacks by one side to the howling indignation of the other side. What SIDE theory has found is that the optimum conditions for group cohesion and for the ability to work collectively towards a group goal are either total anonymity of all members or else total transparency of all members. I would argue that transparency is the optimum condition here, as public visibility and public affirmation are powerful motivators, while secrecy may not lead to much positive change.

Groupthink is explicitly linked to persuasion and compliance, both of which can also be seen at work on social media. Persuasion is where one person is convinced by another to engage in a certain behaviour, often coexisting with attitude change by the person engaging in the new behaviour. Compliance is an external, obvious change in behaviour in response to a direct request. There is no change in the person's actual attitude, but the behaviour is amended. Obedience involves compliance with the wishes of an authority figure, while conformity is a change in attitude as a result of pressure, such as peer pressure. Internet users can often underestimate the power of groupthink and persuasion. The dangers are clear to see in, for example, the recruitment practices of terrorist organisations. They have successfully used online approaches to persuade young people of their beliefs and worldview and then get them to comply with their suggestion that the young person leave their family and join the terrorist cause. This is a particularly chilling example of the insidious power of the internet to connect with and control remote lives, but it is also a very real possibility and one that users should always be aware of.

The 'minor' cybercrimes, as we are calling them, and which many of the general population engage in, can carry on regardless because to a large extent the law has not yet caught up with the online realities. When you consider trolling (the deliberate act of posting controversial and provocative messages online in order to create discord, argument and dissent), hacking and revenge porn, which are the most common questionable behaviours the internet community is involved in, you can see the Routine Activity Theory (RAT) at work. In its simplest form, this posits that most criminal acts require the co-presence of three elements: a motivated offender, a target and an absence of guardians. On the internet, this co-presence is easily available, which can lead people to move from thinking bad thoughts to carrying out bad actions. In the case of revenge porn, for example, the internet provides a deceptively simple way of teaching an ex-lover a lesson. This is the new face of the 'crime of passion', whereby the person who feels themselves to be wronged (a motivated offender) wants to rid themselves of those negative feelings by pouring them in the direction of the source of their torment (the target) and realises that an online campaign provides an anonymous outlet for their vitriol. Alone in their room with the laptop or phone, there is no voice of reason to tell them otherwise. From their point of view, they have a totally level playing field on which to play out their revenge. This sort of 'freedom' is how people can become unfettered from their own common sense, leading them into actions they might regret for a long time to come. (They overlook the fact that there are heavily resourced cybercrime units in the UK and in Ireland devoted to tracking crime, tracing IP addresses and targeting malevolent and illegal behaviour. That feeling of privacy is completely erroneous and misleading.) It is plain that the underlying psychological motive here is to move from feeling small and slighted to feeling like the big, bad wolf – menacing, in control, always with the upper hand. These are powerful feelings and motives that can be hard to control and rationalise.

Similarly, trolling has become an everyday norm for internet users and very much part of our daily vocabulary. It often stems from that same sense of grabbing back control, exerting control over others and enhancing one's own sense of self. Just like the fairytale troll, who hid under bridges waiting for an unsuspecting victim to terrorise, online trolls lurk on the periphery of discussions, waiting for an opportune moment to pounce with a provocative comment, then sit back and watch the sparks fly. This is the preserve of anonymity again, allowing people to draw a line between 'online me' and 'offline me', thus facilitating all manner of hurtful actions. The 'cloak of anonymity' can have a dehumanising effect, making users feel detached from the emotional effects of their words and actions. The resulting disinhibition skews behaviour away from what would be normal for that person in face-to-face interactions. This loss of self-consciousness, stemming from the removal of the threat of confrontation or rejection, is akin to deindividuation, which occurs when our personal identity becomes subsumed into a group or social identity, which can in turn lead to antisocial behaviour – think of the gang that prowls the streets in a pack, looking for mischief, egging each other on.

To date, there hasn't been much research into trolling, but that is changing. One of the first studies conducted into it found that trolling was largely the result of boredom, attention-seeking and revenge. Trolls derive entertainment from prodding others into explosive reactions. To them, what they are doing is fun, a contest of verbal dexterity and wit, and if anyone is upset by it, it is that person's problem. The internet becomes a mask to hide behind, a new persona to try on, one big game with the troll holding the winning hand. What they fail to realise is that their actions can have consequences. I have seen many of these consequences, such as expulsion from school, relationship break-up and loss of employment. These are serious, life-affecting events that can be hard to overcome, especially when they are unforeseen and unexpected.

One of the most high-profile issues to emanate from the internet is that of cyberbullying, which is rightly receiving a lot of attention and discussion. This is like trolling taken to a new level, with a corresponding new level of consequence. With bullying, the victim quickly realises they have a permanent intruder in their

home in the form of their tablets and devices. This is one of the
key facets of cyberbullying – that it follows you home and refuses
to leave you alone for any minute of the day. This is proving to
be a huge problem in Western countries, in particular, with
reports of suicides as a result of sustained bullying campaigns. In
the US, the name of Tyler Clementi is now well-known after the
eighteen-year-old university student took his own life because his
room-mate filmed him on webcam – without his permission or
knowledge – in an intimate moment with a fellow male student.
In Ireland, there have been a worrying number of teenage suicides
attributed to cyberbullying. In an article on this growing trend,
The Irish Times (22 September 2015) reported that 'two thirds
of young people said online victimisation was worse than face-
to-face', while one in four reported they had been the victim of
cyberbullying and just over 50% of respondents identified it as
a bigger problem than drug abuse. Those who had experienced
it reported feelings of helplessness and feeling very alone, while
others had suicidal thoughts as a result. The fact is that reading a
damaging text often evokes a stronger emotional response than a
face-to-face insult or even negative imagery. It has a big and lasting
impact.

The statement in the article to the effect that cyberbullying
is worse than face-to-face bullying is very interesting. It reminds
me of the groups described earlier who work to safeguard the
Web, who must view deviant material, because they often tell
me that witnessing images is less upsetting than reading through
text descriptions. They feel that an image can be quickly pushed
from the mind, but they find reading text allows them to build a
narrative around the victim, which makes that person more real to
them and causes them to empathise with that victim at a deeper
level. I think it must work this way with cyberbullying, too. If
someone writes something about you in a text or in a chatroom or
on Facebook, it creates a new narrative about you, and that is very
threatening. You could compare it to the gossip-mongers of old,
who could rewrite your personal story without your permission

and you were powerless to prevent it. Someone, somewhere would inevitably intone that 'there's no smoke without fire' and that would be your reputation shot to pieces. In the modern age, bullies can now do this to horrible effect by making something seem very real by virtue of putting it in writing. This is compounded by what the media can do to an individual's reputation, often causing undue anxiety and a sense of resignation to awful, uncontrollable consequences. This is why cyberbullying feels so threatening to the victim – it's persistent, it's insidious and you can never scrub that text or that image from the vaults of the internet's server memory. It creates a sense of something that will never let the victim go, that has control over the victim and thereby destroys the victim's sense of autonomy, control and well-being. The common reaction I have seen among victims is a paralysis of thought and action – they can't get past what was alleged about them, but they have no idea what to do about it. For the adolescent, this is particularly difficult to deal with because it combines public exposure and ridicule with a helpless feeling that it can never be undone, can never be escaped from. For a person in this sensitive age of psychological development, it is understandable that such thoughts can lead to anxiety, depression and suicidal thoughts, especially at a time of important identity formation.

I dealt with just such a case, which involved a young man. Matthew came to see me with his mother, and it was immediately clear they were both very anxious and upset. I had read the book of evidence, which described the charges against Matthew: sexual assault of an underage person. Looking at the awkward, well-mannered young man sitting opposite me, it seemed impossible he should be capable of such behaviour. But as we talked, he told me that he was pleading guilty to the charge.

Matthew told me about his life, how he found it difficult to make friends and fit in. He had never had a girlfriend or felt like he wanted one, but the reason for this hadn't presented itself until recently – when he met the underage person who was pressing charges against him. They met at school, where this other boy was in a lower class to Matthew because he was younger than him. Matthew sent the boy a message via Facebook and they chatted about various things. Then Matthew asked the boy if he liked girls, to which he replied that he wasn't sure. That immediately gave Matthew hope that he might in fact like boys, might in fact like him. Feeling his way carefully into this possible relationship, Matthew told this boy that he liked him and asked him to meet him outside of school. Up to this point, the two boys' stories matched, but here they diverged.

The two boys met in a local park, where they talked and got to know each other. After a time, they shared a kiss, which Matthew said was consensual. They progressed onto oral sex, each boy performing it on the other. Again, Matthew said this was fully consensual; the other boy said he was forced and that it was a sexual assault. The problem was that the other boy didn't allege this to his parents or a teacher or to the police: he posted it on Facebook. Matthew's mother's whole body trembled as she described the effect of this action on their lives, once everyone in the school and local community had read the accusing post. I felt very sorry for Matthew and his mother: they had been accused and judged by their peers before ever being able to have their side of the story heard. The boy's post alleged that Matthew had abducted him and then assaulted him. As a result, Matthew was taunted everywhere he went with the words 'abductor', 'paedophile' and 'pervert'. The effect on him was apparent – his body was tense with anxiety, he cried throughout our interview and he seemed unable to fully comprehend that this was now his reality. One of the worst outcomes for Matthew was the effect on his relationship with his father, who hadn't known his son was gay. Matthew hadn't told him because he knew his father would have huge difficulty with that, and now his father had to deal with these accusations and an impending court case. The stress on the family was immense.

I asked Matthew why he thought the other boy had done this. His mother answered quickly that it had to be guilt stemming from engaging in a homosexual act. Matthew shrugged miserably, unable to formulate an answer. He reiterated that he was going to plead guilty, even though he didn't believe he had done anything wrong (although he had sex with an underage individual). Ignorance is not a defence in law, so while he was certain of his innocence, he had to plead guilty because the fact that he did not know what he was doing was wrong or could be deemed wrong would not sway the court in any way. When his case came to court, he was convicted of illegal sexual behaviour against a minor and received a suspended sentence, which meant he was convicted but didn't go to prison. He was relieved not to be facing a jail sentence but distressed that he would always carry with him through life a criminal record. The judge also banned him from having a social media presence, which for a young man is an extremely difficult punishment to bear when social media is a lifeline and, in some cases, a way of life.

One of the key psychological concerns about internet usage is the possibility of, level of and effects of addiction to it. At one time, the suggestion of humans becoming addicted to computers would have been laughed at and dismissed, but that's far from the case now. We have all, to one extent or another, become conditioned to reach for the phone, to check for new communications and messages from the wider world. We do it unthinkingly, an automatic response. I have had clients describe how they cannot walk by their phone without pressing the button to check the screen – even if they walked by it just ten seconds before. As social animals, we strive to communicate, looking for good news, looking for affirmation, wanting to know what others are doing, wanting to feel popular. The internet thus feeds into our natural psychological make-up, rewarding us continually with pleasurable feelings of connectivity, usefulness and popularity. It's a very seductive mix, and it's all too easy to succumb to it. Mary Aiken describes it as being 'as powerful and intoxicating as alcohol', which only serves to underline its potential for addictive behaviour.

What we could see in the future is humans regarding sleep as an inconvenience because it disturbs their always-online status.

This is a worst-case scenario, but as more and more of the planet's population become users and crave connectivity, it is very possible it could tip over into psychological addiction. Indeed, it could become a physical or chemical addiction too, given the pleasure chemicals that online activity can release in the brain. There have been some interesting studies recently, using MRIs to track brain activity in relation to connectivity. These showed that our brain activity spikes in response to the buzzing of our phones. At night, as many people sleep next to their charging phone, the same spikes can be seen, even if we don't consciously hear and are unaware of the phone's activity. This suggests we are starting to connect with our devices in both conscious and unconscious ways. This is a relatively new science, so we have much still to learn about the human–machine interface. It seems safe to argue, though, that the overlapping of social media, brain neuroplasticity and neurolinguistic processing will change how we understand the world and therefore how we interpret it and communicate it to others. This will be integral to the study of psychology over the next thirty years, and young psychologists should see this as a new world of opportunity for research and practice. I will follow each new stage with great interest and fascination.

CHAPTER SIX

SELF-MEDICATION AND WHERE IT TAKES YOU

W hen talking about addiction of any kind, it naturally broadens out the discussion because addiction is so prevalent among humans, and not just in the criminogenic population. It cannot be compartmentalised as 'those who are addicted' and 'we who are not'. In truth, addiction is a core part of human existence and it would be fair to say that the majority of people are addicted to something, be it alcohol, narcotics, prescription drugs, sex, power or external validation through peer approval. It is an extremely common behaviour that crosses all social divides. The key distinguishing factor is whether the negative behaviours resulting from the addiction are deemed to cross the line or not. That said, submerging ourselves into anything with disregard for all else – be it exercise, food, religion, routine habits – leads to a blinkered and counterproductive situation that does not benefit the health of the mind. Therefore it's truly a case of not casting stones, because there's a very good chance you have sinned too.

In psychological terms, addiction is a process disorder, which in this regard essentially means that the person has an inability to process difficult emotions and experiences, which leads to negative behaviours, often self-destructive behaviours as much as aggressive behaviours. Substance abuse is a common way to self-medicate, in an attempt to protect the mind from those emotions and experiences. But of course substance abuse is unpredictable, and each person is unaware of how the substance will affect their behaviour until they've crossed that line – by which time it may be far too late. When it comes to alcohol and many drugs, there is a very fine line between pleasure and chaos. For example, a food addiction can lead to obesity, while an addiction to managing food and a fear of failing to do that can lead to eating disorders. The outcomes are starkly different, but the motives derive from the same source: a need for biochemical arousal, the pleasure principles and brain neuroanatomy.

As well as being a process disorder, alcohol and drug addiction are likely to occur with comorbidities, meaning they occur in conjunction with other challenges, such as depression, low self-esteem, self-loathing. The addiction will always have both a mental and a physical aspect because it is directly linked to both thought and behaviour. The behaviour is what you are confronted with – the drunk and angry person, the high and unpredictable person: this is the outward manifestation of the addiction. The thought is the hidden element, but it is the cause of the behaviour, which is why psychological intervention is so important in treating addiction successfully. If it goes untreated, alcoholism, in particular, can lead to death, usually via cirrhosis and brain deterioration, which can give rise to dementia. It is a slow, debilitating and undignified process of wasting, affecting mind and body equally. If a person has reached this chronic level of alcohol addiction, they are unable to stop drinking, it has become a way of life and the withdrawal symptoms are by now so debilitating as to effectively bar the person from making any efforts to do so. The alcohol, in effect, takes over and takes control and the person becomes powerless to stop it.

The process of addiction is generally similar in most people who present with it: they start drinking or taking drugs to escape from something inside their own minds – a memory, an emotion, a bad experience, something they cannot think past on their own. They don't seek help and instead self-medicate by using substances to blur their thinking and soften the sharp edges of what they remember and feel. As time goes on, their body builds tolerance, so they need to take more to get the same high as before. They begin to realise that when they don't take the substance, they experience horrible withdrawal symptoms combined with cravings, which takes away any desire to stop using the substance. Often, the person knows there is a problem in their life and doesn't enjoy the addiction anymore at this point. But even so, they feel it is now a necessity to get through each day. The spiral has also begun into behavioural addiction, which occurs when we perceive an external locus of control, such as alcohol, to be capable of relaxing us, capable of unravelling our stress and making us feel better. When it reaches this stage of united thinking and behaviour, it's only with outside help that the spiral can be halted.

Most of us classify our drinking habits as 'normal' and 'not worrying', but you might be surprised to learn of the approach to alcohol use disorder (AUD) in the DSM-V. It lists eleven questions and your answers indicate if there is a potential or existing addiction problem. The questions are as follows.

In the past year have you:
1. Had times when you ended up drinking more or longer than you intended?
2. More than once wanted to cut down or stop drinking, or tried to, but couldn't?
3. Spent a lot of time drinking? Or being sick or getting over other aftereffects?
4. Wanted a drink so badly, you couldn't think of anything else?
5. Found that drinking – or being sick from drinking – often interfered with taking care of your home or family? Or caused job troubles? Or school problems?

6. Continued to drink even though it was causing trouble with your family or friends?
7. Given up or cut back on activities that were important or interesting to you, or gave you pleasure, in order to drink?
8. More than once gotten into situations while or after drinking that increased your chances of getting hurt (such as driving, swimming, using machinery, walking in a dangerous area or having unsafe sex)?
9. Continued to drink even though it was making you feel depressed or anxious or adding to another health problem? Or after having had a memory blackout?
10. Had to drink much more than you once did to get the effect you want? Or found that your usual number of drinks had much less effect than before?
11. Found that when the effects of alcohol were wearing off, you had withdrawal symptoms, such as trouble sleeping, shakiness, restlessness, nausea, sweating, a racing heart, or a seizure? Or sensed things that were not there?

According to the DSM, if you answer yes to at least two of these questions, it indicates an alcohol use disorder. If you answer yes to two to three, that's classed as mild disorder. If you answer yes to four or five, that's classed as moderate disorder. Six or more affirmative answers indicates severe disorder. This might prove a sobering thought for many people, but it's important to reflect honestly on those questions and your answers to them.

The effects of substance abuse and addiction are wide-ranging – it will usually be the case that while I'm dealing with a single individual who is before me because of the adverse consequences of their addiction, there is a wide pool of people also adversely affected by this person's behaviour. It's the stone in the pond effect – addiction ripples out, on and on, hurting everyone in its path. For the people around the affected person, they might have to deal with that person's violent behaviour, depression, self-harming, constantly letting down family members and breaking promises, the dispiriting 'one step forward and two steps back' of attempts to give up the substance, the chaos that emanates from the addict and affects all areas of personal and family life. It can be a life sentence of its own, to live with and attempt to care for someone who is engaged in substance abuse.

For the addict, the effects are no less awful. In terms of mental health and well-being, this is the first thing to be compromised. I would commonly see social withdrawal, irritability, poor mood, a total lack of interest in life and living, social apathy, despondency, depression, chaotic lifestyle that makes the person vulnerable, anxiety, aggression and poor interpersonal relationships. All of this can lead to disordered thinking, which allows the vicious cycle to keep on spinning, trapping the person inside it. Of course, the person has usually started this addictive behaviour out of some sort of disordered thinking or mental health challenge, so it stands to reason that substance abuse exaggerates and greatly worsens those disordered states, even if the person's hope is that it will help them.

A good example of this is cannabis use, which users enjoy because it gives a state of alternate lucidity or relaxation or feelings of pleasure. We see the world in a different way after smoking cannabis and it gently disinhibits the user. The problem is that continued and persistent use leads to the periods of real lucidity, outside of the cannabis bubble, becoming shorter and shorter and the person's 'norm' becomes the thinking they experience while under the influence of the substance. This norm is, in fact, an impaired reality, which is the definition of psychosis. Research isn't conclusive at this point, but studies conducted thus far have shown a link between cannabis use and psychosis in males. (Men tend to use substances at a higher frequency and concentration than women.) It can happen that long-term drug use can lead to psychosis or to episodes of hypomania (mild form of mania, characterised by elation and hyperactivity) and hypermania (severe form of mania) later on in life, after the age of forty-five.

Physically, the effects of addiction are also very detrimental. I have encountered patients with malnourishment, cirrhosis of the liver and brain deterioration that would appear to be linked to excessive substance use. (These long-term physical neuroanatomical effects on the brain have yet to be researched in detail, but in my work I do see repeating patterns that suggest a link to the substances abused.) Substance use can wreck the general health of the user because it is all part of not caring for themselves and not caring about what happens to them.

So having read all that, the obvious question to ask is: why? Why do people engage in behaviours that are clearly bad for them and that they generally end up not even enjoying? There are many different reasons, but genetics and self-medication are probably the two most common ones that I encounter in my work, both with criminals and with the general population. In terms of genetics, it has been proven that if you are the child of a parent who suffers from alcoholism, you are four times more likely to develop an addiction. Undoubtedly this isn't solely a genetic cause-and-effect: it can also be simply environmental. The child has grown up in a disordered, chaotic house where the care-giver/s continually plunge into denial and cope with life through substance abuse, making that seem normal and possibly also inevitable. The child's life is made unpredictable and fragile by the actions of the parent/s, which creates the right conditions for disordered thinking, difficulty in processing emotions and thereby desire to blot out certain things from the mind. So the child gets caught up in the parent's vicious cycle, which normalises this learning for the child, leading to substandard problem-solving being understood as 'standard' for the young learner.

The desire to escape from one's own self could be described as a behavioural addiction – the person craves the 'time out' they feel alcohol provides, so they drink to achieve that. Substances can quickly generate chemical addiction as well, because they can cross the blood–brain barrier so fast and so effectively. Addictive substances generally increase the secretion of norepinephrine, adrenaline, dopamine and serotonin, which are the pleasure chemicals responsible for giving us a sense of well-being. The problem is that the more these and other pleasure neurotransmitters are used, the more numbed we become to their effects over time, requiring greater amounts of the substance for the same hit. And of course withdrawal stands waiting at the gateway to wellness, bringing with it tremors, emotional upheaval, nausea, vomiting and lethargy. It's no surprise that addicts find it so difficult to break out of the prison they've built for themselves.

The effects are different for different addictions, but at the bottom of them all is a desire or need for disinhibited behaviour. So for the sex addict, sex is more about control (of themselves or others) than affection or emotion. Power can be to do with the thrill of the chase (such as closing a big deal) or arousal through risk-taking or the need for affirmation by becoming a leader among others. Narcotics and alcohol, as we have seen, are very much related to each other and the desire to get away from oneself. The desire for external validation and affirmation through peer approval is often found in the criminogenic population, especially when a person starts as a juvenile delinquent and goes on to commit crimes into adulthood. The common thread running through all forms of addiction is a transgression in order to gain affirmation through power over ourselves, others and the environment, which is a self-serving motive.

I deal with cases of addiction and its consequences very regularly and, as I said, both in forensic and general practice. Addiction takes no notice of social divides, education, wealth or success; it can be found in so many different lives and personalities. One of the notable things about addiction in Ireland is how often it is enabled by those who are closest to the addict. This can be particularly true of alcoholism. I think this is because, on the one hand, there is shame attached to it and people don't want to acknowledge that it's part of their family and, on the other hand, because Irish people do tend to have a sort of friendly tolerance for alcohol and binge-drinking. The Irish have long been known as drinkers, but it's always dressed up as funny and charming and just a little bit naughty – not actually bad. Alcohol is an outlet that we all collude on, silently agreeing that it's necessary and acceptable. That creates an environment where addiction can flourish. There is a shared national trait among the Irish whereby we don't like to think that we have to stop. This makes for admirable resilience and determination when it comes to surviving a recession or emigrating into a new culture, but it's a disaster where alcohol is concerned. I also wouldn't underestimate the effect of the climate on personality, odd as that may sound. From years of observation and listening, I have come to the conclusion that mood is definitely affected by weather and light, and of course mood in turn leads to behaviour, whether positive or negative.

There was a parental capacity case I worked on that brought home to me the extent to which disordered and addictive behaviour can be tolerated in Irish families. I was asked by social workers to meet and compile a report on a man called Eoghan, who had been denied access to his children via a care order. They wished to know if the order was warranted or could now be revoked. It had been put in place because of violent behaviour by Eoghan towards his wife, which had led her to take their children to a refuge on a few occasions. The police had invited her to make a statement to facilitate a prosecution, but each time she declined. Recently, she had sought and received a barring order against her husband, but the social workers felt he was still spending most of his time in the marital home. It seemed his wife lacked the will to take the steps that would lead to real and sustained change.

I read the reports and arranged for Eoghan to visit me at my office in Dublin. He lived outside Dublin but was eager to be seen to be helpful and engaging fully with the process, so he quickly agreed to make the journey. When he walked into the room, I could sense that he was nervous, on edge, but at the same time his eyes betrayed that he had taken something. My first question was: have you taken something this morning? At first he repeatedly said no, but I was insistent, and he finally admitted that he had taken a Xanax tablet to calm his nerves. He also mentioned the sleeping tablet he had taken the night before to ensure a good night's sleep in preparation for the session. Watching me for a reaction, he quickly said that he had given up alcohol and that he desperately wanted to be with his family again. He seemed full of remorse and a desire to change, which I felt was genuine and an encouraging sign, but then he could also be switching prescription drugs for alcohol, which would be a problem in terms of living with his family again.

As we talked, I asked about his children and he smiled broadly, talking about them with great affection and pride. It was obvious that he was very involved in their care and knew exactly what was going on for them at school and in their extra-curricular activities. He spoke particularly of his son's talent for martial arts and how he accompanied him every weekend to events, waiting patiently through long tournaments in order to cheer him on. I told him this was wonderful to hear and it marked him out as a devoted father, but then I mentioned his forensic history – the beatings he had given his wife, plus an earlier conviction for violent behaviour. This went against his desire to provide a good home for his children. He agreed but said it was only when he drank that he became violent and that, even then, he had never harmed any of the children – 'only' his wife. Having read the reports, it seemed to me that this was possibly more down to the Trojan efforts of his wife to keep the children from him.

By the end of the session I felt unclear as to the best course of action. Here was a man who seemed to be a good father, but there was potential for destruction – and with children involved, I had to be very sure of the outcome. In order to glean more insight, I arranged to travel to meet with Eoghan's family and hear their side of the story. I travelled to their home to meet the family: his wife, Molly, and his four children, two boys and two girls, all aged between three and sixteen. Molly was an instantly likeable person – down to earth, humorous and full of energy. It was hard to imagine this strong, articulate woman accepting life with a man who beat her. There was nothing at all to cause alarm or suspicion – it was clear the whole family loved Eoghan, wanted him home and were willing to work around those drunken blind spots in his behaviour. There was huge loyalty towards him and from what the children said, they missed him terribly when he wasn't at home. Molly, too, was obviously still in love with her husband and wanted to get their home life back on track. She exhibited no bitterness towards him for the times he had hurt her, bearing it all with a 'chin up' attitude and a very clear-eyed focus on the children's well-being. The formulation of Eoghan was that of a high-functioning parent with an apparent inability to restrain himself from negative behaviours that were equally damaging to his family as to himself. His behaviour posed challenges to the family, but his daily parenting and presence were important enough to make up for those challenges.

I asked the social workers to bring in Eoghan then, so I could watch the family interacting together. That only served to confirm the conclusions I had reached that this was a happy family with a good and healthy dynamic – apart from the nights when Eoghan came home drunk. I asked his eldest child, a sixteen-year-old girl, what she would like Eoghan to change in order to come home for good. She looked surprised to be asked but then looked over at her father and said: 'That he promises to stop drinking.' Eoghan nodded solemnly and told his family that, this time, he had given up for good. 'I've had an epiphany,' he told them. 'I've promised God.' I kept my face neutral, but it seemed an entirely unconvincing promise. I looked over at his daughter and she rolled her eyes and shook her head. Clearly, she shared my thinking. Looking around the room, I felt that no one believed this grandiose statement, not even Eoghan himself.

It was both a simple and a difficult case. I could see that the family wished to be together and that the children bore Eoghan no ill-will and were not frightened of him. Molly had reason to be fearful, but she clearly cared deeply for him and didn't want him to lose the children from his life. They all confirmed that when he drank Eoghan did become aggressive, but that aggression was always directed at Molly, never at the children. I thought long and hard about Eoghan's situation before making any recommendations. Like his family, I concluded that I'd have to work around his blind spots, too, because depriving this family of their father wasn't going to deliver any optimal outcomes. My final recommendation was that Eoghan could have supervised access for a set period during which time he would have to abstain from alcohol completely. If he did that, it would then move on to unsupervised access, until eventually he had proved himself enough to be allowed move back home.

While the case had a fair outcome for Eoghan and Molly and their family, it did make me think about the Irish attitude to alcoholism. At only sixteen years of age, Eoghan's daughter was already resigned to lies and broken promises. That seemed a very sorry state of affairs to me. And while I greatly admired Molly's resilience and focus on her family, it was also sad to see her accept Eoghan's behaviour and choose to live with it. My hope was that the recommendation would see Eoghan finally give up alcohol for good, but conquering addiction is never easy and rarely straightforward. But so far, Eoghan and his family are doing very well. This is the result of a combined-services approach, including addiction counselling, parenting support, respites and close supervision by social work and legal authorities alike.

In Eoghan's case, his family had adopted a 'for the greater good' attitude, trying to accommodate his alcohol-fuelled behaviour and contain it within the generally positive family dynamic. In another case I worked on, it was shame and fear that defined the family dynamic. This is another common facet of the Irish family, whereby addiction is ignored, never spoken of, brushed under the carpet, so that the family need never acknowledge there is a problem. This is a particularly insidious response to an obvious mental health question and can lead to tragedy – as it almost did for Catherine.

Catherine was sent to me by her employer because she had turned up for work one Monday morning drunk and unable to participate in an important meeting that was scheduled. She was a patient in my general practice, the embodiment of the high-functioning alcoholic. When she walked into my office, she seemed groomed, poised and very much in control of her life, but as she began to talk, that façade fell away and it quickly became apparent that life was very much a struggle for her. I listened as she detailed the raw emotions of sibling rivalry and parents seeming to favour one child over the other. In this case, Catherine was the high-achiever, but her efforts and achievements were never recognised or applauded. Instead, her parents were consumed by caring for and dealing with her sister, who became pregnant at eighteen and whose life had always been dramatic and chaotic. Catherine felt ignored and, at base, unloved, a feeling that had been undermining her mental well-being for years, even if she had never recognised that fact.

Our sessions were interrupted by the Christmas break, and when we resumed, Catherine seemed more anxious than before. I had encouraged her to talk to her family about her drinking and tell them that she was trying to deal with it positively through regular sessions with a psychologist. Their reaction was far from helpful. Her parents had strongly resisted her description of her life, insisting there was no alcoholism in their family. They had blanked out her efforts to be honest, which caused a lot of hurt to Catherine. It reinforced for her the feeling that they didn't love her enough. She had also had to share Christmas with her sister and her brother-in-law, whom she hated to be around. As we discussed those strong feelings she held towards him, she confessed that her sister had come home one day with a black eye and her baby and belongings, saying she was leaving her husband for good. Catherine was delighted, encouraging her to stay away from him and giving full vent to her thoughts about him. Her sister then went back with him and told him all that Catherine had said about him. A few nights later, one of his friends had turned up at Catherine's house, drunk and raving about her disrespectful behaviour, and he had then tried to rape her. Catherine managed to fight him off only because he was so drunk, and she pushed him out her front door. This incident had a huge effect on her, which had contributed to her need for alcohol. She was drinking to feel in control of her emotions, to separate herself from her family and to blank out the memories of that night.

We made good progress thanks to Catherine's honesty, but then came an evening when I got a phone call from her boyfriend, concerned for her safety. She had decided to go on a retreat, to reflect on her life and think things through clearly, but her phone was turned off and he couldn't contact her. I urged him to drive straight to where she was, which he did. He found Catherine hungover and upset – she had planned to commit suicide. This, to me, was a perfect example of both high-functioning alcoholism and also how self-medicating with alcohol is an extremely dangerous thing to do. The combination of her own difficult emotions and the effects of alcohol almost made Catherine decide to do something she didn't actually want to do. The alcohol had clouded her thinking, blinded her to her options, which had led to disordered thinking and suicidal ideation, making her think she wanted to cross a line that normally she wouldn't even consider. Now that her life has moved on and she is no longer addicted to alcohol, Catherine is very glad that her plan that night did not succeed. Now that she is sober, Catherine has been able to reassess her abilities and the contributions she can make and the potential for success in her life, both personal and professional. Once she rid her system of alcohol, it crystallised her ability to assess herself and her potential accurately, which has allowed her to make good decisions, to focus on what she really cares about and to make sustainable choices regarding her personal life and her career. She is now becoming the person she wanted to be all along.

I have come across many people, particularly those who have committed criminal acts, who have used alcohol or drugs to explain their behaviour. I don't think they drink in order to allow them to commit the act, but once it has been committed, they are happy to point to the substances and name them as the direct cause, bypassing their own culpability. A good percentage of crimes feature a perpetrator who is drunk or high or who is engaged in the activity in order to procure such substances, but I think the role of those substances in these crimes is often overestimated. I think that, very often, it has crossed the mind of the perpetrator that such a crime may take place, but instead of examining that thought rationally and making a choice, they numb the feelings associated with the risk or fear of being caught by using substances. The reason for drinking or taking drugs is the key consideration here. The person might think that what they are doing has no bearing on what they will do next, but they fail to factor in the level of disinhibition that alcohol and drugs promote. They are not fully aware of its effect on them and what they might be capable of doing when under the influence. Normally, I find that this understanding comes only with hindsight, as they piece together why something happened.

I had a very interesting case to deal with where the piecing together was the key to the different outcomes. It concerned one crime but two different perpetrators, which gave a good foundation for comparison of the outcomes. The crime occurred at a house party, when a group of young men targeted one man, beating him so badly that he later died of head injuries. The investigation was necessarily broad and lengthy, so it was three years later that I was asked to assess two of those accused of delivering fatal blows to the victim. Jeremy was now twenty years of age; Giles was now twenty-three. I agreed to interview both men, having read the reports and book of evidence in detail. Neither man was still in contact with the other and each was unaware that I was interviewing his co-accused – a fact that I never divulged, of course.

I saw Jeremy first and was immediately struck by his demeanour – he was accused of murder, yet he seemed distant and unconcerned. He described his home life, which was marked by an absent mother and a father who drank regularly, sometimes becoming violent as a result. Jeremy had previously faced charges of drunk and disorderly and criminal behaviour, and he had charges against him since the incident we were discussing. Again, he seemed detached from all this, as if it didn't affect him one way or the other. I asked him to describe the night of the attack, and he described it in a dismissive way, saying he didn't know the victim and had just taken part and kicked the man in the head, but that was all. I reminded him that the victim had died of head injuries, but he looked disinterested. I reminded him that he was accused of murder as a result of those fatal injuries, and he shrugged, telling me that he didn't feel like he'd committed murder because he'd been drunk at the time. His attitude was almost as if he hadn't been there. He didn't see his decision to kick the man in the head as a decision at all – it was something the alcohol had decided to do. His complete inability to accept responsibility for his actions, combined with his behaviour since the incident, were proof that he was at high risk of reoffending. If he offloaded all of his decisions and actions on to whatever substance he was taking, then he was incapable of examining those decision and actions, feeling remorse and changing his ways.

By contrast, Giles turned out to be a very different personality. His part in the crime was similar to Jeremy's – he didn't know the victim, wasn't interested in having a fight, but when he passed the fight on his way out the door to go home, he threw a punch at the victim. It caught him under his right eye, after which Giles continued on his way and went home, thinking no more of it. When he learned of the man's death a few days later, he was very upset but didn't feel it was anything to do with his action. He was interviewed by the police and was helpful, answering as comprehensively as he could. He told the police that his behaviour that night – punching someone – was uncharacteristic, but he had been grieving the then recent death of his father, to whom he had been very close, and finding it difficult to handle his mother's grief as well. He wasn't himself that night, as Irish people like to say.

As we talked it over three years later, it became clear that while Jeremy also felt he wasn't himself that night and had taken that thought to a preposterous conclusion – that he wasn't to blame for anything – Giles had confronted the events of that night and accepted that blame was attributed to him. Yes, he had been suffering from grief, but he quickly realised that his behaviour that night was wrong. As a result, he cooperated fully with the authorities and with me, and when the case came to court he pleaded guilty. As he had remorse and accepted responsibility for punching the man, and because he had lived a crime-free life since that night, my report recorded Giles's likelihood of reoffending as very low. He had accepted what had happened and taken steps to change his life, particularly through training and employment, and also by giving up alcohol entirely and settling down with his partner. Unlike Jeremy, I felt Giles would go on to lead a good life and would put this incident behind him eventually. It was a difference of perspective, but it was crucial to how their lives would play out into the future.

The existence of a mental health challenge prior to addiction is very commonplace. This comes back to the idea of self-medication, where people see substances as some sort of saviour, able to deliver them from the hellish spaces inside their own minds. This is an entirely incorrect thought, and I have seen it again and again lead to unhappiness, destruction and often the crossing of the line into illegal behaviour. There is another argument here, about the inadequate resources available to those with mental health challenges, an inadequacy society pays for dearly when it leads to criminal behaviour. We have seen this too much recently with the advent of 'lone wolf' terrorism, such as the attacks in Nice and Orlando. When a person is experiencing great difficulty in their thinking and processing of the events that have affected them, it can lead to extremely disordered thinking.

I have worked with many people who fall into this category, where substance use was their preferred coping mechanism for other problems they couldn't discuss or sometimes even admit to. After working with them, what emerged as the base cause of their trouble was self-hate. They would point to alcohol or drugs or 'bad company', but we would drill down into the behaviour and discover self-hate at the base of it all.

Sean was a good example of this process. His life featured a number of different experiences that had destabilised his mental health, but it took him a long time to realise that. When we met, Sean was thirty-seven years old and had been in prison for the past six months. He seemed to be coping well with prison and was able to appreciate the fact that it meant he couldn't drink alcohol, which was having a positive effect on him. He described the crime he was serving time for: drunk and needing cash to drink more, he broke into a house – chosen at random, without thinking about it – and threatened the elderly woman who lived alone there. In order to scare her into giving him cash, he threw furniture about, broke things and threatened to kill her. She had no money to give him, so in the end he took a few euro from her handbag and some bits of jewellery, then ran away. Having made no effort to disguise himself or proceed with caution, he was quickly identified by the police and arrested.

We talked about his life before this nasty incident, and he described how family life had been great – until his dad developed a drinking problem. That cost him his job and his marriage, and Sean's mother struggled to keep the family going. When drunk, his father would beat him, and Sean said this happened two or three times a week until he was fifteen, when his father left the family home for good. Sean had trained as a chef, had girlfriends, tried to get on with his life, but he was addicted to cocaine and cannabis. At the age of twenty-three something happened that changed everything for him. He was driving four of his friends in a car one night, when he crashed. One of his friends was killed. Sean had been brought very low by remorse and guilt, unable to believe that he had caused the death of a friend. He turned to heroin to block out those horrible feelings, which in turn wrecked what he had built up in his life. He was filled with self-loathing and unable to forgive himself. He described himself to me as 'a murderer'. The drugs were the only way he could go on living, but of course it was no life. It had led him to this point, terrorising an elderly woman for a few euro. I applauded Sean's efforts to be drug-free and recommended regular psychotherapy sessions, both one-to-one and group. It was clear it would take a lot of sustained work to break through the hatred he held towards himself and all the things he regretted.

Declan's story echoed Sean's, in that a crash had been the watershed moment in his life, too. His case also illustrates the process disorder at work, whereby a person can become stuck on a particular idea of themselves. In Declan's case, he had become stuck on the idea that he was 'useless', and that thought had almost destroyed him. It's a testament to the power our thoughts hold over our behaviour and well-being and how we can be held hostage by negative thinking.

I was asked to see Declan because he was accused of committing arson, compounded by wasting police time. He would get drunk, set fires in derelict buildings, then ring the local police station to report the fire. He would not set fires to hurt people – it was always empty buildings – but he got a thrill from calling the police, from being the one to alert them, from feeling like he was someone useful. When we met, he was facing four counts of arson and seven counts of false reporting.

We talked about his home life, which was busy given that he had seven siblings. His parents had worked hard to provide for them and, while money was scarce, they all got on well and he was happy. But when he was around eight years old, his mother's brother began to sexually abuse him and threatened him with all manner of consequences should he tell. The young boy was in a terrible situation because his uncle was a well-loved member of the family, often asked to babysit. At this time, his schoolwork plummeted and he was held back a number of times. Eventually he left school in first year, when he was fifteen years old. He saw no connection between the abuse and his inability to concentrate and work in school. Instead, he had branded himself 'useless' at everything, which became a self-perpetuating thought. He found solace in alcohol and cocaine, which quickly became all-consuming. He lost his girlfriend and access to his daughter and ended up living in a hostel. It was from there he had made his calls about the fires.

Declan had to learn to recognise the pattern of his past life: how his uncle's actions had derailed his thinking, leading to harmful behaviours and self-hate and, finally, self-medication with drugs and alcohol. He had to learn to forgive himself for what he'd done through understanding why he'd done it. I felt he was on his way to this self-understanding, thanks largely to a new girlfriend, who loved and supported him with great devotion, and volunteer work he was engaged in with the River Rescue services. Through these two positive lenses, he was learning to see himself from a fresh perspective, which was enabling him to stay off the substances that had led him into trouble.

Declan benefitted hugely from a psychological approach to his behaviour, allowing him to eventually recast himself in a new, more positive light. The question of how to tackle addiction has been examined across a spectrum of experts, from GPs to psychiatrists and from occupational therapists to forensic psychologists. In Ireland, the UK and beyond, psychologists have provided leadership for the development and delivery of various psycho-social approaches to addiction and its negative behaviours. These approaches are mainly derived from cognitive, social learning and motivational theories, but now are also increasingly influenced by neuroscience and genetics. The nature of addictions, what they are, is important in terms of how we deal with them, both in the general population and in the criminogenic population. For all addicts, it is essential to form a robust therapeutic alliance and to conduct functional analysis of behaviour in order to correctly identify the cause and treat it. This brings in the role of mental health, which often underlie the addictive behaviour. An interesting study by Weever, in 2003, found that 44% of attendees at a London community mental health facility reported problematic drug and alcohol use within the previous twelve months. Another survey, this time of those in treatment for dependence and related problems, showed that about 90% of participants met the criteria for one or more mental health problems, such as psychotic disorders, anxiety, severe and minor depression, and personality disorder. I find this particularly frustrating as minor and severe depression, and even anxiety, are eminently treatable through CBT and psychopharmacology. We should be aiming to treat these primary disorders in order to prevent the secondary disorder of addiction from occurring at all.

In terms of the approach of the justice system in this regard, a baseline for tolerance needs to be identified – we cannot ignore that drugs and alcohol are associated with so much crime yet we are not allowed to factor in consideration of evidence – there must be a distinction drawn between what is an altered mentality and what is hedonism. In other words, while the substance may play a role in how the personality developed or how brain function was depleted, no court or judge will, correctly, accept a defence that only the substance was directly responsible for the offending actions.

In my own work, I have found active listening and CBT to be the most useful methods for treating addiction. It provides the supported self-examination that is necessary to understand one's own thinking and be able to work to change it. When treating addiction, it is essential to understand the motive governing the behaviour. If a person is drinking because of an emotional or psychological attachment to, and therefore reliance on, the substance, then it is far more likely to become a problem. What it is necessary to understand – and what I feel needs to be disseminated far and wide – is the message that it is not a life sentence: people can and do recover from addiction by tackling the underlying subjects that have allowed it to flourish.

I dealt with a young man who became a good example of how addiction can be overcome, even when it has a strong motivating factor. On the face of it, Patrick's story sounded depressingly familiar: a young unemployed man who needs money for drink and decides to break into a house to steal the money. He and another young man, also a heavy alcohol and drug user, performed a very amateurish break-in that quickly saw them apprehended and arrested. Reading the report, I wouldn't have been surprised if Patrick had described a household marked by parental absenteeism, alcoholism and physical abuse, but when he sat down in front of me and started talking, his story was very different.

I visited Patrick at the prison where he was being detained, but even before I got to that meeting, I received a phone call from his father, who was anxious to meet me. It is unusual for parents to be so involved, but I felt this was a good sign. I told Patrick's father I would meet with him after talking to Patrick first. I was led into an interview room, and Patrick immediately stood up to shake my hand. He explained that he had pleaded guilty, that he felt terrible about what he had done and that he was awaiting sentencing – which is where my report came in. His home life was very good; he had left school early but went straight into an apprenticeship that he enjoyed and was leading an enjoyable life. Things took a bad turn when he crashed his motorcycle. It was a severe crash, leading to six months of rehabilitation for Patrick. He now wore dentures as a result of the accident, and he had very obvious facial scarring; I noticed that he kept turning his head slightly away from me in an effort to present his 'best side'. He lost his job, suffered a lot with pain, broke up with his girlfriend and took to staying at home, smoking cannabis. The night of the burglary, he was trying to get money to pay off the drug dealer he owed. He had never been in trouble before in his life.

Neither Patrick nor his family knew how to access mental health supports, which is why his condition deteriorated to such an extent. When I met his father the next day, he expressed huge regret that they had not realised the extent of Patrick's depression sooner and got some help for him. His father vouched for him in no uncertain terms, telling me that Patrick was a good person but the scars and the loss of his normal life had caused him huge anxiety, which he had tried to quell with alcohol and drugs. But if the accident hadn't occurred, he knew Patrick would be thriving and living a good life. Having met Patrick, I felt the same way. My report recorded that the likelihood of reoffending was very low and that he required extensive psychological support to overcome the negative emotions that were controlling his behaviour. I recommended psychotherapeutic intervention, CBT and addiction counselling, further recommending the support and participation of his parents in this, given their high level of care and involvement. According to forensic research, being convicted and serving any prison sentence automatically increases risk of reoffending to moderate-to-high. Patrick would have to serve a sentence, given that he was pleading guilty, but we could begin this work pre-release, and that coupled with his compliance might negate some of the duration of the sentence. Post-release, the top priority would be to get Patrick back into his apprenticeship training and give him the supports needed to succeed and go on to find employment.

As usual, I didn't hear any results from the court trial, but given that Patrick was pleading guilty, it was inevitable he would serve some time in prison. I was very pleasantly surprised to receive a call from his father a few months later, telling me that Patrick had received a three-year sentence, suspended to ten months. They had feared a much heavier sentence, so they were very pleased with his outcome. His father asked if I would administer the CBT and psychological supports I had outlined in my report, which I was very happy to do. I felt that, with such strong parental support, Patrick had every chance of turning this situation around.

After his release, Patrick had a fortnightly session with me for almost twelve months. We addressed all of the negative thinking that had plagued him since the accident, especially with regard to the facial scars. We talked about how everyone bears scars, some visible, some not, and that it is our scars that allow us to learn, empathise, adjust and develop. Through these CBT-led discussions, Patrick slowly came to accept what had happened to him and learned to like himself again. He formulated a new vision for his future, one that was far from being house-bound and drug-addicted. Once he could see this new future, he began to take steps to live it. By the end of our year of treatment, Patrick was once again enrolled in vocational training and he felt far more in control of his life. It remains one of the major success stories of my work – to see a young man shift so far from negative and harmful thinking and behaviour to coping well, living fruitfully and being much happier. I hope that will serve as an inspiration to others who are in the midst of the darkness of addiction. Once you seek out the supports you need and engage fully with them, it is entirely possible to free yourself of addiction and the line-crossing behaviours it brings with it.

CHAPTER SEVEN

LOSING CONTROL? ANGER AND VIOLENCE

When did you last get angry? When you remember it, do you feel ashamed or secretly pleased with how you handled yourself? Do you feel you taught the target of your anger a lesson that had to be taught? Do you feel guilty that you got angry? Do you feel wholly justified?

Your answers are probably not simple and are no doubt even more complicated than you realise. Anger is a complicated emotion. It derives from the many psychological layers that go to make up your personality. The angry moment isn't a single, standalone incident, it's a compilation of different moments and feelings from across your whole life, quite likely involving emotions and memories you do not consciously recall or attribute meaning to. What makes us angry and how we channel that anger have a lot to say about the kinds of people we are and the kinds of inner resources we may have or lack.

Whatever happened to trigger your anger, your physical reaction will have had a role to play in what happened next. Anger releases adrenaline – the 'fight or flight' chemical – and it raises blood pressure and increases heart rate, all of which makes it difficult to think clearly. Inside your brain, the limbic centre lights up. Whereas the cerebral cortex is the seat of thinking, the limbic centre is the seat of emotions, meaning it's more primitive in its understanding and has scant regard for consequences. So when those anger buttons are pushed, the limbic centre beats the cortex into submission and releases a wave of hormones – adrenaline, norepinephrine, stimulants – into the body that can take up to twenty minutes to dissipate. You are now in an altered physical and mental state that is unpredictable. People often describe getting angry as 'losing control', and in the moment it can feel like you've been possessed by an emotion that's bigger than you. But thinking back to your own last outburst of anger – did you lose control, or did you allow yourself to lose control? Was it a case of 'offence is the best defence', and you let loose before the other person did? Did you feel the anger rising and there was a split second when you could have gone either way, but you decided, at some level, to give vent to it? It can be very hard to be honest about such incidents – sometimes because we don't actually understand ourselves in that moment, but also because it means confronting the darker side of ourselves, which can be disconcerting. It's the conscious versus the unconscious, taking responsibility versus lying to oneself – anger can represent strength or it can reflect a weakness, an insecurity, emotional fragility as opposed to strength. Anger can have different sources.

There can be a very positive aspect to anger – it is an energy, just as John Lydon (aka Johnny Rotten) insisted it was. When channelled and used properly, a certain amount of anger can translate into determined action, ambition and concentration. For example, when I'm working with patients who are suffering anxiety regarding upcoming presentations or exams, I advise them that getting a bit angry about what they have to do will settle their nerves and allow them to focus more clearly. Anger is, after all, a normal human emotion, a manifestation of extreme emotion (generally arising from a threat to your person) that can be an important survival tactic. It is also a social emotion that connects us to each other, because anger always has a cause and a target. As a result, we often experience righteous anger (now we're with Samuel

L. Jackson in *Pulp Fiction*), where we feel completely justified in our anger because the target has created the circumstances that gave rise to it. That, too, can be a good feeling – we are angry, and we are right. In its own way, that can have a positive psychological effect by lending focus to concentration, allowing us to block out extraneous requests and deal succinctly with the matter at hand.

As with all things, the positive aspects can flip into negatives if the anger becomes uncontrollable, irrational, frequent and out of all proportion to the triggers. When this happens, the person can develop an anger disorder. The key to understanding the disordered thinking behind the anger is to know that the anger is a secondary emotion – it is the primary emotion that is the real cause, and that must be deciphered if the person is to change their destructive behaviour. When anger becomes a habit, and is combined with psychological or psychiatric disorders, it can lead to crossing the line into criminal behaviour.

The sources of anger can be complex and difficult to unravel. In my work, I very regularly hear anger attributed to substances – 'the drink made me do it'. This is a very common defence after the anger has subsided and the consequences are beginning to be felt. The truth is usually that the substance use is the result of a primary disorder, and once the person self-medicated against that disorder, thereby failing to process that disordered thinking, they inadvertently gave free rein to other deep-seated emotions, such as anger. Anger and violence never occur in isolation: they are the outward manifestation of something buried much deeper. The person perceives a threat of some kind – be it physical, mental or emotional – and responds by lashing out to disable that threat. It is a form of self-protection, even if it is very often wildly misdirected.

One of the most powerful sources of anger that I have encountered is the need to be heard, or rather the feeling that no one is listening and no one cares. That feeling of neglect and disregard can lead to cognitive distortion as the person builds a case against the world, identifying myriad 'cons' that embody the attitude of the world towards them and justify their opinion of themselves. It's a form of paranoia and once it takes hold it can lead to all manner of disordered thinking and behaviour. I worked with a young woman, Alice, who repeatedly explained her aggressive behaviour with the words: 'nobody's listening to me, they don't get what I want and need'. This feeling led to such aggressive behaviour against her family that when I met her she was the subject of a safety order, which required her to maintain a certain distance from her home. She was only twenty years old, intelligent, a university student with a love of music and languages, and yet she was capable of being so angry, her family could no longer trust her to be in the house with them.

Her aggressive behaviour had started at the age of thirteen, manifesting as temper tantrums. These outbursts occurred only at home and were mainly directed against her mother. When she was sixteen her father died of cancer. Before his death, he asked her to make an effort to control her behaviour, a request she complied with while he was receiving hospice care at home. Soon after his death, the pattern of aggressive behaviour erupted again and included biting and thumping. She was both physically and verbally aggressive towards her mother. When her mother asked for help and care workers were assigned to the case, Alice would often detain them in her house against their will. The police had to be called in to deal with these situations a number of times.

When I was asked to assess Alice, she presented as an articulate young woman with a strong desire to be part of a social group, to have friendships, a boyfriend and a good career. When she described her life to date, it was clear that those desired things had eluded her until now – she had no friends in school or college, found it difficult to initiate conversations and connect with people and therefore had no social network. It became clear that these shortcomings caused her huge frustration, which had been transferred on to those closest to her, leading to her aggression towards her mother and family. To Alice's mind, the fact that her life wasn't as she wished it to be was the fault of other people, who either 'don't want to talk to me' or 'don't get me'. She used anger to deflect blame and externalise it, keeping herself safe from those negative thoughts. This frustration and the poor cognitive processing of it was exacerbated by a poor level of empathy and ongoing disinhibition of her negative behaviour against others. When asked about her mother, Alice clearly didn't comprehend the damage that she had caused through her behaviour. Her belief was that anger was sometimes the best solution, so she wilfully engaged in it. Her sense of loneliness and isolation led to self-sabotaging behaviour that only increased those emotions as a result. Again and again she asserted that 'no one listens to me'. She made me think of Edvard Munch's painting, *The Scream*, ranting, screaming and tearing the world apart in a misguided attempt to make it work better. Alice clearly illustrated the fact that anger is a secondary emotion. What I and the other clinical supports had to help her discover was that the primary emotions were frustration, sadness, loneliness and low self-esteem. As she was an Arts undergraduate and interested in culture, I recommended music, art and equine therapy alongside counselling and CBT. It took time, but Alice slowly began to understand herself better, which led to a marked decrease in her angry outbursts.

The other very common source of anger that I have encountered is aggression as a learned behaviour. This relates back to social learning theory and the proposition that what we witness as children we often replicate as young adults and adults. A child who is raised in an environment where aggression and violence are common occurrences is deeply affected by what they see. This behaviour teaches them that anger is the only method of conflict resolution and getting what you want. They aren't given any insight into emotional language, so they grow up without that essential psychological vocabulary to express themselves and find alternative ways to solve problems. What often happens is that the things they have witnessed as children mark them deeply, but they are unable to process them. They carry with them complex emotions that they cannot name or recognise, which means they never come to terms with them. Those emotions are generally negative and difficult. Anger, on the other hand, can be pure and simple and energising. It therefore becomes the default emotion because it feels like control. Anger is their coping mechanism, and it allows them to mask and hide from other, more unmanageable feelings. They won't be aware that this is what is happening, but it is a dangerous psychological situation that often leads to them crossing the line into illegal acts.

There was a young man who had caused untold grief through his actions, hurting many people, but I nonetheless felt a great degree of sympathy for him because so much of what was happening was beyond his ability to consciously control and process. I was called in to assess Austin for a case at the Central Criminal Court, where he was facing a disturbing number of charges. The charge sheet included theft, assault, property damage, false imprisonment, threatening behaviour and possession of a weapon with intent to harm. Austin had admitted responsibility for the offences and was pleading guilty, so my report would go towards the judge's final sentencing decision. Austin was already in prison, so I met with him in an interview room the size of a bathroom, containing just a desk and two chairs. The walls were painted glossy green, reminiscent of a hospital ward. I noted the silver button beside the door at my back, which would ring a bell and switch on a light over the door, alerting the guards if I wanted, or needed, to exit, as I was locked in.

In the book of evidence the man presented was a dangerous criminal offender, and a repeat offender at that. The man I met was young, in his early twenties, and appeared nervous and apprehensive. He made every effort to answer my questions fully, but his memory surrounding the crimes was poor and he struggled to describe exactly what had happened. He was calm, though, and able to discuss the impact he had had on his own life and prospects and on his family's lives. He felt regret that he had caused pain and embarrassment to his girlfriend, mother, brother and grandmother, in particular. His understanding of what constituted negative behaviour was skewed, but I felt he did experience guilt for his actions and some degree of sympathy for his victims. He had also been engaging with the services on offer in the prison, taking part in anger management workshops. He was able to describe to me what was wrong with his previous ideas of conflict resolution and also new methods he had learned in the workshops for responding to stressful situations.

Austin clearly wanted to be different, but there were elements in his psychological make-up that militated against such change. He came from an impoverished background, one of four children with a hardworking and ever-present mother who did her best for them. Austin had never met his biological father, but his mother's partner of twenty years was the key male role model throughout his childhood. This man was involved in criminal activity, so violence and drug activity were commonplace in Austin's childhood, both at home and in the disadvantaged community in which he lived. When Austin was ten, their home was petrol-bombed on account of his stepfather's associations with criminals. The house was destroyed, and Austin's dog perished in the fire. The family moved to a new location, where Austin, now aged fifteen, witnessed the attempted murder of his stepfather, who was shot but survived the attack. Within the house there was domestic violence and physical abuse of Austin and his siblings, in spite of his mother's efforts to protect them from their stepfather. It was striking that when I asked Austin if he felt his childhood experiences had contributed to his high levels of anger and aggression, he felt they had not because his childhood had been 'normal'. To him, that was just the way life was and he believed many people lived this way and shared these experiences.

As a result of all he witnessed and experienced, Austin's emotional and psychological development were disrupted and negated. He developed high impulsivity, poor empathy, learning difficulties, high levels of aggression, clinical depression and high anxiety, culminating as a presentation of ADHD in school. To this was recently added post-traumatic stress disorder, including nightmares, irrational fears and tremors, after Austin had witnessed the death of a fellow inmate by heart attack. For Austin, this psychological and emotional deficit led to aggressive behaviour from the age of eleven. He also became withdrawn and isolated, not wishing to discuss his problems with anyone. He left school at thirteen, which began a life of unemployed drifting, drinking, drug use and, eventually and inevitably, criminal behaviour. Austin was working hard to take responsibility for his actions – by pleading guilty and by engaging with workshops – but it was an uphill battle for him because he had huge difficulty expressing emotion and displayed emotional incongruence, which is a conflict between what one feels and what one understands or displays. For example, I feel happy but I get angry – this is because I perceive happiness or contentment to be uncomfortable feelings that I am not willing to accept and internalise. His emotional development had effectively been halted and moved in a negative direction that was affirmed by poor role-modelling and replaced with unhealthy beliefs about 'normal' behaviour, which included using anger and aggression as coping mechanisms. In doing this, he was replicating the behaviour of his stepfather, which had become his norm. His upbringing had left him with very low self-esteem, which manifested as anger against others in his environment, regardless of whether he knew them and whether they had done anything to make him angry. For Austin's victims, here was an out-of-control man, aggressive and violent and completely detached; for Austin, he was acting out rage emotions that had been created in him by his environment in the past. He was trapped in a cycle of anger and violence because it had developed so strongly in him that it became the hub around which the rest of his personality revolved.

The common reaction is that the person doesn't see or understand how certain poor developmental aspects in their life have contributed to deficits in their personality – they simply don't register cause and effect in the course of their lives. This in turn is related to how ignorance and detachment cause anger and emotional upset without the person actually being conscious why that has happened. In order to stimulate understanding, I very often recommend anger management via psychotherapeutic intervention as the most effective way of educating the person about where their anger comes from, one likely source being attachment disorder, for example. Cognitive behaviour therapy can identify the sources or triggers of anger and how it begins to develop. Once that identification has been made, the client and I agree a strategy to redirect the anger in a different way that avoids hurting others. This might involve leaving the immediate environment, punching a boxing bag or rechannelling the emotion elsewhere to avoid harm. Anger is a difficult emotion to manage and a difficult behaviour to change, so this therapy often takes years to complete. It requires dedication on the part of the client and extensive work on the self. I have found that group CBT is very effective in this regard, where the subject can be questioned by peers and forced to respond in a non-violent manner, with the support of the group facilitator, who will be a trained psychologist or an expert in group CBT. In my own practice, this method has proven the most effective way to tackle anger and its problem behaviour. I recommended group CBT for Austin, for example, and although he was slow to respond at first, eventually he began to understand the chain of events and emotions that underlay his anger, which was a crucial first step towards changing that behaviour. He is still engaged in CBT but starting to feel the benefits of committing to understanding and changing his own behaviour.

Psychologists categorise anger leading to aggression as one of two types: impulsive or instrumental. Among the non-criminal population, instrumental anger is not as common. This is 'dish served cold' anger – a calculated act that is designed around a particular goal or agenda. It reflects the person's own anger and frustration through being methodical, premeditated and without remorse or care for any consequences. This sounds psychopathic, but it does not fall under that category. Anger alone does not qualify someone as a psychopath. If, however, it exists with other presentations with an effect on the environment (described in Chapter 9) then it can be a psychopathic trait. It is self-serving anger born of a sense of oppression. Examples of this would be things like the campus shootings in America or 'lone wolf' acts of terrorism, like that which occurred in Nice in the summer of 2016. The person who is capable of instrumental anger usually exhibits a marked lack of guilt and empathy, which is why psychopaths and sociopaths will engage in this type of aggression. Impulsive anger, on the other hand, is the type most of us are familiar with – the 'blowing your top' anger that flares up in response to a trigger. This is a reactive response to an event that makes us so angry, we want to lash out and hurt someone. Someone who is impulsively angry will usually be described as 'quick-tempered', having 'a short fuse'. Those around them learn to handle them with a certain amount of care in order to avoid triggering an outburst. Episodes of impulsive anger would include smashing objects, shouting and hitting – there is a strong outward manifestation of the feelings rampaging around inside the person. This rampage is aided by hormones in the body, such as testosterone. A person can live their life and be prone to impulsive anger but never cross the line into illegality. The progress of impulsive anger to violent aggression is very often related to mental health, to psychological disorders and to having more negative factors in one's life than positive factors. Those extra burdens can turn impulsive anger into something far more uncontrollable and dangerous.

I believe, too, that there is a mix of the two types of anger, which is most commonly seen in the psychopath. This is marked by an impulsive rage that is harnessed to become chronic, with long-lasting temper marshalled into a personality that will become a human weapon against everyone who disagrees with them. This type of anger demands patience and a degree of self-control until the ultimate outburst of grave violence against another or against many others. This mixing of the temperaments is a dangerous cocktail that can have disastrous consequences.

The most common personality disorder among humans is borderline personality disorder (BPD). This is essentially a mood disorder that affects the ability to interact socially, read visual and environmental cues and respond appropriately, but is also often self-destructive, even when support and love are provided to the person. The angry habits are so deeply entrenched that positive influences are dismissed and sabotaged, leaving the person isolated, lonely and with a tremendous feeling of rejection, albeit caused by their own actions. Borderline personality disorder is classified as a mental health condition, but it often goes undiagnosed and the person lives with it and its consequences without ever understanding themselves properly. When I meet a person with BPD, very often I find that the cause is attachment disorder, which we examined in Chapter 3. The lack of healthy attachment to the mother or primary care-givers gives rise to distress, anxiety and feelings of worthlessness and anger. As noted above, anger provides a very effective mask to threatening emotions. This is why the triggers for anger can seem so innocuous to the onlooker. The 'threat' need not be physical at all, though: it can be the threat of being shown to have limited intelligence or success, the threat of being called 'useless' or 'stupid' or 'worthless', the threat of being laughed at, rebuffed by the opposite sex, humiliated, belittled. If a situation presents any of these possibilities, the person with BPD can react violently in an effort to stave off the feelings this will give rise to. At base, fear and anger are intimately linked, and it is fear that gives rise to the greatest anger. In the case of Alice, above, her angry outbursts seemed as irrational as they were frightening, but they were triggered by her fear of being lonely, of being dismissed, of being considered immature or selfish. For Alice, those were powerful triggers, strong enough to cause her 'fight or flight' response. She chose to fight – attacking those who loved her most in an effort to contain and control the difficult emotions.

One of the common effects of impulsive anger and of BPD is self-harm. And one of the common coping mechanisms people use to live with anger and self-harm is self-medication. Both addiction and self-harm are manifestations of anger at oneself – like a punishment the person metes out to him/herself every day. Addiction is anger against oneself; self-harm is violence against oneself; both are self-medication to dull the emotions. The self-harming teen, covering their arms with long sleeves, has become a staple of popular culture and young adult films and books. That familiarity can lead people to overlook the seriousness of self-harming and its potential to lead to suicidal ideation. If a person is cutting their own body, scarring their own skin, that speaks of an extreme anger that they are living with day in, day out. They require immediate and specialist help to break the cycle of deep anger followed by the relief of self-inflicted violence.

I have worked with a number of self-harming individuals, but Scott seemed, on the surface, an unlikely candidate. On paper his life was stable and healthy: he had a happy childhood, a loving mother and strong sibling relationships, and he had reached all the normal milestones. Even though he was in trouble with the law, his family continued to support him. His siblings were successful in their lives and there was no forensic history among his family members and no genetic psychological disorders or alcoholism. A brief overview would describe Scott as entirely 'normal', yet here he was, sitting opposite me, being prosecuted for drunk and disorderly behaviour, possession of a knife and shoplifting. He presented with a long history of alcohol addiction, drug use, expulsion from two schools and various arrests and court appearances. His mother attributed his troubling behaviour to getting 'caught up with the wrong crowd'. Clearly in this case, appearances were deceiving.

During our interview, Scott was sociable and friendly, able to talk and speak for himself. He was very upset and regretful at the distress he had caused his family, but he attributed the entire cause of his behaviour to alcohol addiction. He could neither see nor admit to any other source for his anger and aggression. Scott had begun drinking alcohol at the age of fifteen and quickly became addicted. The only outward reason I could discern for this was the anxiety produced by his 'family mantra' of not discussing emotions and always presenting a perfect image to outsiders – neighbours and the local community. While this did not seem to weigh heavily on his siblings, Scott described it as causing him to feel pressure and anxiety, which affected his mood and self-esteem. He had self-medicated with alcohol. This sequence of negative emotion and addiction had led in turn to self-harming – cutting along his wrists – social isolation, low mood and difficulty managing emotions. The constant turmoil inside his mind eventually resulted in outward manifestations of anger and aggression – in reality, Scott was wrestling with and punishing himself, but he had no understanding of that at all. He could not see any connection between his alcohol use and his psychological challenges.

The reasons Scott gave to explain his behaviour – alcohol, family expectations – and that his mother gave – falling in with the wrong crowd – seemed slim and vague, but as we talked more, it became clear that there was far more at work here than he understood. This is a common factor in anger and aggression cases – the person does not understand this part of their own psychology/personality and is mystified by their own feelings and actions. This separation from their own thinking and behaviour makes it very difficult for them to change it, because change requires understanding. As Scott talked about his life, it was easy to see that he had very low self-esteem and struggled to understand and express his emotions. What he described as his 'normal state' was in fact depression and mental health instability and inconsistency, with possible learning difficulties as well, leaving him with no strong tenet of thinking upon which to build ambition or feel affirmation. When these unrecognised challenges to his emotional well-being were coupled with alcohol and drug use, it had exacerbated the negative emotions and his inability to understand them, leading to negative and self-destructive behaviours. His strongest emotion, perhaps, was regret and guilt that he had caused his family shame and disappointment. Regret and guilt are tsunami-like emotions that can easily overwhelm, and anger proved an effective way of blotting them out for a while. My conclusion was that it was highly likely that Scott presented with BPD, based on his addiction, self-destructive and isolated behaviours coupled with guilt, shame and depression. This was the source and cause of his addiction, despondency, low self-esteem, suicidal ideation, self-harming and emotional regulation difficulties. Taken altogether, his case suggested a complex of mental health challenges, none of which had been diagnosed to date, leaving Scott defenceless against them.

The key feature of anger and aggression was very apparent in Scott's case – that anger is a secondary emotion, coped with through the outward aggressive behaviour. Behind it lay the truth, but Scott was incapable of recognising or accessing that truth on his way. This is a presentation I see again and again, especially with regard to violence – the person simply cannot explain why they did what they did. They are divorced from their own thinking and fall headlong into the gap between thought and understanding. People immediately relate violent behaviour to men, but that isn't reflected in my practice. I have assessed and treated many women for violence and aggression as well. There is no gender split here – men and women are equally capable of experiencing this divorce from the self and responding to it with extreme behaviour.

Sally-Anne was a young woman of just twenty who was facing the serious charge of intent to endanger life. She had pleaded guilty, so I performed the assessment for the purposes of sentencing at the Central Criminal Court. The violence she had perpetrated was disturbing and severe – on a night out with friends, she had pointed out a woman in the pub and said something to the effect that she was going to 'get her'. Sometime later, Sally-Anne had smashed a glass against the table, then used it to attack the other woman. She hadn't just jabbed wildly with it; instead she had dragged the jagged glass down the woman's face, causing maximum damage and scarring. She was lucky to have missed the carotid artery, which could have caused her victim's death.

When I walked into the interview room, Sally-Anne was smiling and friendly. I sat down and explained who I was and what the process of assessment would be. I began to ask my opening question, but she interrupted me, stating loudly that she had ADHD and that was why she had attacked the other girl – 'It's not my fault. I didn't do it.' It was the externalising of blame that I had heard from so many other offenders before her – 'I did it, but it's not my fault' – a contradictory statement that belies a marked lack of self-understanding and awareness. ADHD involves poor attention, fleeting responses to environmental cues, hyperactivity and high impetuosity, often impulsively communicating or acting out of anger or any emotion. But while it might cause frustration and inappropriate behaviour, it is often not violent at all and could not be expressly designated as the sole cause of violent behaviour. I got to ask my original question about her childhood and she described a difficult background. Her father was the adored focus of her affection but often absent because of periods spent in prison. Her mother was a recovering alcoholic who had suffered severe post-natal depression, so her mothering was supplemented by the support of Sally-Anne's grandmother. From a young age, Sally-Anne had been troublesome and troubled.

Sally-Anne had left school at fifteen, given birth to a daughter at seventeen and never had a job. Her daughter she had given into the care of her own mother, who was now raising her. When I asked why she had made this decision, she cited her ADHD. She had moved to London, which was where she had met her husband – a man with a forensic history not unlike her father's. They had married just a few months before the night out that led to her arrest. Sally-Anne had received her diagnosis of ADHD at the age of thirteen, following years of hyperactivity and defiance at school. It seemed to be a label that she was embracing, like a shield against honesty and responsibility.

I asked her why exactly she had attacked the woman in the pub. She said the woman had made a remark about her skirt, describing it as 'tarty'. Sally-Anne reiterated that ADHD and alcohol were the cause of the attack – that she couldn't even remember doing it, like she wasn't really there. I often hear this explanation, that an altered mental state is responsible for the action, that the person wouldn't do it in their 'normal mind'. It's a curious idea, that we have two minds – one normal and one malicious, the 'not-us' mind. This splitting of self and responsibility is often put forward as justification for extreme behaviour, but it's not real. We each have one mind – yes, it has many layers and some can be conflicting, but it's not possible to assign some behaviours to the 'real me' self and other, unacceptable behaviours to the 'not really me' self (unless realised in schizophrenic or dissociated identity personalities, which are very, very rare). That's a semantic argument, not a psychological argument.

As we talked about her sense of being dissociated from herself that night and her feelings about her victim – which seemed vague and detached – she pushed up the sleeves of her top. There were scars along the inside of her arms. When I asked about them, she quickly covered them over again, told me they were 'nothing'. Her self-harm gave insight into a high level of psychological disorder with a correspondingly low level of self-esteem. I began to understand why Sally-Anne had reacted violently to the woman's criticism. Sally-Anne had low self-esteem and self-worth, anger about her father's absences and her mother's incessant attempts to tell her he hadn't lived his life well, she was lacking in education and prospects, impulsive and all of this led her to feel unable to care for herself or others – which was why she had readily given up care of her daughter. Her reasoning was skewed by her disordered thinking, which meant other people posed a very real and fearful threat – even if only through their words. Sally-Anne felt those words as a direct attack, which was why she had attacked right back. And afterwards, guilt, regret and responsibility had been handily dismissed by way of ADHD and alcohol. It was as if Sally-Anne saw her diagnosis as permission to behave badly – that it was expected of her and beyond her ability to control. It was a stark illustration of how labelling can have adverse effect on some people – especially young offenders – by giving them a means of abdicating responsibility for their own actions: 'I did it, but I'm not to blame.' This is not to say that they don't have a legitimate diagnosis or indeed very real feelings, but the behaviours are not always consistent with the conditions or the emotions.

Another case provides an interesting comparison. Josephine shared some of the characteristics of Sally-Anne's case. Their crime was similar, although Sally-Anne had behaved more violently. In Josephine's case, she had been on a night out, drinking, and another woman had made a disparaging remark about her career. Josephine was already disinhibited by the alcohol and the remark triggered an outburst of impulsive anger. She pushed the other girl violently; the girl fell backwards and hit her head on a table corner. She bled profusely and was scarred as a result. This was a first offence for Josephine, who had no forensic history and had never behaved in such a manner before that night. Her solicitor suggested she wasn't 'able to handle alcohol' – obviously the offender's prime defence has gained a foothold in wider thinking.

Josephine turned out to be an Australian woman in her early thirties. She was strikingly thin and was very upset about the situation she found herself in, crying throughout the interview and wringing tissues in her hands as she talked. She was eager to talk about what had happened and seemed open and warm during our interaction. She was distraught to be facing a charge of assault and violent disorder. She confirmed that she had never done anything illegal before in her life. She was a care worker, a job she loved and had been working in for ten years. She had met an Irishman in Australia and, even though the relationship was faltering, two months previous she had decided to accompany him home to Ireland, believing it would improve matters for them. Once here, she was seized by homesickness and loneliness. She found it difficult to make friends and had no one to talk to about her feelings. She admitted that she had always found it difficult to make female friends. Since the age of sixteen she had been in a series of relationships and always treated her boyfriend as her closest friend. This led to huge dependency, which would subsequently undermine the relationship. She seemed unable to stop this cycle. I asked about her relationship with her father, and she described how he had left the family when she was a child.

I asked why she had attacked the other woman and, like Sally-Anne, she described a single comment that pushed her over the edge. The woman had asked what she did for a living and Josephine had described her job. The woman reacted disdainfully, talking about her as if she was a 'skivvy', Josephine said. This came on the back of Josephine's loneliness, her boyfriend ignoring her that night in favour of his friends, her drinking more than usual as a result, and then the one thing that was going right in her life – her work – was belittled by this woman. Josephine had 'seen red', as she said, and pushed her. She had not foreseen the potential of that push to become a more serious accident.

(An interesting parallel here is that Australia has initiated and promoted the 'One Punch Campaign', alerting people to the potential for a single punch to cause serious injury and even death. This arose after a number of incidents of young men, normally on nights out drinking, throwing one punch that led to tragic consequences and arrest. Like them, Josephine had lashed out in a split-second attack, but it had far-reaching effects on her victim's life. She had never intended to maim the woman, it was a purely impulsive lashing out, but it had dire consequences. The effects of anger can be far wider and larger than we ever intended.)

Unlike Sally-Anne, Josephine did not have a history of anger or aggression. She was a woman in a particular set of circumstances who put in motion a chain of events that she believed she couldn't stop or control. (Control is a perception often tainted by our own myopic viewpoint.) I felt sorry for her. She hadn't pushed the woman out of malice or a desire to hurt, instead it was a purely emotional reaction, pushing away the source of pain and hurt. She expressed huge guilt and remorse for what had happened. She did say that alcohol had led her to behave as she did, but crucially she accepted responsibility for drinking and for her subsequent violent action. She didn't excuse her action as the result of alcohol: she simply knew that alcohol and disinhibition were part of the cause.

In my report I concluded that she was of moderate to low risk of reoffending and recommended that she needed twelve sessions of psychotherapeutic intervention and to cease drinking. However, Josephine also needed external validation in her life and family support – she needed to go home to Australia. Unlike Sally-Anne and other aggressive offenders I had dealt with, I felt that Josephine was highly unlikely to offend again because it was out of character, she had accepted responsibility and she understood to a large extent the true source of her actions that night. When her case came to court, she was convicted of assault and received a twelve-month prison sentence, but suspended on parole with a view to probationary review.

When an offender is apprehended for a violent act, especially if it is their first such act, I always regard them as fortuitous. This is because those who don't get caught or reported will go on to offend again, whereas those who are apprehended have a chance of becoming enlightened about the causes and consequences of their actions, both for the victim and themselves. The crime where I see this occurring most often is with regard to sexual violence. If a man or woman commits a sexual offence but the victim doesn't report it and there are no consequences to the action, the offender is easily able to distort the facts in order to justify that behaviour. This allows them to repeat the behaviour, which they will keep doing until apprehended. Statistics prove that violent sexually offending men nearly always reoffend. If violence has no adverse consequences for the violent offender, he or she will regard it as acceptable behaviour – they are given no reason to think otherwise. So if a young man sexually assaults a woman and the expected knock on the door never sounds – the police never become involved – his thinking is bolstered by this evidence that he did no wrong. It further skews his thinking, making him highly like to reoffend.

Actual physical violence remains the most criminal line that can be crossed with regard to anger and aggression, but there is a non-physical form that can also be incredibly destructive and therefore is worth citing here. This relates to the behaviour of the passive-aggressive personality. This personality type is characterised by subtle aggression, often enacted verbally through insults and demeaning comments, or else via sly actions that are bullying but can easily be argued not to be, making the victim feel wrong-footed and unsure of what is actually occurring. The passive-aggressive trait often stems from bipolar disorder, depressive disorder, anxiety disorder or personality disorder, often being a manifestation of features such as impulsivity and unhappiness. The passive aggressor is more likely to be sociopathic – utilising social means to facilitate a personal vendetta. This form of abuse is subtle, erratic and can be volatile, and it usually affects the victim deeply because of the emotional upset it causes. As the victim often ends up wondering if they are simply being paranoid, it plays on their mind and causes a depletion in self-esteem, poor confidence and incompetent decision-making. Many different behaviours and scenarios could be described as passive-aggressive, but examples would include adultery, where the offender ably justifies his/her actions without taking account of how deeply these actions have affected their partner, and also preventing a colleague's promotion or success by subtly or underhandedly blocking their attempts to progress within the organisation.

Passive-aggressive behaviour can be more harmful than an overt act of violence and can have long-lasting emotional effects. It may not be considered illegal and it is not quantifiable by the law, but it is common in households across all social divides. This is a line that many people cross, but because it's not punishable by law, many don't regard it as a significant or severe action. But it most certainly is.

I have given treatment to many victims of adultery, very upset and let down about their partner's actions, unsure of their own emotional state and worried for family and friends, as well as for themselves. The common reaction is a gross cynicism about the human race and universality about its future demise, believing that the whole world is against them. I dealt with a case that typified the effects and depth of emotion that can follow on from passive-aggressive behaviour. Martin was a successful man in his mid-thirties who looked to have a wonderful life. He had a good job, home, wife and disposable income to enjoy it all. However, his marriage wasn't as perfect as it looked from outside, and he had privately been worried about it for some time. He tried to talk to his wife about the distance between them, suggesting couples counselling in order to re-establish the emotional connection they had once shared. She didn't feel counselling was necessary. When things didn't change, Martin blamed himself, believing his emotional inadequacies and personal shortcomings were causing the rift. He then found out, quite by accident via text and email messages, that his wife was having an affair. She had been engaged in a close and committed emotional and physical relationship with his friend for the past three years. She had never owned up to this, never allowed Martin to make the choice to leave her; instead she had taken the passive-aggressive route of doing what she wanted to do until she was found out.

Martin was understandably distraught when he found out that he had been manipulated and deceived to this extent. He couldn't accept that his wife could have let this situation carry on for three years without ever feeling the need or the confidence to talk to him about it. The marriage ended, but the fallout for Martin was low self-confidence, great sadness and an inability to trust people anymore. He lacked focus on what the future would hold or how he could become fulfilled again, through work, relationships or anything else. Mostly, he struggled with the hypocrisy of his ex-wife's statements over the years – she had repeatedly said that they should never hurt each other and always endeavour to communicate honestly, even if things should turn out badly as a result. Her actions had undermined his fundamental personal principles, calling his beliefs into question. He found himself at the mercy of his moods, switching quickly from anxiety to sadness to anger, which affected his concentration and attention span.

Martin was effectively stuck in a cycle of grief for a number of years after the break-up, which led to him becoming socially isolated. When he finally sought help and came to me, he described himself as 'a shadow of myself' – he felt insubstantial, without purpose or meaning. We talked about his situation over many sessions, and he eventually was able to reconcile his feelings and process them without the extreme emotional flux. He developed a new vision of his future and his needs, which led to his decision to work for some more years, save money, then emigrate in order to live a quiet life in a secluded spot. It was a stark illustration of how deceit, dishonesty and manipulation by one party can deeply affect the personality and life of another. Martin's ex-wife settled down happily with his friend, but Martin was the victim of their lies and his life was changed forever and indeed far more radically.

The force and effects of anger, in all its forms, are powerful and often far-reaching. It is important to understand this and also to understand our own anger – its triggers, common type and manifestation. This requires a good deal of honesty, which may only be achieved through therapy with a trained psychologist. However, there are questions you can put to yourself to ascertain if anger and aggressive behaviour might be having a negative effect on you, your family and your life.

- Do I become irritated more than five times per week?
- What makes me angry?
- How do I communicate anger?
- Has anger led to aggressive outbursts against myself or others?
- Has anger negated my decision-making ability?
- Have others commented on my anger during the last year?
- When I am unhappy, do I become angry?
- Do I use crutches, such as substances, to dull my anger?

If you answer 'yes' to these questions, it is fair to say that anger is a challenging emotion for you and is likely causing difficulties in your life. It is possible to tackle these problems and change your behaviour, however. The best interventions I can recommend are CBT, sport and healthy distractions, such as hobbies. The key thing is to identity the triggers of your anger and learn to avoid them. It's the ABC approach that we have discussed before: identify the antecedent (trigger), alter the behaviour (alternative coping mechanisms, such as leaving the room or counting to ten), improve the consequence (the outcome of your actions is in your power to control). Anger, be it aggressive or passive-aggressive, can destroy lives. This should be the guiding thought to our behaviour and we should invest energy and time in understanding, modifying and controlling our behaviour accordingly.

CHAPTER EIGHT

SEX: IDENTITY, DEVIANCE AND DISORDERED THINKING

D id you check through the contents list at the start of this book and turn to this chapter first?

You are most certainly not alone if you did. Sex is a small word that packs a very big punch. It is a siren's call – we have to look, we have to listen, we cannot look away. Humans are sexual beings, it is our primary drive, instinct and need, which is why we are drawn to it, in all its forms, and endlessly fascinated by it. It is the thread that knits through our lives, weaving together the multifaceted aspects of us into our sexual self – how we sexually behave in our private lives and project ourselves publicly. Our gender, our sexual identity, our sexual orientation, our ways of having and enjoying sex, these are the things that decide so much about our thinking, our behaviour and the lives we lead, from birth to death.

The terms surrounding sexuality are constantly in flux as each generation examines, discusses and labels the sexual phenomena it encounters and prioritises. For example, before the ground-breaking work of Alfred Kinsey, traditional approaches to sexual orientation identified just two options: heterosexual and homosexual. In the 1950s Kinsey added bisexual to this spectrum in an effort to reflect the actual complexities of sexual desire and attraction. Since then, the 'sexual revolution' in scientific and cultural thinking has led to an explosion of labels and possibilities, with a new focus on 'fluidity' in relation to gender, sexual identity and orientation. The once unquestioningly accepted idea of being a particular gender and orientation for all of one's life is now being rewritten, with research suggesting that we are far more fluid and that we can travel up and down the spectrum over the course of our lives. That spectrum runs from purely heterosexual to purely homosexual, but in between lie a plethora of options and variations, allowing people to readjust their sexual identity as and when they wish.

In psychological terms, sexual identity is how we identify our sexuality, shape it, describe it and live it. This is how we choose to be sexual, who we choose to be attracted to, who we want to have sex with – the answers to those erotic questions combine to create our sexual identity, which we are free to choose. Sexual orientation, on the other hand, is our primary focus of desire. So while we might primarily be attracted to, say, men, we might choose to identify as bisexual and conduct sexual affairs with men and women. We are aware of the primary orientation, but we can choose how closely we live by it. Orientation is, therefore, more inflexible than identity, which is flexible, fluid and chosen freely. In spite of being a natural and essential part of our make-up, scientists still don't know what exactly determines each individual's orientation. When it comes to our sexual make-up, we remain, in many ways, a mystery to ourselves and sexual identity can cause us to choose to be alone.

Sexual identity is deeply interesting to psychologists because some argue that it is chosen, but others state it to be pre-determined. It is wrapped up in our emotional expression and self-confidence, but it also relates to what makes us aroused and interested in others. Sex and sexual behaviour are not, however, simply about acts or physical emotions: they are far more to do with emotional control, affirmation and power with and over another. Sex is the most intimate moment, where one person becomes completely secure with another or, alternatively, completely powerful over them. A good and healthy sexual identity, to my mind, revolves around not taking oneself too seriously but being constantly aware of a sexual drive that may or may not be inhibited. The inhibition of sexual desire when necessary is important, but the disinhibition of being able to be warm and close to someone, be openly sexual, is a very important medium by which we express our emotions. It's about the fascination of the unknown, the desire to get to know another person, feeling a degree of connection to them or wanting and finding affirmation of one's self. Sex is a portal through which we escape the everyday, the daily stressors – and sometimes even ourselves. It is a moment of pure communication, which is, at base, what humans desire most. I have found that the common denominator among sex offenders with whom I've worked is that they don't have an emotional language to allow for healthy communication and they haven't experienced that deep connection to another person that complements the development of communication. Many sexual offenders describe a sex act that consists of one, or very few variances in, body position, powerful thrusting of hips and an aggressive need to ejaculate. The end of the act is prioritised over the actual act of sex itself. This is often accompanied by denigration of the victim. Paedophilic sex offenders, for example, are aggressively self-serving. The underlying problem is that many men perceive anger, strength and control as inherently sexual and therefore as something that should be displayed by them, at the expense of physical closeness and mutual enjoyment. For female offenders, they most often cite the need to be without inhibition, to clearly voice their desires and to be able to control others as sexually gratifying.

The psychology of sexuality necessarily brings us right back to Sigmund Freud, who conducted so much research and devoted so much time to this primary instinct. His work centred on the psychological triumvirate of the id, ego and superego. Briefly, the id is the death instinct and the life instinct, which is aimed at self-propagation and survival, and it is governed by the pleasure principle; the ego, which he proposed emerges at six months old, operates on the reality principle, the foundation of which is concern with personal safety; the superego is the formation of the moral principle, which guides and criticises our actions. Freud's theory is that we are born with the id already present – a mass of biological drives that motivates and defines our behaviour. As the person develops, the id demands warmth, food and sex. Its energy Freud called the libido, which he considered to be the driving force permeating our entire personalities and propelling us through life. In his earliest formulations, Freud described the libido as entirely sexual, with other aims and desires arising by some modification of the libido. Nowadays, Freudian therapists use the term libido to refer to the idea of drive energy – the energy we invest in achieving a goal. Freud saw the life instinct as the primary drive, but it could be affected by the death instinct, which he described as the state to which humans are instinctively drawn, a state in which all tension is dissipated. (This echoes *la petite mort* – the name often used by poets as a euphemism for the orgasmic climax.) The self-destruction impulse of the death instinct is tempered by the life instinct, which causes that aggression to be focused outwards, into the world. Aggressive instincts are an important component in our behaviour because a measure of aggression is necessary to achieve our aims.

It is the interplay between the id, ego and superego that shapes our personality and behaviour. Freud's theory was that sexual life begins at birth and progresses through a series of psychosexual stages of development, each of which corresponds to an erogenous zone. So we have the oral stage – breastfeeding, sucking fingers and soothers – and then the anal stage – toilet training and fascination with faeces, with gratification deriving from gaining control over the sphincter muscle – and then phallus stage, which should more rightly be called the genital stage because both males and females become more aware of their genitalia at that point, with consequent curiosity and anxiety around sexual differences.

That's a very quick trip through the fundamentals of the development of sexual identity and the key Freudian theories, but I think every adult is aware of and can chart the development of their own sexuality. We can have different degrees of awareness in this regard, but it is clear that our sexuality is the foundation of our self, bound up in all our ways of thinking and behaving. When healthy development occurs, which is aided by parental role-modelling and care, it is marked by personal, emotional and sexual growth, empathy for others, the ability to perceive the emotional, physical and sexual perspectives of others, use of sex for physical joy as well as emotional connection, comfort with one's own and others' bodies, generosity, contentment, fantasy and imagination. The person has self-confidence in their sexuality and sexual choices; they enjoy sex because they have experienced it at their own pace of maturing and have learned what they do and don't like and their partners have respected these preferences. A healthy sexual identity is one that recognises the huge enjoyment and benefits to be derived from having tactility and responsiveness with a willing partner. If those stages have been reached and embraced, the person will have a desire and an ability to communicate physically with a partner in a mutually enjoyable manner. They will also exhibit sexual security, which is an appreciation of the closeness, tacility and sexuality of feminism or masculinity. When a person has such security, it translates as a happier and healthier sexual lifestyle. As we get older, sex may become the cornerstone of emotional acceptance and life satisfaction, whether that be upon reflection of our own sexual journey or how we relate to others – partners, family and offspring.

Sexual deviance has traditionally been viewed as a warped or 'wrong' sexuality that culminates in deviant behaviour, with deviant being defined as 'dangerous', 'humiliating', 'perverse' and 'unnatural'. However, this whole area is now changing hugely as cultural norms shift and the question of sex and sexuality is opened up to a much wider debate. So where once deviance was condemned as lying beyond normative sexual behaviour, this line is becoming far greyer and far more blurred. What was considered sexually deviant twenty years ago is not considered so now. Sexual deviance can involve consensual adults engaged in entirely legal acts, such as sadomasochistic behaviour, cross-dressing and numerous sexual partners. Across popular culture and into psychology, there is a huge amount of focus on redefining sex for new and future generations. I think the next generation of psychologists will be very interested in transgender and gender-fluid research and discussions, which will no doubt prove to be a very pertinent paradigm in psychology over the coming years.

So if sexual deviance has largely come in from the cold, how do we assign the labels 'unhealthy' or 'wrong' to sexual activity? It remains the case that interrupted or disrupted psychosexual development can lead to processing difficulties with regard to sexuality and sex. Where unhealthy development occurs, this can lead to social isolation, being uncomfortable with others, hypoarousal (the 'freeze' response) and hyperarousal (the 'fight or flight' response) during sex, emotional upset when physically close to another, little sexual expression, numbed affect, poor sense of self-identity, fear of intimacy and disclosing of emotions to another person. The common causes of disrupted sexual development are negative parent role-modelling, experiencing sexual or physical abuse, witnessing abuse and watching pornography at an impressionable age.

One of the early cases I dealt with involved a woman who exhibited inappropriate sexual behaviour that stemmed from disrupted psychosexual development and mental illness. I was a master's student at Leicester University at the time. As such, I was assigned to shadow a professor to study his working methods and learn from them. On this particular day, I accompanied the professor as he went to interview the woman, Anthea, at the hospital where she was confined, having been brought in for prostitution and wilful exposure (defined as demonstrating sexual acts, such as masturbation, in a public place). She had been transferred to a hospital because she had received a diagnosis of schizophrenia, which my professor was now investigating. It was the first time I had encountered the effects of unhealthy development, and at the time it shocked me. Anthea answered the professor's questions about her mental state, her general health and her medication in heavily intoned monosyllables, but at the same time she reached her hand down inside her leggings and began to masturbate. The professor's expression never altered as he continued with his questions. I noticed that he changed tack to explore her emotions, asking leading questions about her emotional state. When we finally left the room – which I must admit I was glad to do – and were alone together, I asked him why Anthea had behaved in such an inappropriate manner. He explained that while we couldn't be exactly sure of what the behaviour signified for Anthea, he felt it was a way of making a social connection, of expressing her emotions – that was why he had attempted to explore her emotional state because he felt that in the aroused state she might be more expressive. The alternative was that she was emotionally incongruent and was actually feeling acute anxiety during the interview but hid it behind the sexual act because that was the only way she could mask her inner emotions. Anthea had received unhealthy role-modelling as a child, witnessing violence between her parents, and this had adversely affected her emotional development. The effect was to stunt her psychosexual development, leading her to confuse anxiety with arousal and to be incapable of adequately understanding her own emotions and needs. This made her a very vulnerable person, open to exploitation.

We saw previously, in the case of Alistair, how witnessing violence against women – in Alistair's case, his father's routine violence against his mother – leads to imitation of that behaviour. Alistair's deprived and violent childhood saw him convicted as an adult for rape and murder. This is a common occurrence among the offenders I deal with who as children witness criminal behaviours in the home. A child is incapable of processing such experiences rationally, which leads to emotional upheaval, shutting down of the painful emotions and memories and, as a result, an inability to achieve the psychological and emotional milestones. This in turn leaves them vulnerable to negative thinking and, ultimately, asocial behaviour. When parents fail to provide adequate care and decent role-modelling, it impacts enormously on the developing child and adolescent. I have seen so many cases of nineteen to twenty-five-year-olds who are emotionally compromised due to poor parenting. For example, neurotic parents who display emotions in a pressured, uneasy fashion can cause anxiety in children, often leading to emotional dysregulation in the young adult, which fuels the need for relaxation through self-medication, substances and sex.

One case that illustrated some of these principles was that of a man called Edgar. He hadn't been subject to wanton violence as Alistair had, but he had experienced disruption of his emotional development, which eventually led to him crossing the line into criminal behaviour. Edgar was in prison for burglary, to which was now to be added a custodial sentence for unlawful and carnal knowledge of an underage female. I went to interview him at the prison, as his solicitor required an assessment of him with regard to the new charge. The book of evidence described how Edgar – a man of almost forty with a long history of drug abuse – had had a sexual relationship with a girl of sixteen. While pleading guilty because the girl's age was incontestable and therefore their sexual relationship fell into the category of statutory rape, Edgar was vehement that it had been consensual and therefore 'not wrong'.

As we talked about his past, it quickly became apparent that Edgar had spent his whole life seeking his father's approval and not receiving it. He described his sisters as the 'golden girls' who could do no wrong, exceeding his father's expectations on every level. He, on the other hand, had never managed to meet his father's expectations let alone exceed them. His father harboured high hopes for his educational achievements and career, but Edgar struggled in school and at home was made to feel useless and worthless as a result. The wound caused by his father's lack of love and affection had never healed, making Edgar vulnerable to further damage. He had moved out of the family home at the age of fifteen, moving in with his aunt. She was a heroin user and she introduced her young nephew to the drug, which started his lifetime of drug abuse. When his father found out what had happened, instead of being angry with the aunt and extricating Edgar from her influence, he disowned Edgar, as if this behaviour was the fullest confirmation of how worthless his son was. This final cut went deep, leaving Edgar reeling emotionally, seeking any means of self-medication to blot out the hurt and anger.

In what can be a relatively common outcome, as an adult, Edgar had visited his hurt and anger on another vulnerable child. The sixteen-year-old girl in question was also a vulnerable child, also a drug user, and they had first become friends through buying and sharing drugs together. After a time, this friendship had become sexual. Edgar assured me it was consensual and wanted on her part, but her age and vulnerable status contradicted his view. Instead of helping her, supporting her and acting in the manner of a responsible adult, Edgar had – like his aunt before him – encouraged the girl's drug use and then exploited her emotional frailty. He imitated and replicated the behaviours to which he had been subjected, disrupting the girl's psychosexual development in the process. It was a vicious cycle of damaged people seeking to damage others. This is what happens when parents or care-givers fail to facilitate healthy development – the repercussions ripple out through the generations, one infecting the next.

Alongside role-modelling and witnessing/experiencing difficult scenes as a child, we also mentioned pornography as a source of disrupted development. There has been much debate surrounding the potential effects of viewing pornography as a child/adolescent, with often vociferous arguments being put forward by those on opposite sides of the fence. From my own work, I am convinced that viewing pornography has a detrimental effect on the emotional development of children, their understanding of sexual desire and

sex, and their opinion of and beliefs regarding the opposite sex.
The advent of the internet means that pornography is now very
easily accessible. It used to be the case that 'soft porn', as peddled
by publications such as *Playboy* or *Hustler*, was the widest available
type of porn, with many men never proceeding beyond that border.
Now, however, the lines between 'soft porn' and 'hard porn' are
increasingly blurred, with every taste and fetish catered for online,
a situation that is, interestingly, in tandem with the ever-evolving
notion of what is sexually acceptable in society. There has been
much focus recently on 'rape culture', with feminists pointing to
pornography, especially violent pornography, as being responsible
for an increasingly aggressive attitude towards woman, especially
those in the public eye – as evidenced by the proliferation of death
and rape threats via online platforms.

For my own part, I would come down on the side of
pornography having an unhealthy effect on the developing mind,
emotions and thinking of a child or adolescent. This opinion
stems from working with male adolescents, in particular, who feel
that pornography is their only means of 'feeling' sexually but who
develop shame and guilt for having viewed it, negating their ability
to communicate with sexual partners in the future, usually because
they fear or believe any future partner will think them 'disgusting'.
I think that social networking will change the evolutionary make-
up of the human brain, resulting in a lowered capacity to restrain
ourselves because of the constant stimulation on offer online. The
ability to access all types of sexual energy that are misleading,
fantastical and absolutely not rooted in any communication skill
will have a deleterious effect on future sexual identity. Having sex
merely as an impulse only serves to fuel aggressive behaviour and,
to my mind, will predetermine more crime against women, men
and children. I think it will also lead to blunting of relationships
and sexual identity, which means difficulty gaining sexual arousal
with a partner after spending so much time immersed in online
sexual activity.

I worked with a young man called Grady who required counselling for addiction to pornography. He was sixteen years old, an introspective young man who enjoyed school, particularly languages, a passion on which he hoped to build his future career. He had many friends, a solid family background, with good relationships with his parents and siblings, who all shared an excellent quality of life. There was no forensic or psychiatric history in the family. And yet his parents had brought him to me because he was exhibiting severe anxiety, worrying constantly about his future. He was self-medicating for this with cannabis, which he smoked every evening. His parents were obviously concerned and wanted to help him get past whatever obstacle was ruining his peace of mind. What they didn't know, and what he confessed to me in our first session, was that he was feeling lonely and inadequate, with a crushing sense that this would be the case for his entire life. He confessed that he used porn to become aroused and masturbate but felt shame and guilt for this – feelings I suspected were derived from his religious background and dominant maternal influence. He had had two sexual partners thus far, but then fell in love with a girl his own age – the first time he had experienced such strong feelings. They were together for a while, but she left him, citing her own 'psychological challenges'. As a result, he was grieving for that relationship, and as he had no sexual outlet and didn't want anyone else, he was engaging with pornographic material more and more regularly. It had got to the point where he couldn't achieve arousal without the use of visual broadcast via porn. He felt completely incapable of pursuing any new relationships because his 'secret activity' had left him feeling disgusted about his own sexual habits, a feeling he felt all other girls would share and denounce him for. This was all raging inside him but the shame and guilt meant he hadn't been able to share these thoughts and feelings with anyone else, which had only made them worse. It was a good illustration of how the easy accessibility of pornography in the digital age can lead to mental conflict and, ultimately, social isolation.

The area of viewing as a direct precursor to doing is still undergoing research, but studies conducted so far suggest that viewing pornography or violent acts does lead the person to try to act out what they have seen, whether through curiosity or because it normalises such behaviour. The other precursor to sexual offending is disrupted sexual development, which can lead to a person experiencing inappropriate, immature or violent thoughts and emotions. If they witnessed sexual or violent activity as a child, that also predisposes them to re-enacting this behaviour as an adult. When these factors join together, and whether they know it or not, the person becomes capable of committing a sex crime because their understanding of sex and love is so skewed it does not give them the ability to interpret sexual and emotional behaviour correctly, or else it fills them with fear and anger with regard to sex, which again puts them in danger of taking out these feelings on a sexual partner. A sexually coercive person is one who will use force, alcohol, drugs or persuasion to have sexual contact with another without their express consent.

During my time working in Australia, I assisted on a case of sexual coercion. The lead was taken by my supervisor, Alessia, when we interviewed a woman accused of coercing a fifteen-year-old boy into having sex with her. The woman, Amanda, was in her thirties and a secondary school teacher. The boy was one of her students, and he had reported to his parents that Amanda had had sex with him. She was friendly to him in school, she said she found him to be 'good company' and she invited him to visit her at home one day, which he did. She insisted he wanted her, that it was consensual and that the boy 'made the first move'. Amanda was pleading guilty to sex with a minor, but she insisted to us that she was not, in fact, guilty because it was entirely consensual. She could not see that there was anything wrong with her actions and in this she was probably aided by the sometimes perceived social construct that tells us women have sex 'done to them', while men are the active and initiating participant. There is also a wide misconception that an erect penis implies male consent.

As we discussed her background, Amanda admitted that she had been abused by her father, which had led to the ending of her parents' marriage and the loss of contact with her father. It was striking that she talked about her abuse in ambivalent terms, not condemning it as wrong. It seemed that being a victim of abuse and struggling to process and rationalise that abuse had led to a cognitive distortion, whereby she rewrote abuse as love. In her mind, she had shared a deep connection with the young student she had seduced; to our minds, she had groomed a young boy and subtly coerced him into having sex with her. The fact that the boy had reported this afterwards pointed to his belief and feeling that it was unwanted sexual contact. Alessia asked Amanda why she had moved jobs three times in the last five years, but Amanda simply muttered vaguely about liking change. During the trial it transpired that two other boys had come forward with the same accusation. The abuse and cognitive distortion it gave rise to since Amanda's childhood had resulted in her becoming a serial sex offender, confirming the direct link between experience, distorted thinking and criminal sexual acts. (It should be noted, however, that Amanda's case was rare. The risk factors for perpetrating sexual coercion are a learning disability, experience of abuse prior to sixteen years of age and being male – Amanda fulfilled only one of these risk criteria, which made her offending unusual.)

Sexual coercion is a crime, but victims rarely report it, usually because they are unsure what occurred and what their role in it was exactly. It is a consent grey area and, for example, the UK's 2013 *National Survey of Sexual Attitudes and Lifestyles* showed clearly that while one in ten women and one in seventy men had been the victim of sexual coercion, more than half never spoke of it to anyone. When coercion involves force and a very clear lack of consent, it is rape, which has higher reporting and conviction rates, although still nowhere near 100%. Rape is a sex crime, and it is often caused by significant psychological disturbance in the person carrying out the crime. What is commonly argued by defence barristers is that the rapist is suffering with post-traumatic stress disorder (PTSD), which led to cognitive distortion and, ultimately, the rape crime. The defence here is that PTSD gives rise to chaotic and out-of-control thinking and behaviour. The following factors are used to support a PTSD-related criminal defence:

1. The act represents spontaneous unpremeditated behaviour, uncharacteristic of the individual.
2. Coherent dialogue appropriately related to time and place is lacking.
3. The choice of victim is fortuitous or accidental.
4. The response is disproportionate to the provocation.
5. The act is rationally inexplicable and lacks current motivation.
6. The act recreates in a psychologically meaningful way elements of the original traumatic stressor.
7. The defendant is unaware of the ways in which he or she has re-enacted traumatic experiences.
8. The act is precipitated by events or circumstances that realistically or symbolically force the individual to face unresolved conflicts.
9. There is amnesia for the episode.

If we look back to the case of Alistair, we can see how the recreation of a psychological stressor did take place: the woman he approached in the bar rejected him and he felt humiliated, which echoed his experiences with and feelings for his own mother. The victim could have had no idea whatsoever that this is what was occurring, but in Alistair's mental and emotional landscape her innocent request to be left alone triggered a huge upheaval, throwing him back to overwhelming memories and feelings. This in no way excuses his actions, but it does seek to provide context for aetiology and behaviour, to explain how a person can become a rapist, how they can be so detached as to be entirely indifferent to the suffering they are causing another human being.

When a person has a lack of empathy – usually because they were not taught empathy by their parents or failed to develop it due to adverse psychological environments, events or congenital disabilities – this in turns means they have little inhibition. In Freudian terms, the superego was never switched on, so they don't have a guiding moral compass by which to make their decisions. It has been proposed that punishment of a child can lead to emotional detachment and deficient empathy, which we have seen in a number of cases throughout this book, where severe punishments have warped the mental and emotional development of the child. A deficiency in inhibition is one of the hallmarks of sexual aggression. It has been proposed that sexually coercive people exhibit higher arousal to rape stimuli. This has been supported by phallometric studies, which measure the response of the penis to descriptions of foreplay and consensual sex acts. Most men are aroused by such descriptions. However, when scripts describing force, pain, distress and fear on the part of the woman are introduced, sexually coercive men exhibit sexual arousal at these descriptions, whereas the arousal of non-sexually coercive men is inhibited. So the psychological distortion among the coercive population has a physical effect, which is what leads to crossing the line into sexual crime.

The case of Anthony illustrated this distortion all too well. He was an older man who had fallen on hard times, was unemployed and had been living in an impoverished state for a number of years. I assessed him pending sentencing for rape. He had a history of alcoholism and when we discussed this he described how he was the child of an alcoholic. His father was hypercritical of him and often absent from the family home, while his mother was an alcoholic with mental health challenges. Her inability to care for him properly turned into outright rejection over the course of his childhood. She would regularly withhold food from him as punishment, and he was forced to steal food to survive. His troubled upbringing had marked his adult life and in the past year he had become homeless. He was taken in by his paternal aunt, a woman in her sixties who wanted to help him start over. She set one condition: that he would not drink alcohol in her house and would endeavour to quit altogether. He continued to use alcohol in her home, hiding it from her. He then began to steal small items in order to buy alcohol. One evening she confronted him about the alcohol and the stealing, which sent him into a rage. He raped her, then ran away. His aunt was in extreme distress, but once he left she managed to call the police, who picked him up soon after. He was later convicted and sentenced to twelve years in prison. For Anthony, the abuse he had suffered in childhood was dragged to the fore when his aunt confronted him, just as his mother must have done so many times. His response was to hurt her sexually, seeking to abuse her in return. It was a particularly sad and traumatic case, involving as it did the serious sexual assault of a lady in her sixties. It seemed it was a trajectory Anthony had been on for a long time, and she was unfortunate enough to be the one against whom he directed his anger and aggression.

The most common sex crime committed in the world is incest, and the most common incestuous relationship is between brother and sister. The perpetrator typically normalises their behaviour by defining it as connectivity, love and friendship. They do not see it as a sexual act but rather as a platonic and emotional activity. The dynamics of such abuse mean that the abused can become an abuser later in life, acting out the scenes they were once subjected to, but this time cast in the role of perpetrator. (Recent research suggests that, generally, episodes of sexual abuse that take place against a child under the age of fourteen feature in approximately 5% of current abusers' backgrounds.) It has also been found that this is a key reason why people seek out child pornography: they want to see what happened to them from a different angle, see if the child's reaction is comparable to their own or not. It seems to create a need to re-enact the abuse and reconstruct the scenarios in order to study them and perhaps understand them better. The abuse of a child creates a long chain of events, each colliding with the next and causing more and more damage to all those concerned.

When working in Australia, I assessed a man who stood accused of incest with his daughter. Raymond was accused of raping and sodomising his daughter regularly when she was between the ages of eight and fourteen. His daughter hadn't directly reported him for this, but during a conversation with a classmate when she was fourteen, she had divulged that she slept in her father's bed every night. The classmate asked if her father ever touched her, and Raymond's daughter had replied that he did, that their relationship was 'special and unique'. The classmate reported this conversation to a teacher, who in turn contacted social services. Raymond had been arrested on suspicion of sexually abusing his daughter and was now awaiting sentencing. I was asked to supply a psychological assessment for the court. He had no previous forensic history, no prior arrests, no interest in child pornography and had never presented as violent or disorderly.

Raymond described to me his relationship with his daughter and their life together. Her mother was an alcoholic who had lost custody of her daughter years before, when the marriage broke up. Since then Raymond and his daughter had lived together, with little interaction with other families. He ran a recovery service for vehicles, which was demanding work with long shifts. He told me that this was why he had to have his daughter in his bed. Pressed to explain this line of thinking, he described how he regularly had to attend at the scene of car crashes, often seeing dead or badly injured bodies of both adults and children. He found it very difficult to witness such traumatic scenes, so when he came home after work, he sought the comfort of a body in the bed beside him, which was his daughter's body. He told me that he was traumatised by his work, that he loved his daughter and she loved him, that she never once told him to stop, that she didn't mind, that he needed her care and attention because of his job, that it didn't affect her at all, and he reiterated the very words his daughter had used, saying their relationship was 'different', 'unique' and 'special' and others simply didn't understand it. In short, he gave me a long list of justifications – all the things he repeated to himself as evidence that what he was doing night after night wasn't in the least bit wrong. He had no inkling of the impact this might have on his daughter

– he took her acquiescence as consent, as enjoyment, in fact. In his distorted view of the situation, what they were doing was an act of love and care and comfort, nothing more, and it wouldn't affect his daughter or her future life. Like many paedophiles and abusers, he placed the onus on his victim: 'she only had to say, to tell me not to'. He completely discounted his role as the adult, the care-giver, the authority figure, the parent. His was a complete abuse of his daughter's trust in him, but he struggled to accept that. It was a stark illustration of the level of cognitive distortion humans are capable of in their bids to justify their actions.

One of the personality types that is associated with incest is the narcissist. The narcissistic personality views all of the world's activities, all people's actions and their own actions as being wholly concentrated on their personal evolution and outcome. It is the extreme of selfishness and as such it causes distorted processing and thinking. The narcissist is therefore capable of engaging in acts purely for their own pleasure and hedonism, without factoring in the impact on the other person, the object of their attentions. Raymond falls into this category because his actions were entirely self-serving, without any care or understanding for how they affected his young daughter. He was able to turn the world towards him, making the entire situation about him and his needs. A child with a narcissistic parent is often affected psychologically and emotionally by this behaviour, especially when it tips over into a sexually inappropriate behaviour, as epitomised by Raymond and his use of his daughter's body for his own needs. The narcissist essentially feels that he is above everyone else and that the normal social and legal parameters do not apply to him – as Raymond insisted, we just 'didn't understand': in other words, the fault lay with us, not him. It's akin to delusions of grandeur – narcissists see themselves as simply more important than others, the most important person in the room, always.

Interestingly, incest between mother and daughter is very rare, but incest between father and daughter and mother and son both feature regularly in forensic psychology. Outside of forensic psychology, people are often astonished that there are female sex abusers. Those who are convicted of such crimes are usually well-known because the offence is shocking, such as Myra Hindley and Rose West, and alongside being labelled an abuser, they are also labelled as deviant and evil. Because women are expected to be matriarchal, kind and more emotionally adept to other people's feelings, the public outrage is almost of disappointment. In this way, the semiotics of their crime is used to set them apart from all other women, as if they exist in their own, separate sphere, beyond and away from the rest of womankind. Those inside forensic psychology know this is not true. There are and have always been female sex offenders, who have committed crimes every bit as chilling as their male counterparts. The psychology of the female abuser also has much to do with affection and control, like the male abuser, but generally has more links to the perpetrator's relationship with her father as well as her mother. It can also link to their view of men and of sex. While male offenders account for a far greater number of convictions, it has been researched as likely that female offenders commit such acts with their own babies and pre-verbal children. This means the victim doesn't know the offences occurred and very often only recall these incidents through treatment or regressive exercises to recover repressed memories.

I dealt with a case some years ago that was deeply disturbing and upsetting and involved a whole family in a degrading sexual abuse dynamic. It can be hard to understand how a parent could hurt their own child, but this particular case showed how that could happen. If a person has been dehumanised by someone else, especially someone they trust and ostensibly love, it can fracture their psychological self and cause radical disruption to their thinking and behaviour. When I met Sylvia to discuss her case, it proved to be a graphic illustration of this cause-and-effect scenario.

The case as it was presented to me was one of parental capacity. Sylvia and her former husband had five children, and it was alleged by the children that their father had sexually and physically abused them. Sylvia insisted she had no idea he was engaged in such behaviour, but she was found guilty of child neglect, which resulted in the children being placed in care and Sylvia being given a short prison sentence. She had since divorced her husband and was now in a new relationship. Just before she was imprisoned she had given birth to a baby and, while she and her new partner seemed delighted and happy, her social workers had questioned if this baby should also be taken in to care. There was a suspicion she might still be in contact with her ex-husband and, indeed, be involved directly in abusing the children, or at least not be protecting them against the sexual behaviour of the father. I was asked to assess her, to determine her capacity and to make recommendations accordingly.

In preparing to interview Sylvia, I studied the book of evidence and the many reports into her case, which was disturbing in the extreme. The family lived in large mobile home that was docked in a dark laneway in a rural location. The husband was both physically and sexually abusive. He regularly beat Sylvia and controlled her movements. He watched pornographic videos with his children, regularly raping his teenage daughter and another younger daughter. At the same time, he would order his teenage son to have sex with his sister. The scene the reports depicted was bleak and unremitting. This was a traumatically dysfunctional family in which everyone was engaged in hurting someone else, all at the instigation of their father. What struck me when reading the descriptions was how unlikely it seemed that Sylvia could have had no knowledge whatsoever of what was happening. It was a mobile home, after all, with limited private space. It was in a quiet area, where it would have been hard to hide the noises of such abuse. Sylvia had intimated to the social workers that her children were making up their allegations and that the abuse had never taken place. Could that be the truth of the matter?

I met Sylvia in the interview room at the prison. She was a woman in her forties, attractive and well groomed. I noted that when she sat down on the chair opposite me, she adjusted her skirt in order to show more of her thigh. It was a small movement, but coupled with her opening, flirtatious remarks, I recognised that her overt sexuality was likely a mask for more difficult emotions. She was behaving in a strongly sexual manner not because she was aggressive but rather, it seemed to me, as a non-verbal statement of vulnerability. We began to discuss her own background, and she quickly spoke of the fact that her father had physically and sexually abused her. She said this in a matter-of-fact way, as if it hardly mattered. However, when she spoke of her ex-husband, she assumed the demeanour and language of a victim, describing herself as constantly afraid of him, that he was 'violent and sex-mad'. She claimed he raped her, but only when he had been drinking and became 'out of control'. I asked if he had done the same to their children, but she strongly denied this, saying she simply couldn't believe it was true. I reminded her that his guilt in relation to their children had been clearly established, and she shrugged. I asked her the question that had been bothering me all along: how could you not have known? Avoiding eye contact, Sylvia launched into a breathless tirade, saying it could not have happened because she wouldn't have allowed such things to happen. She would have saved her children. Her impassioned denial was very convincing.

I had been asked by the social workers to meet Sylvia's new partner as well, which I went to do once I'd completed the interview with her. He was a big man physically but seemed gentle and soft-spoken. He had a good job, strong family connections and spoke with anticipation of Sylvia's release from jail, when they could be a proper family. I asked him what he knew of her first marriage, and he spoke angrily of the first husband's violence and temper, that Sylvia was lucky to be out of that situation. I asked about Sylvia's five children from that relationship and he seemed surprised. He didn't know she had five children, and he didn't know they were all in care. He believed she had been incarcerated for tax fraud. He looked at me in bewilderment, and I looked at him with growing concern. It didn't bode well that Sylvia had lied to him about such an important part of her life, especially when she was planning to marry him and raise a family with him. Lying to one's partner isn't a crime, of course, but it does exhibit inconsistencies in the communication between 'committed' partners. So when I wrote up my report I concluded that Sylvia's risk of harming or neglecting her baby was moderate, due to previous neglect of her children combined with conviction and incarceration, therefore I recommended supervised access, building up over time to full reconciliation of the family.

Six months later, I received another call regarding Sylvia. Unusually, another report was requested – on the basis that new information had emerged. This turned out to be an allegation by her twelve-year-old son that Sylvia had had sex with him. I returned to the prison, ready to interview Sylvia once more, this time determined not to allow her to use displays of emotion in order to withhold information. As before, her behaviour was overtly sexual towards me, aiming for kittenish but in fact coming across as nervous anxiety. It was definitely a blocking mechanism, her way of trying to control the conversation and the dynamic between us. I immediately told her I had met her partner and that I was surprised he knew nothing of her five children who were in care. She shrugged; it didn't matter because their baby would never be taken into care because he was a good man. Her lack of appreciation for the need to be honest in a trusting relationship pointed to distorted thinking around adult relationships and expectations. It suggested the damage wrought by her father's abuse of her had led to inadequate coping mechanisms, which was in turn leading to potentially harmful behaviours.

I brought her back to her first family, in the mobile home. I described the scene, evoking it, encouraging her to see it from a non-distorted point of view. She immediately tensed up, snapping at me that she wasn't there when bad things were happening, but I pressed on, talking her through the scenario, through the impossibility of her living there and being completely oblivious to the traumatic abuse her children had recounted. She held herself tightly, as if the words themselves were hurting her. Quietly, in a gentle voice, I told her that her children would suffer psychologically for the rest of their lives because they had not been protected from their father. I noted that it would affect their future relationships and happiness, that it would affect them when they had families of their own. I told her that the only way her children could get any help for what had happened to them would be via honest confrontation of what had occurred. That understanding was their only hope of somehow moving on from all they had endured. The slow, sure narrative approach worked – Sylvia broke down, sobbing and shaking. She finally admitted that her children were telling the truth, that the abuse had taken place. Through tears, she told me that she loved them, but her husband had threatened to kill her if she intervened or told anyone, and she fully believed he would carry out that threat. As a result, she had 'kept out of the way' whenever the abuse started. She made herself deaf and blind to what was going on right in front of her because it was the only way she felt she would survive.

This was a huge breakthrough, for Sylvia to admit the extent of what had happened to her family, but I had to broach her son's allegations. Using the same gentle, non-threatening tone of voice, I told her that her son had alleged that he had sex with her, at the instigation of her husband. She clenched her fists in anger and told me that it was a lie, that it had never happened. I told her that her son was highly sexualised, which wasn't normal at the age of twelve. She denied it again. I told her that her son needed her to be honest about this. She denied it again. So I changed tack and told her that, in that case, it appeared her son was exhibiting troubling behaviour, making serious false allegations against his own mother. She stared at me in defiance and shouted that her son was not a liar. I held her eye, steadily, saying nothing. It was a moment of choice for her: tell the truth or know her son would be branded a liar. I suppose it came down to her or him, and in that moment Sylvia chose him. She hadn't chosen to protect him or her other children back in the mobile home, but now she made the right choice. She closed her eyes, slumped in the chair and admitted that she did have sex with her son. It was a terrifically difficult thing for her to admit, because it meant she would never have unsupervised access to her baby with her new partner. That admission would change and haunt her life, and I'm sure she knew it. I was very glad to have the truth out in the open for all concerned, even though it would have a negative impact on her hopes to start a new family.

I called an emergency meeting with the social workers to inform them that Sylvia had admitted to having sexual intercourse with her son. It had happened under duress, stemming from her deep fear of her husband and the warped dynamics he had put in place in their home, but she had nonetheless engaged in an act of incest, which put her into the sex offender category. I was asked to deliver the news to her new partner, which I agreed to do. I drove to his home and appraised him of the situation and of his new position – that if he welcomed Sylvia home upon her release from prison, their baby would be taken into care immediately. He was deeply shocked and wept for a long time, but when he composed himself he stated that the relationship was over, that he would bring up the baby alone. It had been a difficult case from start to finish, but it was the best outcome in the circumstances for Sylvia's partner and baby. She had been pushed to the edge by her father's abuse and then her husband's abuse, but she nonetheless had to take responsibility for her choice to cross the line into sexual offending.

Incest is an example of a sexual disorder, other examples of which are paedophilia (under which term incestuous behaviour often falls), bestiality and necrophilia. These occupy the far end of the sexual spectrum and are classified by the DSM-V as paraphilic disorders. It defines these disorders as: 'intense and persistent sexual interests outside of foreplay and genital stimulation [between]… consenting adults … The definition is broad enough that there are dozens, even hundreds, of identified paraphilias and paraphilic disorders, all of which are replete with ambiguity and controversy, but the DSM-V specifically identifies only eight: voyeuristic, exhibitionistic, frotteuristic, sexual masochism, sexual sadism, pedophilic, fetishistic, and transvestic disorders.' In my own work, I haven't dealt very much with bestiality or necrophilia, but I have interviewed many paedophiles about their behaviour.

Paedophilia is not classed as a sexual orientation, rather it is a sexual disorder and it is illegal. It is defined as sexual fantasies about children through to grooming and sexual contact with children, 'child' being categorised as under eighteen years in some countries and under sixteen years in others. In the modern age, paedophiles are vilified and reviled, with the full weight of the law brought to bear on them if they are convicted. This has not always been the case, however. Far from it, in fact. The name itself comes from the Greek *paidos* – child – and *philia* – love. This is apt given that in Ancient Greece buggery between a man and a boy (pederasty) was regarded as a relatively normal part of sexuality, on a par with homosexuality and transvestism. Brothels dedicated to boy 'prostitutes' were available in every Greek city and men of the free-born social class kept slave boys with whom they would conduct sexual relations. The sodomy of boys was regarded as a normal social interaction for men.

The history of paedophilia is very interesting for what it tells us about social and cultural norms and expectations down through the ages. It has been present from earliest times, with opinion regarding its 'normality' or 'criminality' changing from time period to time period. Up until the nineteenth century it was largely tolerated, indeed children could be prosecuted as willing participants who embraced 'unchastity'. In eighteenth-century London there was a belief that sex with a child would cure venereal disease, so men engaged freely in sex with minors to avail of this 'cure'; it is interesting to note that the same belief prevailed in Africa in the late twentieth century with regard to AIDS. A study of court records further shows that child abuse often went unpunished because children were not deemed credible witnesses at trial and because often the blame was bestowed onto the mothers of victims, who should have taken better care of their charges. (Again, it is slightly dispiriting to find a ready twenty-first century example of this same thinking in the *#worthlessmother* trend in May 2016 after a young boy climbed into the gorilla pen at Cinncinati zoo.)

The first time we encounter the labelling and discussion of paedophilia is in *Psychopatia Sexualis,* the 1886 study by Richard Krafft-Ebing. There, he defined it as 'a psychosexual perversion' but recorded his belief that it could be cured. By contrast, in modern psychology paedophilia is classified as a divergence of personality, normally the result of psychological damage sustained in childhood. It was the twentieth century that saw the growing awareness of the adverse effects of sexual contact on minors. Alfred Kinsey was a notable advocate of child welfare, recording in his 1953 study of female sexual behaviour that 25% of girls under fourteen years had experienced some form of abuse. Interestingly, when Kinsey published these findings, the public wasn't remotely interested – although they were excitedly focused on his findings with regard to premarital sex and adultery. It was the second half of the twentieth century that saw a new and high-level focus on paedophiles and their activities, culminating in 1996 with the protest march in Brussels that saw 250,000 people take to the streets to condemn the handling of the Marc Dutroux case. Now, sexuality is understood as part of psychological, emotional and physical welfare, with a desire to protect it from those who would use it to their own ends. Hence the widespread concern about paedophiles on the internet and the rise of social tools such as the sex offenders register.

The question people always ask me in relation to paedophiles is: how could they do that? The idea of being sexually attracted to a child is repulsive to most people and they regard paedophiles as almost sub-human, too perverted to be able to relate to in any way whatsoever. I have sat in interview rooms with many paedophiles over the course of my career, and their crimes never get easier to hear, but there is a clearly discernible pattern and personality type that perpetrates such sex crimes. Typically, the offender gains affirmation from the sense of purpose and control gained from grooming the victim. The key thing is that they categorically do not see their actions as completely criminal or wrong. I have never yet had a paedophile say to me, 'Ian, I love young children and I don't know what's wrong with me.' That is not a sentence I have ever heard, and I don't expect to ever hear it. They normalise the behaviour for themselves, justify it, neutralise their actions, blame others, never take responsibility. They do understand that the behaviour must be covert and hidden from public scrutiny, but due to society's 'intolerance' and not their own deviant behaviour. It is necessary to understand that this is possible because of their strength of mind. It takes huge mental fortitude to groom and abuse a child. It requires steadfast determination to attain that level of contact and, once attained, the abuser must be able to withstand the child's distress and confusion. When I work with the staff of firms responsible for investigating online paedophilic behaviour, as I described earlier in Chapter 5, it is striking that every employee – both male and female – cites the same aspect that haunts them in their waking and in their sleeping. They tell me time and time again that it is the face of the child in the abusive images they must view – it is the child's realisation that something is amiss, then their deep distress, confusion, anxiety and pain. It is the eyes of the child that they cannot forget. That illustrates for me the level of detachment of the paedophile – to be able to be in the room with that distress, causing it and yet having the mental determination to ignore it, rewrite it and continue on. That is the truly chilling aspect of paedophilia.

During my time in Australia I dealt with an offender who provided a clear illustration of the profile and offending nature of paedophiles. I met with Gregory at the medium-security prison where he was being held pending assessment and sentencing. When I arrived, there was no interview room available and the guard suggested I come back another day. After a back-and-forth exchange, the guard finally agreed that I could use the canteen and he would ensure no one would enter during the course of the interview. I got myself a coffee at the counter, then sat at a table and waited to meet Gregory. He was brought in a few minutes later by two guards. He was of slight build with wispy grey hair pulled back in a ponytail and was wearing a tracksuit. He placed a flask on the table between us and launched into a tirade on the evils of coffee drinking. One of the key features I have noticed in paedophiles is the tendency to hold extreme views, and Gregory was no different. His flask contained a gloopy green juice, which he sipped slowly throughout the interview. He told me, 'You are what you drink,' averring that he never consumed anything solid – all of his food was pureed, like baby food. To his mind, this liquid diet bestowed on him a strong physique and aura – it actually made him powerful.

I asked about his background and although he deflected my questions and tried to continually bat them back to me, he did concede that he'd had a difficult childhood. He had been placed in foster care as a child, where he had been beaten regularly. He had never been sexually abused, but he had never been shown warmth or affection of any kind. There was a chasm within him where familial love and care should have been. This also corresponded with what I have since come to regard as one of the defining marks of paedophiles – that they are pathetic individuals. In psychological terms, patheticism is the inability to access one's own emotions or discuss one's own challenges and behaviours. It causes great difficulty in forming relationship with others and leads to choice of a poor social peer group and degraded social interactions in general. Pathetic individuals often feel they have had a history of bullying, which leaves them trapped by feelings of resentment and anger. This is why engaging with a child in sexual contact makes them feel better about themselves and gives them perceived positive interaction and a sense of power that's been missing all through their lives. Gregory lived on his own and had no significant relationships. Although he had forged a good academic career, he was nonetheless defined and confined by his early experiences and his need to rout them through a feeling of power. We might be inclined to think of sexual predators as aggressive and detached, but in reality – and like bullies – they are more often prey to their own emotions, unable to control their thinking and behaviour.

We went on to discuss his offences, which had been perpetrated against the children of his relatives. There were three different families involved, and he babysat regularly for all of them. Two of the families had one child, the third had two children, and Gregory's relatives were delighted to have a trusted relative minding the children while they were out. One of the children began wetting her bed and her school questioned why she was suddenly moody and tearful, but her parents had no idea why her behaviour had changed. The crimes only came to light by accident: one evening the parents of one of the children arrived home unexpectedly early and found the sitting room empty; they found Gregory in their child's bedroom, in the act of performing oral sex on her. Once the police were involved, the extent of Gregory's activities became apparent. He had abused all four children, forcing them to give and receive oral sex and also forcing penetrative sex on them. He was arrested and charged with child rape and assault. I listened to his account of what he had done and it was clear that he felt neither remorse nor guilt. I asked about his victims, if he thought they would suffer the after-effects of his actions into the future. He shrugged, his demeanour displaying no empathy whatsoever, and told me again he had been teaching them – 'my fluids will give them power'. His extreme views were part of the rationalising of his behaviour.

Gregory was an intelligent man in academic terms, with a good level of education. This fed into his grooming of the children, giving him the insight to coerce them into sexual acts. Grooming is the key trait of child abuse, especially with children over the age of eight. It is extremely rare to hear of 'snatch and grab' assault by a paedophile, as you would hear of such incidents being perpetrated against women by male rapists. Once the child attains the age of six to eight years, the sex offender abandons the idea of spontaneous sex offending and focuses determinedly on grooming and planning for contact. That is part of the gratification for the paedophile – the planning, the gradual attainment of what he desires. Grooming can take one of two routes: the befriending route, which relies on building trust and dependence and then exploiting it; or the threat route, which uses threats specific to the child to terrify them into compliance. The former approach is very often used online, where offenders attempt to engage children in chat and present themselves as a trusted friend. To do so, they often use childlike language and some psychologists argue that in doing so they are regressing to a childhood personality type, in order to feel free and without the woes and worries of the world around them. Gregory chose the latter route, using lots of different threats to ensure the children never told their parents, or anyone else, about the abuse they were experiencing. It is a common trait among abusers to demand secrecy, but Gregory enforced it in a disturbing manner. He showed the children lurid images of bestiality and warned them that would happen to their pets should they tell. Again, this is a very common ploy by abusers, to make threats against beloved pets to instil fear in their victims.

As with every abuser I have worked with, Gregory was adept at justifying his actions so that he never had to feel guilty about what he was doing. He kept insisting that he was 'teaching them', passing on his power. I asked who was responsible, and he immediately laid the blame at the parents' door, telling me they drank alcohol and didn't guide their children appropriately. He described aberrant parents and willing children, vacating himself from the picture entirely. In doing so, he displayed elements of narcissism – a chilling level of self-obsession that saw him as the centre of the universe, and no one else mattered in the slightest. This conformed with the profile of the paedophile, who often displays attachment disorder, poor emotional expression and distorted cognitive processing. The fact that these elements are the result of adverse childhood experiences does little to evoke sympathy for the offender – I certainly couldn't feel any sympathy for Gregory, who had twisted the world to his view and his service, basking in his 'power' and the notion that he was sharing it with others. It was a disturbingly distorted justification for his crimes.

I encouraged Gregory to talk in great detail about what he

had done, listening intently to every single aspect of his narrative. This is very important when assessing sex offenders as the details can hold important clues as to the psychology, motives, desires and cognitive distortion at the base of the offending. During interviews, I question such offenders very closely, allowing them to tell me about their offences at great length. I do this in order to glean every piece of information possible and in order to create a rapport. I choose my words very carefully – for example, I always refer to 'young person' instead of 'child' or 'baby', to avoid any sense that I am judging them. The rapport established through close and careful questioning means I can deliver a comprehensive report, which serves three distinct purposes: first, it helps the State decide what level of punishment to administer; second, it illustrates what level of trauma the victim experienced, perhaps aiding in their treatment; and third, it provides insight into what treatment the offender requires should they be considered a candidate for rehabilitation and early release. In short, the detail I compile ensures I perform the public service part of my job to the highest level.

Once the interview process was complete, I had to draw up my report on Gregory and his likelihood of reoffending. He had no forensic history, other than the minor charge of 'wilful exposure' (a common precursor to sex offending) arising from an incident where he had masturbated in his car. This was not unusual, however, as sex offenders tend to be very careful and move very slowly, working towards their offences methodically and with a view to not getting caught. So his lack of forensic history did not necessarily mean he had not offended before. It is also the case that sex offenders tend to view pornography first, taking time to move on to contact offending, which is the biggest line for them to cross. Given the nature and extent of Gregory's offending against the four children, this suggested it was not his first contact offence. Accordingly, I pieced together the information and my own formulation and concluded that Gregory was at high risk of reoffending, especially given his lack of guilt, empathy, remorse or insight. I therefore recommended that, as a high-risk offender, he should be transferred to a high-security prison and should receive an intensive level of ongoing psychological treatment. I later found out that he received a sentence of twenty years, with no parole. Eight years into his sentence, Gregory applied to participate in a 'sex offender treatment program' but was declined a place due to his 'gross cognitive distortions, no insight or remorse and willingness to attain treatment solely to create the opportunity for early release'. He remains in prison.

I am often asked if treating paedophiles is possible, if they can be 'cured'. This isn't what treatment aims for in the sense that it is understood that paedophile tendencies can't be made to disappear. However, through CBT, it is possible to modify behaviour and change perspective, which can greatly reduce the likelihood of that person offending or reoffending. CBT is considered the optimum treatment modality for paedophilia, along with 'solution and emotion focused therapy' in group and individual settings. The Australian and Canadian penal systems, for example, offer programmes in separate prison units where the paedophile offenders live for up to twelve months, receiving treatment within the group four days per week, eight hours per day, led and supervised by at least two very experienced psychologists. Once the full programme has been completed, they return to the prison fold, with the eventual aim of being moved to medium and minimum security prisons where they participate in 'refresher' sex offending treatment programmes, which are less intensive but nonetheless last up to six months. Upon full release from prison they must attend a community-based programme for two hours weekly, indefinitely. Reoffending rates are thought to decrease by up to 20% as a result of such intervention, but it is by no means a 'cure'.

The focus of treatment for paedophilia is to provide knowledge and awareness that enable the offender to avoid abusing anyone else, with the hope that the learning will provide habituation to readily avoid contexts that may contribute to the risk of further sex abuse. The therapy will seek to identify each person's 'triggers', allowing them to monitor their own behaviour and notice when behaviours are creeping in that suggest a slide towards sexual contact. Once the triggers are noticed, the person can then request help to pull their behaviour in the opposite direction. It is acknowledged that they may still experience sexual desire for children, but the whole focus of the treatment is to make them unlikely to act on those desires. It is difficult work to undertake, there's no doubt about that, but it's important for society that we try to make a difference and facilitate the integration of socially acceptable behaviours in sex offenders.

Cases of sexual crime are treated with the utmost care because the impact on the victim is so severe. Sexual aggression is one of the most intimate, destructive and hurtful aggressive tendencies against another person. It normally results in post-traumatic stress disorder in the short-term, but in the longer term it can also cause emotional regression, stunting and a deep fear that permeates the victim's life and future relationships. A sex crime is, therefore, one of the worst crimes a person can commit, regardless of the motive or reason behind it. The problem is that so many victims don't come forward to report their experiences, through fear, shame or a feeling of loneliness and vulnerability that blinds them to the notion that they could receive help, that they are worthy of receiving help. In cases of incest, the emotional impact is even more severe because the pain and humiliation are visited upon the child by those who are meant to love and protect them. It is a deeply traumatic abuse of trust and the natural order by which parents are meant to take care of their offspring. As the cases above have shown, it is very often the situation that the victim accepts the distorted justifications offered by their abuser, investing in the narrative that says 'this is okay, it is normal and I'm doing it because I love you'. As a society, we must work to get out the message that all forms of sexual coercion are wrong and unacceptable and that help is available if you have been the victim of such a crime. If reporting and conviction rates go up, that would act to some extent as a deterrent. It is essential for victims that we deliver a coherent and consistent condemnation of any sexual behaviour that transgresses consent, respect and care for another.

CHAPTER NINE

THE PSYCHOPATHIC SPECTRUM

Are you picturing the beautiful Janet Leigh in the shower, screaming in terror? It's hardly surprising if you are because Alfred Hitchcock has largely hijacked the whole notion of what a psychopath is and what he does. Hitchcock's 1960 film *Psycho* (based on the 1959 novel by Robert Bloch) remains the iconic depiction of the psychopathic personality and has added to the many misconceptions and exaggerations that surround the personality disorder of psychopathy. From his taxidermy to his mother fixation to his transvestism and propensity to murder women he finds attractive, lead character Norman Bates is the living definition of 'psychopath' in many people's minds. It is necessary, therefore, to start by unravelling the misconceptions and saying what a psychopath is not.

The first common assumption I often hear is that *all serial killers are psychopaths.* This isn't strictly the case. A serial killer who kills impulsively and randomly, with little planning and restraint, is probably not a psychopath. On the other hand, a serial killer who enacts killings that are very cleverly and very clearly premeditated and methodically planned might well come under the criteria for psychopathy. It's not a given that all serial killers can be assigned this personality disorder. This links to the second assumption, which is that *all psychopaths are physically violent.* Again, some are, but it is by no means a defining characteristic. The personality traits of psychopathy, such as lack of guilt, lack of empathy and poor behaviour controls, can lead to violent outbursts, but it's just as possible that a high-functioning psychopath could lead a successful life and cause no physical harm to any person. In fact, many doctors exhibit psychopathic traits, and they spend their lives reducing physical harm.

This again links to the third assumption, which is that *all psychopaths will cross the line and commit crimes*. Some do, some don't. Again, it's quite possible for a person to live out their life without anyone knowing they score high for psychopathic traits. This is one of the reasons why it's so difficult to define psychopathy in a simple manner: it's so complex both in cause and in effect. The other factor to consider here is the psychopath's level of intelligence, which can often be high. This means it is quite possible for them to cross the line and never get caught. Or they might cross other kinds of lines – not into illegality but certainly into manipulating others and causing emotional harm. But it's not the case that a presentation of psychopathy will inevitably lead to jail time – a psychopath can exhibit a preponderance of some traits and very little of others.

I have on occasion heard people posit *a link between psychopathy and autism*. This is a dangerous assumption in that anything that miscategorises a mental disorder is unhelpful and possibly harmful. I don't think there is an association between psychopathy and autism or autism spectrum disorder. The actions of the autistic person might suggest a similarity – actions such as the tendency to be socially withdrawn and uncommunicative – but I think this comparison is down to a misunderstanding of what psychopathy is and is not. It is important to examine the context of the person as well as the exhibited traits. The dynamic between the individual and others or with his/her environment is as important to categories when diagnosing as is the core presentation – this is not so important when formulating a medical diagnosis of physical illness, but very significant when considering mental presentations. It is also important to remember that any diagnosis is only as useful as the treatment solutions it provides.

It's also often claimed that *psychopaths are insane*, and we might have to blame Norman Bates for that assumption too. Psychopathy doesn't necessarily mean insanity. In legal terms, insanity is assessed via fitness to plead, and while a diagnosis of insanity means the person cannot be tried for their crime, a diagnosis of psychopathy would not excuse the accused from a criminal trial. Fitness to plead assesses the individual's: ability to understand the evidence, ability to instruct counsel, ability to question legal advice, ability to understand jury selection and generally to have the mental competence to actively help themselves during a trial through legal instruction. If the individual does not have one or all of these abilities, they are 'unfit' to plead under the Insanity Act. However, that does not mean that they are insane, at least not what the layman considers insane. Insanity, to my mind, is a misnomer, an outdated term that isn't specific or helpful. More useful is 'psychosis', which is an impaired perception of reality. Those who are psychotic don't see the world as it is, which is very relevant in bipolar disorder with states of mania. Psychopathy has been considered a feature of insanity, especially in American law, but even there it does not necessarily mean a person is governed as insane and completely unfit to plead. Other factors, such as those listed above, must also be considered. In Ireland and Europe, psychopathy is not documented in legal annals as a key feature of insanity and therefore does not preclude fitness to plead. It is a broad term, becoming ever more complex as culture changes more than the condition changes.

The sixth common assumption is that *all psychopaths have a dark fixation on their mother*, to an extreme and extremely dangerous extent. In *Psycho*, this is a key part of Bates's character and behaviour – his love for his mother is so all-consuming, he kills her to keep her pure and him alone. This level of dramatic obsession obviously plays well in a thriller, and it's not entirely untrue, but it exaggerates the point. What can be said with regard to the mother–child relationship commonly seen among psychopaths is that there is attachment disorder, stemming from a poor relationship. As set out in Chapter 3, attachment disorder can have serious consequences, and one of them is to create fertile ground for a powerful sense of rejection and grief. When this happens in the life of someone with psychopathic tendencies, it can lead to negative behaviours, especially against loved ones or those considered important role models.

The next assumption is that *all psychopaths are male*. This is a cultural construct, probably stemming from that other cultural construct of the virtuous female. Throughout human history women have been raised onto ideological pedestals, and one of these sees them idealised as being essentially and fundamentally 'better than men' and 'less criminal than men'. This isn't true. It makes for good, shocking drama, though – think of the public reaction to Glenn Close in *Fatal Attraction* or to Sharon Stone in *Basic Instinct*. The idea of the female psychopath is presented in popular culture as utterly sensational and unnatural. However, the full spectrum of psychopathy does occur in both genders, so there are definitely female psychopaths. But as with most disorders, the tendency in women is to exhibit internalised symptoms, such as depression and anxiety, while men typically exhibit externalised symptoms, such as aggressive behaviour. However, an interesting study conducted by Robins et al. in 2003 found that there were gender differences in violent behaviour that allowed for this idea of women as intrinsically less violent. They found that women tended to be violent in the home, towards their own family members, inflicted less injury than male counterparts and were less often reported or arrested following their violent behaviour. Other research found that women with antisocial personality disorder (APD, the umbrella term under which psychopathy falls) were more likely than APD men to be physically violent towards their sex partners and children. So it seems to be the case that female psychopaths are adept at keeping their offending behind closed doors.

A final common assumption: *it would be impossible to fall in love with a psychopath.* This, unfortunately, is not true either. It's all too possible to be swayed by the outward charm and emotional manipulation of the psychopath. One of the key traits of psychopathy is telling lies, but a clever person can lie and manipulate and always seem to be in the right. A psychopath is less capable of feeling love or deep attachment, but they can feign it very well when it suits them. This is the key aspect: love is always exhibited for their own benefit. But nonetheless, as they can simulate love convincingly, they can make people fall for them.

So where does that leave our iconic psychopath, Norman Bates? If I were to diagnose Bates, I think I would describe him as having schizo-affective disorder, with hypomania and features of psychopathy and narcissistic egocentrism. But I suppose that wouldn't make for a catchy film title.

Those are the things a psychopath is not, some of which might come as a surprise. Describing what a psychopath is can be very difficult. The lack of precision and clarity on this topic is reflected in the various terms used and the conflicts between key diagnostic tools. Is a sociopath very different from a psychopath? Does a psychopath definitively have antisocial personality disorder, or does APD lead to psychopathy? Part of the reason for the lack of specifics is that this area of diagnosis is relatively new and research is still relatively light, albeit ongoing. The term 'psychopath' was first coined around 1900 and applied to people with no sense of right or wrong. In the 1930s the term sociopath was preferred, because of the social damage wrought by psychopaths. In 1941 Hervey Cleckley developed an important list of traits describing the psychopathic personality, which included things like incapacity for love and antisocial behaviours. But now we have returned to using the term psychopath, and we distinguish between 'primary psychopathy – genetically caused psychopathy – and 'secondary psychopathy' – produced by environment. When we refer to sociopaths now, we mean people with APD who could have been law-abiding and productive citizens given consistent and confident parenting. The fact that they received poor parenting triggered their APD characteristics to develop into sociopathic tendencies, which are characterised by inadequate socialisation, conduct disorder and oppositional defiant disorder, with an unsocialised character due primarily to parental failures. By contrast, psychopathic tendencies are described as a genetic peculiarity, usually a peculiarity of temperament.

The key manual with regard to defining and diagnosing is the *Diagnostic and Statistical Manual of Mental Disorder* (DSM), which is published by the American Psychiatric Association. It didn't include psychopathy until its third edition in 1980, and when it did, it included it under the umbrella term of antisocial personality disorder. It gave the following criteria for a diagnosis of APD:

•   Pervasive pattern of disregard for and violation of the rights of others occurring since the age of fifteen years.

The criteria are broader than the core definition of 'psychopathy', which is essentially a lack of the restraining influence of conscience and empathic concern for others. This lack means the psychopath has very low levels of fear and anxiety, which makes them capable of behaviours that non-psychopaths would find very difficult. For example, the classic factor of animal torture as a child would form part of the make-up of the psychopathic personality, but that's an ability the vast majority of children do not possess. It would be very difficult for the average child to carry out acts of torture on an animal – it would feel like breaking a very significant taboo. Unfettered by empathy or guilt or anxiety, the child with psychopathic tendencies finds it incredibly attractive and easy to hurt defenceless animals.

It's not yet possible to answer with certainty the question: what causes psychopathy? There are certainly cognitive factors that contribute to it, which is the genetic basis. Brain research has shown specific differences in the brains of psychopaths, with abnormalities in the grey matter of the prefrontal and temporal lobe and in the white matter of the corpus callosum, the fibres of which connect the two hemispheres. At base, there is a peculiarity in the psychological make-up of the psychopath that can manifest in many different behaviours. To my mind, in order to examine the factors that contribute positively or negatively to psychopathy, one would have to focus on empathy, conscientiousness, harm-avoidance, agreeableness, impetuousness, impulsivity, anger, disinhibition and socialisation, both prosocial and antisocial attitudes. What we can say is that while psychopaths will share some characteristics, there is no 'typical' psychopath to whom we can point as the embodiment of the disorder. It's simply not as simple as that.

These terms and umbrella terms and associated terms are all quite confusing, but thankfully we have to hand the diagnostic checklist compiled by Robert Hare in the 1970s and then revised in the 1980s and 1990s and which remains the undisputed scale for assessing psychopathy. The Hare Psychopathy Checklist-Revised (PCL-R) is a twenty-point list of the traits of a psychopathic personality. Hare took issue with the DSM approach described above, because his research showed that a person who scores a rating for psychopathy will also rate as having an APD rating, but, crucially, an APD rating does not necessarily mean the individual qualifies to be a psychopath. So to lump psychopathy in under APD is misleading, as far as Hare is concerned. He devised a checklist that is specific to psychopathy.

The PCL-R is the key tool of the forensic psychologist because, properly used, it provides a reliable and valid assessment of the clinical construct of psychopathy. I would also use the PCL-YV (Youth Version), which is a similar checklist but adapted specifically for use with adolescents. The twenty points on Hare's checklist also provide us with a comprehensive insight into the personality of the psychopath.

The Hare Psychopathy Checklist-Revised (PCL-R):
1. Glibness/superficial charm
2. Grandiose sense of self-worth
3. Need for stimulation/proneness to boredom
4. Pathological lying
5. Cunning/manipulative
6. Lack of remorse or guilt
7. Shallow affect
8. Callous/lack of empathy
9. Parasitic lifestyle
10. Poor behavioural controls
11. Promiscuous sexual behaviour
12. Early behaviour problems
13. Lack of realistic long-term goals
14. Impulsivity
15. Irresponsibility
16. Failure to accept responsibility for own actions
17. Many short-term marital relationships
18. Juvenile delinquency
19. Revocation of conditional release
20. Criminal versatility

Each item in the PCL-R is scored on a three-point scale (0, 1, 2), according to the extent to which the administrator judges that it applies to a given individual. Total scores can range from 0 to 40, reflecting the degree to which the individual matches the prototypical psychopath. In North America a score of 30 is typically used as a cut-off score for the research on psychopathy. I also use this score when assessing, but there is latitude depending on the presentation and experiential history. I usually rate anyone less than 10 as a 'low' presentation of psychopathy, 11–29 as 'moderate' and 30–40 as 'high'.

I wouldn't be in full agreement with Hare's view of the DSM's way of categorising psychopathy under antisocial personality disorder. I don't think that antisocial behaviour is a nuanced variable or that a psychiatric diagnosis will be hampered by including it in the construct. I think that antisocial personality is a characteristic feature that helps us to differentiate psychopathy from other psychiatric syndromes. For example, individuals with histrionic personality disorder are flamboyant, insincere and shallow, a schizoid personality disorder is characterised by persistently shallow affect and a person with attention deficit hyperactivity disorder displays behavioural dysregulation. However, none of these mental disorders runs the risk of being confused with psychopathy because none of them has antisocial as a characteristic feature definitively conributing to their classification. In addition, analysis has shown that antisocial tendencies are especially important indicators of psychopathy in the non-incarcerated community.

So this, then, is the key with regard to psychopathy – it is not a collection of specific behaviours: it is a set of personality characteristics that give rise to often negative behaviours; although there is one defining characteristic, which is being antisocial. The media portrayal of 'the psychopath' is often one-dimensional and sensationalist. Who can forget the image of Hannibal Lecter, from *Silence of the Lambs*, in his restraining mask? And he was a forensic psychiatrist – as well as a serial-killing sadist. Those images end up taking precedence, and the actual disorder gets lost in the hyperbole. Psychopathy is not often about wild extremes: it is a spectrum of characteristics and behaviours and generally environment and nurture will have a large part to play in where on the spectrum the person with psychopathic tendencies ends up. That spectrum is very wide as well, with people on it you wouldn't expect to be connected by a mental disorder. For example, people who are regarded as having a psychopathic tendency but who didn't develop a full spectrum pathology include Sir Winston Churchill, the African explorer Sir Richard Burton and Chuck Yeager, the first man to fly faster than sound. If you can believe Robert Caro, his biographer, Lyndon Johnson exemplified the psychopath. He was fearless, shameless, abusive of his wife and underlings and willing to do almost anything required to attain his ends.

These men, who are recorded by history as courageous, charming, successful and wealthy, are bedfellows on the spectrum with Hitler and Stalin, both relatively fearless, clever men unconstrained by guilt or pity, whose ruthless rise to power would not have been possible had they felt normal degrees of caution or conscience. Studies have suggested that psychopaths are also to be found in abundance among business people, investors (risk-takers), counsellors, media personalities, actors and entertainers. This was the subject of Robert Hare's 1993 study, *Excellent without Conscience*, in which he traced the psychopath through many different fields and found psychopathic tendencies to give great advantage in certain professions and situations. If you are looking for the slick madman, you'll miss the psychopath who's right under your nose.

The opinion that many business people fit on the spectrum is not new. Indeed, I have encountered it in my own work. It is often said that white collar crime is the work of the successful psychopath who can't help pushing the risks that bit further, which ends up being his undoing. I was asked to assess a man called Edmund, who was facing a charge of fraud. It's actually surprising how little of this sort of work I've been asked to do, given the amount of white collar crime going on in Ireland during the Celtic Tiger years and then in the recession that followed it. This stands in contrast to the norm in the USA, where forensic psychologists are very often involved in these sorts of cases. The statistics on white collar offenders show that they tend to be clever and manipulative risk-takers who score high on the PCL-R.

Edmund was a highly successful businessman in his mid-sixties, who had enjoyed a Midas touch with regard to his businesses. It was important to him that his family had a comfortable home, material wealth and status, and he provided for them extremely well. During the boom, his wife decided to end the marriage. Their four children opted to stay living in the family home with Edmund, and it was all very amicable. Edmund had plenty of money and wanted to acquit himself well with regard to his wife, so he gave her a large sum in settlement, enough to set her up in the lifestyle to which she was accustomed. Then the bubble burst, the economy hit the skids and Edmund found himself in the alien situation of having a paltry bank account and owing huge sums of money to creditors. He responded to this by making fraudulent tax claims. I asked if he had asked for financial advice before breaking the law, and he conceded that he had not. He felt he knew more than the advisors, that he could safely do it and not get caught. He thought, in other words, that he was of a superior intellect to everyone else. He reckoned the Revenue authorities wouldn't have any idea what he was doing and that he'd sell some assets and get back on the straight and narrow again. It hadn't worked out that way.

Now, Edmund was suffering from anxiety. He had lost his appetite and wasn't sleeping and claimed to be deeply affected by the pending court case. He did feel remorse, but I felt there was an irritability with the situation that was likely the strongest emotion. He couldn't believe he had been caught out; he was still struggling to accept that outcome. He had invested fully in the notion that what he was doing was 'temporary', was not really wrong and didn't actually deserve punishing – certainly not the three- or four-year prison sentence with which he was threatened. He measured himself by a different yardstick from everyone else, as if he deserved special treatment and handling. This narcissistic view is common among psychopaths, along with the belief that they know more than anyone else and therefore never require help. Taking into account the fact that he had been making efforts to pay back the money and that he was suffering from anxiety, I recommended community service work that would utilise his particular skill set. I felt he might learn more from that experience than from a stint in jail.

Edmund scored high on the psychopathic scale, but clearly he had been able to function well in the world and be successful and high-achieving. He wasn't incapacitated by his disorder: he was able to use it to his advantage, but he had negated his obligations to society and affected the social status of his family and, indeed, the community at large. That was also the case for Ireland's most well-known psychopath, Graham Dwyer, although in his case he couldn't keep the mask from slipping because his needs were so selfish and so extreme. Dwyer epitomises the spectrum of the disorder: for many years he led a successful life, qualifying as an architect, marrying, having children and enjoying a 'normal' life. If anyone had guessed at his psychopathic tendencies, they would probably have put him low on the spectrum. Dwyer was very clever in how he set up his life, understanding what he needed to maintain a façade of respectability and 'normality' that would sufficiently hide his sadistic needs and activities. In an 'alternative sex' web chatroom he met Elaine O'Hara, and they commenced a sexual relationship that was sadistic in the extreme. Dwyer would beat her, stab her, draw blood, tie her up – all in the name of his sexual pleasure. Once alone with her, he quickly moved to the high end of the spectrum, releasing all of the frustrated desires he kept carefully hidden from view the rest of the time. He represents the more extreme end of the psychopathic scale, which makes it all the more sinister, but impressive, that he convinced so many people he was a perfectly normal man, especially in such a small community and country.

An important question to explore is, what are the factors that lead to those psychopathic characteristics becoming negative, or indeed extremely negative and dangerous, behaviours? The psychopath has a psychological peculiarity, in that he has little to no fear and little to no anxiety, but this peculiarity is not of itself evil or vicious. However, anxiety and fear are often present in the psychopath, but covert and used, consciously or subconsciously, as building blocks to premeditated malevolent acts. It is when it is combined with perverse appetites or an unusually hostile or aggressive temperament that the individual travels along the spectrum of behaviours towards extremely negative activities and behaviours. So what causes this? Researchers are still investigating the answer to that question, but we can trace it to some causes. One of the deciding factors is the key experiences in childhood. If parents adopt a coercive approach to communicating with and disciplining their child, this can lead to aggressive antisocial behaviour. So, for example, if you have a very active and perhaps difficult infant who is interacting with insufficiently responsive parents, this causes distress in the infant. By the age of two, this will have led to coercive behaviour by the child to create a response, and then by extension to a lack of social skills. If this behaviour goes unchecked, it can then lead on, as the child grows, to ADHD, oppositional defiant disorder and conduct disorder. What the child has learned while growing up is that coercion is the most effective way to obtain things from others and get what they want. The negative reactions of other people to the child's coercive behaviour are likely only to strengthen an antagonistic, loveless, exploitative state of mind. When this effect is layered onto a brain with psychopathic tendencies, it can cause that person to escalate up the spectrum into extremely negative behaviour.

Another aspect of psychopathic development where the environment or nature plays a role is through attachment disorder with the parent. We have already seen how great the impact can be on a person's psychology if they do not form a bond with their mother in infancy. A lack of intimate bonding causes shockwaves through the personality, warping and wrecking the fragile constructs of self-esteem, confidence, resilience and emotional security. Attachment disorder has a deep-seated effect on every personality type, but when it is allied to the psychological facets of psychopathy, it can be extremely damaging. These environmental inadequacies can exacerbate the inadequate levels of fear, empathy, guilt, remorse and anxiety already present in the psychopath, creating a much greater level of detachment and therefore ability to commit extreme negative behaviours. This was evident in the case of thirteen-year-old Conor, recounted in Chapter 4, who was a primary psychopath (genetically caused) but those natural tendencies were enhanced and exacerbated by an abusive father, an overwhelmed mother and an impoverished background. Conor exhibited high-end psychopathic spectrum behaviour from a very early age, which was related to the environment he struggled to cope with living in.

I encountered this same sort of story again when dealing with one of the most memorable cases of my career. It involved a high-achieving American artist in his mid-seventies who was arrested for the transportation of cocaine into Ireland, with intent to distribute. This is a serious offence, carrying with it a mandatory sentence of ten years in prison. When I read the book of evidence, I found it very difficult to understand how a man of such learning, intelligence and experience could have fallen prey to such an obvious and frankly amateur scam. It was only when I met Julius that I began to see what had really happened and why.

I interviewed Julius in the prison where he was being detained pending sentencing. He was a short, rotund man with sallow skin and thinning grey hair. He had a warm, big smile and soft, delicate hands. His eyes were kind and there was an air of vulnerability in the way he spoke, often tilting his head to one side like he was recalling a story or happy episode. He was courteous and helpful, explaining the details of the case clearly and, at times, a little patronisingly, as if my inability to understand his actions was caused by a lack of intelligence on my part. It wasn't that I didn't understand what had happened; it was that I couldn't understand how he had so blindly trusted in all that he was told and complied so unquestioningly and so obediently.

The story started with an email that delivered fantastic news: Julius had been left two million dollars in the will of a distant relative. Julius had never heard the relative's name before nor anything whatsoever of his existence, but they shared a surname and the man was dead and his fortune was waiting to be collected. Julius replied at once, asking to be sent the money. The reply he received detailed a very complicated procedure that would have to be followed in order to secure his inheritance: he would fly to Malaysia, where he would meet some men who would give him the documents necessary to collect the money from the bank. Soon after, a return ticket to Malaysia arrived in the post and Julius set off to collect the money, but no one showed up at the rendezvous point, so he returned home to America disappointed.

Then, another email: apologies about Malaysia, you must fly to Brazil instead, where a contact will meet you and you will then fly on to Dublin. Julius once more headed for the airport with the return ticket his correspondents had posted to him, and he flew to Rio de Janeiro. This time, he was met by the contacts, as promised. They gave him the details about the Dublin bank appointment and gave him an overnight bag to take with him on the journey. They told him the bag was full of gifts for the bank officials, gifts to thank them for completing the transaction for Julius. I asked him if he had found this strange in any way. He told me he trusted them and had no reason to question their motives. I asked if he was aware that one should never carry a bag onto a plane with unknown contents – it is written on every security poster in the airport. He replied that he was a widely travelled man, in demand as a university lecturer, and therefore was very well acquainted with travel protocol. He simply didn't think that it applied to him, it seemed. He told me, 'but people respect me, I am a highly lauded artist', as if that offered a cloak of protection from the criminals of the world. This level of self-regard was the first indicator of a very elevated sense of self-worth and narcissism (even though he cleraly was 'worthy').

The genius painter flew into Dublin with his bag full of 'gifts'. He was stopped by Customs and a chain of events was set in motion that had led here, to this interview room and the threat of ten years in jail. The bag contained two kilograms of cocaine, which pushed the crime into the 'intent to distribute' level, hence the harsh punishment of a mandatory ten-year sentence attached to it. I was aware that an Irish doctor had been asked to assess Julius and I was curious to know what he had deduced. I asked about their conversation, but Julius shook his head and said it had never taken place. I knew that that conversation had indeed taken place, so this was my first inkling that there might be memory loss at work, which would suggest possible dementia. He hadn't met the Irish doctor, Julius said, because there was absolutely no point in him talking to someone with far less knowledge and insight about his mind than him.

I changed tack and asked about his childhood. He described a deprived and dangerous childhood in the Far East with an abusive father who eventually walked out and an overwhelmed, hardworking, desperate mother – a background reminiscent of Conor's. He had managed to get out and clearly saw himself as a breathing miracle for his ability to transcend that very poor start and work up to global recognition for his talents, paintings and intellect. He talked me through his trajectory, describing it as a chain of brilliant achievements and gilded success. His pride knew no bounds – he spoke of himself as a man apart, superior to anyone else he had ever met, a phenomenon that commanded deep respect and authority. It was a paean to himself, and I felt it was well rehearsed, that he must recite this litany of achievements regularly.

We talked about the charge he was facing, and I asked if his wife and children were coming over to support them. He shrugged and clearly couldn't see the point in that. He had, he said, told them not to come, that he was perfectly capable of sorting this out himself. The more he talked about his family, the more I felt he rarely let them have a voice or a presence. He seemed cagey, not wanting me to contact them even by phone. I tried to get a feel for any forensic history or psychiatric background by asking about the health of his wife and children. To my astonishment, he confessed that one adult daughter had died of breast cancer, but he had saved his wife from the same fate. Saved? How? He described, in great detail, how, while painting his wife, he detected a lump in her breast, called a surgeon friend of his and 'got' her treatment: 'Without me she would never have lived.' This revelation went a long way to confirming my suspicion that Julius was a psychopath and that he had fallen prey to the fraudsters because of an unassailable belief in his own greatness. I asked about Julius's mental state, and he said matter-of-factly that he had 'some depression' but that this was typical of a high-functioning person. This was yet another example of his ability to justify challenges and opportunities alike. There was one smooth veneer of greatness that overlaid his whole character. Due to his ability, he was destined to always do the absolutely correct thing. This thinking clearly identified him as a psychopath.

The more we talked, the more I felt convinced that jail was not the correct response to Julius's crime. Yes, he had transported drugs and should have known better, but my instinct was that he was, at this late stage in his life, a victim of his own mental disorder, and he was likely to be suffering early stage dementia as well. His actions were neglectful, but they weren't malicious. I administered various scales, and sure enough Julius scored very high on the PCL-R, which corroborated my own formulation. I knew he had a friend in America who was a psychiatrist and that he was pleading for extradition so that Julius could receive specialist psychiatric care at home. After our interview, I was inclined to agree with him.

I wrote a comprehensive report that detailed Julius's mental disorder, his narcissism, his depression and my conclusion that he was also suffering from early stage dementia, which had exacerbated all of his thinking and actions in this case. Unusually, I was called into court during sentencing to give expert testimony. (I don't normally attend for sentencing, rather for trial.) When testifying, I strongly recommended repatriation and a psychiatric response to this elderly man's situation, arguing that allowing him to die in prison, most likely confused and deluded, would benefit no one and achieve nothing, especially given that he posed a very low risk of reoffending, particularly if his internet use were consistently monitored. This is a case where I remain very proud of the justice system, because it was a rare example of a multi-expert and multi-agency approach where all concerned worked in concert to deliver a compassionate verdict to this man. As a result, Julius received an exception to the mandatory

ten-year term, a five-year suspended sentence, and was allowed
to return to the USA on the condition that he never enter the
jurisdiction of Ireland again. In this instance, the justice system
did its job very well.

In my work, Julius and Conor were exceptions because they
were psychopaths. I would estimate that only 5% or less of the
people I've interviewed were psychopaths; I am far more likely
to meet psychopathic tendencies as part of antisocial personality
disorder. A typical example of how I encounter psychopathy
would be Declan, who was facing a charge of assault. He was
a nineteen-year-old man with a considerable forensic history
as well as a history of alcoholism and substance abuse. Declan's
home life was chaotic and aggressive, with an abusive and
angry father and an alcoholic, largely 'switched off' mother.
This started him out in life with attachment disorder, which, as
we noted above, led to ADHD, oppositional defiance disorder,
conduct disorder, depressive disorder and anxiety. It was a chain
reaction of disorders, one leading on to the next, all exacerbated
by poor parenting and an unpredictable and threatening home
environment. Declan scored eighteen points on the PCL-R,
indicating a moderate level of psychopathy as compared to the
average population. As such, he is a very typical example of the
sort of psychopathy I encounter quite often, where environment
and parenting have caused disorders that combine into antisocial
personality disorder. This then registers on the PCL-R as a
higher-than-normal level of psychopathy.

I think it's clear that while high-end psychopathy is relatively
rare and presents as very different from the normal population,
there is more overlap at the low end of the spectrum, which
presents a complex interplay of various factors that could lead to
high-functioning success or could alternatively lead to giving in to
personal temptation, crossing the line into overt criminality and
likely imprisonment. Very often a psychopath is torn, wanting to
live a certain life that might be accepted by others but giving in
eventually and not caring what other people think. Understanding

psychopathy and APD and other complex disorders is difficult, but it is the responsibility of psychology, psychiatry and health care to strive to acquire more information. Our growing knowledge of genetics, biochemistry and their links to behaviour will help this cause, not only to facilitate treatment of the psychopath but also to harness the positive, productive and progressive aspects of the psychopathic personality.

CHAPTER TEN

A VERY THIN LINE: MENTAL HEALTH CHALLENGES FOR EVERYONE

The information and many cases presented throughout this book have by now made it clear that the line between the criminal population and the non-criminal population is very thin, probably far thinner and flimsier than most people realise. Yes, we have seen crimes that had to be punished and were very clear violations of basic human rights, but time and again we have also seen the dreadful effects of poor parenting, inadequate care and lack of guidance on our most vulnerable citizens: children. What I think has emerged is a bigger picture that brings in the cyclical nature of mental health illness, its effects on the person and on those around them and the generational legacies it hands down and promotes. As medical science evolves we are beginning to understand the extent of the effects of nature/genes on humans, but it is also the case that 'nurture' can ameliorate or exacerbate those effects. For all these reasons, it is essential that the reader takes from this book an appreciation of their mental health, an understanding of or desire to understand our own status in terms of mental health and a desire to proactively protect their mental health into the future.

It's worth investing in one's mental health because good mental health carries with it so many benefits. It is fulfilled by having healthy perspectives, engagement in socialising, interests in various things, occasional training, healthy intelligence, a positive optimistic view and generally contributing to and engaging with one's personal, professional and social environment. When our minds are clear and positive, it allows us to enjoy life, friends, new situations and fresh challenges. We won't be blisteringly happy all the time – that's not a realistic goal – but we can aim to be content and secure and good to those around us. From positive mental health stems kindness, warmth, helpfulness and empathy, which we need in the world more than ever in these troubled times. And when I say 'investing' in one's own mental health, I don't mean by way of expensive treatments or shopping trips. I simply mean by regarding it as a treasured possession that deserves to be thought about, checked over and well minded.

While positivity is the goal, it is the case that mental health problems are experienced by a huge number of people. One in four people will experience a mental health challenge – and that's a global figure, which means 25% of 7 billion people know what it's like to struggle within their own minds. Given that level of common affliction, it seems almost ironic that mental health problems make people feel so lonely. If we could read each other's minds, we would no doubt feel intimately connected and understood instead. But the reality of such challenges remains a sense of isolation, negativity, pessimism and anhedonia (an inability to feel pleasure or joy in anything). When in the grip of such negativity, the person doesn't future plan or have goals or an ambition to fulfil, which in turn limits their environmental interaction. It inhibits both their desire and ability to have friendships and to create loving, demonstrative relationships with families and partners. It could be described as a claustrophobic state of being, locked up inside yourself and wanting to break free but not having the energy or belief that it's possible to do so.

The job of categorising mental health challenges and pathology is an extremely difficult one. While not necessarily always encompassing personality disorders, the presentation can transcend many, many conditions, including personality disorder, depression, bipolar disorder and schizophrenia. In effect, 'mental health' is a very wide umbrella term that encompasses a spectrum of presentations and behaviours that may be environmentally, personally and genetically linked. Sometimes 'mental health' describes the pathology or 'disease', but at other times it can reflect how robustly our mind functions day to day. Then, of course, each heading has numerous other links – for example, a diagnosis of process disorder can be further linked to cognitive information processing, emotional language, academic ability and learning disability. So the links keep going on, incorporating more and more psychological terms and conditions under that bulging 'mental health' umbrella. Indeed, the thickness of the ICD-10 (International Statistical Classification of Diseases and Related Health Problems) book and the DSM-V bears testament to the number of disorders, criteria and categories required in order to make a diagnosis. It's often a tangled web, and it can take a lot of work to disentangle and decipher it.

The symptoms of mental health can be similarly wide-ranging, taking in all manner of complaints from minor transient feelings of depression to sleep difficulties to grief and to more significant psychopathology. The most common mental health problems encountered in the community are depression, anxiety, phobias and somatoform disorders, with dementia also becoming increasingly common in the over-fifties. Somatoform disorders are where there is a physical manifestation of an emotional challenge, often presenting as irritable bowel syndrome, hives, rashes, nervous twitches, fibromyalgia and chronic pain. By now people are keenly aware that depression – which normally co-presents with anxiety – is extremely common, but the key thing to know is that it is very treatable. Over 80% of those who present with acute depressive disorder can be treated successfully within six months. The common symptoms are difficulty sleeping, low self-esteem, social withdrawal, isolation and negative hygiene, which all point to depressive disorder and should be taken seriously by anyone witnessing them in a loved one. There is a very interesting statistic which shows that if the person does not present within four to six months of experiencing symptoms, they are unlikely to do so for a further eight to ten years. That's quite shocking, in fact, to think that a person would suffer for a whole decade simply for the want of owning up to their reality and going to see their GP. That's all it takes: talking to a healthcare professional is the first step, and the help is there and will make a huge difference.

I have talked through symptoms of mental health problems or pathology with a huge number of people over the years – both in general and forensic practice – and it is clear to me that, in spite of all the positive media efforts, there is still a sense of embarrassment, humiliation and shame with regard to mental illness. This is the biggest stumbling block to asking for and receiving help. I think there's a lingering notion of mental health difficulties somehow being related to mental weakness or 'impairment'. This is probably not helped by media reports in the aftermath of tragic events such as the German Wings suicide/homicide or the campus shootings in the USA. These reports often link the words 'depression' and 'anxiety' to the perpetrators' acts, which can serve to muddy the waters with regard to what these challenges actually are. If 'depression' makes you deliberately crash a plane full of people into a mountain, then naturally people feel an instinctive aversion to being linked to 'depression' in any way. I haven't worked with the people in those cases, but I very much doubt their diagnosis was simply 'depression'. There would have to be severe levels of anxiety and aggression, quite likely with a psychiatric illness and major cognitive distortion as well. In fact, mental health is separate and different from mental or cognitive ability. Those cases are at the extreme end of the spectrum, not at all representative of the general cohort of the population in terms of the presentation and effects of mental health challenges.

Throughout the book we have examined different factors that can lead to mental health illness, and how these in turn can lead to criminal behaviour. So, for example, process disorders can lead to substance abuse, which can lead to criminal behaviour to support that habit. It's all about the coping mechanisms and the links those create. Where mental health illness does tip over the line into law-breaking, there are usually other factors present as well to facilitate this, commonly poor understanding and empathy, no family support, unemployment, low socioeconomic status, impoverished nutrition and poor living standards. It's when there is a perfect storm of factors that the behaviour becomes uncontrollable. This is borne out by an examination of the make-up of the prison population of which 60–70% have mental health challenges.

I worked with a young woman who was charged with harassment and who was on the way to becoming part of those statistics: a mentally ill member of the prison population. Collette was a woman in her forties who lived at home and had limited contact with the outside world. The assumption was that she was suffering with some sort of cognitive distortion or mental health problem that had led to the offences committed. The case against her was clear, and she admitted that she was guilty. For a period of about six months, she harassed the victim, a man she stated she had fallen in love with, via social media and Twitter in particular. When I was asked to assess her, it was with regard to sentencing, as she had pleaded guilty. She was liable to receive a sentence of between two and four years.

I met Collette in my office, and it was very quickly clear to me that her mental capacity was limited. I could tell that this was not a case of mental health or cognitive distortion and that there was something far more fundamental at work here. I had to reword sentences and questions carefully so that she could understand what I was asking. As we talked about her actions and the court case, I could see that her levels of comprehension, processing speed, memory and temporal reasoning were all limited. She told me that, while she was happy in her own life, she had felt jealous of the victim because he was successful, and she desperately wanted to make a connection with him. There was no malevolence in her behaviour, but she wanted to reach out into his world and be part of it. She had no understanding of the effects of her actions on this man. This lack of insight, her poor emotional language and naivety, her lack of understanding of the consequences of her behaviour and her disinhibition and impulsivity had all contributed to her offending behaviour. But that behaviour wasn't criminal in the sense that it was poorly organised, benign and with no further intent behind it. She collected mobile phones and opened multiple Twitter accounts because she believed this would connect her to the man more closely. This showed that she simply didn't understand what she was doing.

I administered a series of assessment scales, including the Wechsler Adult Intelligence Scale, encompassing a Verbal Comprehension Index, Perceptual Reasoning Index, as well as scales for working memory and processing speed. The results were indisputable: Collette had a severe learning disability that greatly hampered her ability to understand, to process information and to rationalise. She did not, however, present with any indicators for mental health problems – no mood swings, no trouble sleeping, no low moods. She was, as she herself professed, happy in her life.

I drew up a comprehensive report that set out the true story of Collette's abilities and her offending actions. It included all of the scales and her scores to corroborate the findings from the assessment interview. I recommended that Collette presented with an extremely low risk of reoffending, particularly if her internet access was monitored and supervised. I was extremely pleased to later learn that the case against Collette had been dismissed from the court, based on the content of my report. I felt this was absolutely the correct decision as a prison sentence would have been hugely traumatic for Collette and wouldn't, in fact, have achieved anything. She had no comprehension of her 'crime' and was herself a victim of her limited learning ability. I was also pleased that it allowed the court to understand the crucial difference between mental health and mental capacity – Collette was not, as had been assumed, suffering from a mental health problem. The more we can hammer home these differences, the better. It is important that people – not least our judiciary – understand the differences and treat them according to their true nature.

While externalising mental pain into negative behaviours is very common, there is another equally damaging coping mechanism in the form of turning those negative behaviours on oneself. We have seen examples of self-harm and self-hatred in the cases presented in this book, where a person seeks release from the turmoil in their head through the distraction of physical pain. This was illustrated in the tragic case of Elaine O'Hara, who became the victim of the psychopath Graham Dwyer. I didn't work with Elaine O'Hara personally, but she was diagnosed by her carers with depression and borderline personality disorder. Elaine was plagued by low self-esteem and self-confidence, which made her vulnerable to exploitation. What may have been more significant was her learning disability, which meant she couldn't understand all of the needs or negative influences of her killer. As a result, she was exploited to the fullest, most fatal extent by Graham Dwyer in perpetrating his crimes against her sexually in a sadomasochistic way, ultimately leading to her murder. Reports on her life and death show that she tried to break free of Dwyer's psychological hold over her, but ultimately she was not assertive or able enough to achieve this. She did seek help and she did receive help, but her desire to be connected, albeit in a violent way, during the act of sex kept leading her back to the brink. No one can know for sure what was in Elaine O'Hara's mind on the day she died, but she was extremely vulnerable and that ultimately led to her death.

People often regard the act of suicide as the greatest, most potent expression of self-hatred, despair and defeat at the hands of mental illness. Suicide or suicidal ideation is not always comorbid with depression, but I think it is very often linked to a transfer of anxiety and anger against others and against oneself where the path of self-discovery has reached a seemingly insurmountable roadblock and the person feels deeply frustrated with him/herself, denigrated and unable to contribute productively to the world anymore. This, to my mind, is the key feeling that leads to suicide: feeling useless and hopeless. Those are powerfully negative states, making the person feel they have nothing to offer to anyone and that there is no possibility of that situation ever changing as long as they live. Viewing a futureless life has a deeply negative effect on the mind and on cognitive processing, which can lead to the belief that one would like to die. I have worked with many people who have attempted suicide, and it is very telling that every single one has told me they were glad their attempt had not succeeded. That tells us that the belief guiding the suicidal thought is erroneous and unreal.

It is interesting to note that Japan has the highest suicide rate in the world, caused in large part by the high rate of suicide among people over sixty years of age. This trend is associated with a cultural belief that when one is no longer able to contribute effectively and becomes, instead, a burden on family, killing oneself is the honourable and 'right' thing to do. Again, this shows the overwhelming power of the 'useless' narrative. I was heartened to learn of an innovative program put in place in San Quentin prison, which is in California and is one of the biggest prisons in the USA. Within its walls, two hundred prisoners are engaged in learning how to code software and their work is being supported by Silicon Valley companies. This training leads to qualification but, even more importantly, it creates a solid sense of usefulness and therefore hope. Research has shown that these men have experienced a decrease in their mental health challenges, so the link between usefulness and positive mental health seems clear. This is the sort of approach I would very much like to see adopted by the Irish prison system because I think any type of training or qualification can have a marked impact on mental health because it imparts a sense of purpose, which is crucial for health of mind.

All of this is very persuasive to the argument of investing in and seeking to protect and preserve one's mental health. In the various criminal cases presented here, we have seen again and again the danger of self-medicating as a treatment for mental health challenges. It has been shown clearly that the introduction of alcohol or drugs only serves to exacerbate symptoms and very often leads the person to cross the line into illegal offences. It is essential not to give in to the temptation of blurring or blotting out those emotions and memories that are causing difficulties. Instead, seek help. There is great understanding of mental health among the general medical population now, so GPs are among those who provide a primary source of contact and care. Remember that depression is very treatable – that is a key message to get across. Earlier in the book we mentioned the 'mental health toolbox' to help assess and monitor our own mental health and take appropriate steps if we feel any problems are arising. So if, for example, I'm a movie-lover and regular cinema-goer and take great pleasure in that activity, but lately it doesn't work for me and I no longer want to go, that's telling me something important. When you learn to look for and recognise those messages, it makes you far better able to handle what's happening. It is extremely helpful to be able to delve into the box for activities that give joy and emotional stability. If this isn't possible, if we feel we don't want to help ourselves or be helped, it's essential to recognise that feeling and push ourselves to attain support, either from personal contacts or from professional resources.

When there is a question over the behaviour of someone you love, examine it carefully and look for the key symptoms, as listed above. Encourage the person to talk to you, facilitate open, non-judgemental discussion and present options for approaching healthcare professionals to secure help. I read new research recently that strongly promoted the benefits of dancing and dancing classes in the preservation of mental health wellness and also to keep dementia at bay. Apparently the mix of mental agility (learning and remembering moves) and physical agility required provide an excellent combination to stimulate the brain. There are so many ways to help yourself – sport, talking, learning, playing, listening – it's important to keep trying new things and be open to them.

We must also think of the next generation, as protecting and minding mental health has much to do with education at a young age. I think the introduction of mindfulness and meditation in the classroom, as some schools have done, is a great addition to the curriculum and will stand those children in good stead in future years. There is so much talk now of diet and nutrition and sugar and 'bad' additives, and that is important too, as nutrition is a component of overall wellness, but it is also essential that our children are just as aware of the power of emotions and how to process and cope with feelings. Those are the coping tools they need to get through life. It will be the case that they will face challenges of one kind or another during the course of their life – we all do – but it's how we are educated and understand and choose to cope with those challenges that is the key to mental wellness and well-being. Thinking about and promoting mental health isn't just a necessary exercise, it's the smart thing to do. Working hard will pay dividends, but promoting how robustly we engage our minds to be well is just plain clever.

EPILOGUE: REDRAWING THE LINE

This book has covered quite an amount of ground, but there are some key points that I would like the reader to take away from this wide-ranging discussion.

First, I think that everyone should have a therapist. I am well aware that in Ireland that is a very contentious statement, but as someone who gives and receives therapy, I am convinced it is hugely beneficial and worthwhile. Everybody needs someone to talk to, someone who asks the right questions that allow us to facilitate our learning about our own personal psychology. Therefore, I think children should learn about psychology in school, from around the ages of eight to ten years, so that they learn not only how to study and concentrate, but also how to understand themselves and be smarter. After all, as we have seen earlier, in the brains of Buddhist monks who regularly practise mindfulness, the hippocampus is almost 30–40% larger than in the normal human population. This means that thinking about your psychology and developing it isn't just healthy, it is positively clever and a smart thing to do, allowing us to integrate more learning and acquire more knowledge. I think that in the future this will be understood and accepted as the norm and that we will have computerised holographic therapists that obtain information from us on a daily basis regarding our mood and well-being. Once the algorithms are designed, our verbal, physical and genetic information will generate therapy unique to us, albeit computerised. This would allow us to continually monitor our mental health and give us support as and when needed. The human being is composed of a fascinating collection of genetics, biochemistry, emotions and behaviours, and that is a complex network. We need to treat it as such and mind our mental health and emotional well-being in a conscious and sustainable manner.

From what I've learned from criminal populations, it does no good to put offenders in jail and punish them for ten, fifteen, twenty years. What they learn in jail can be counterproductive, often making them even more self-deprecating and damaging to society. Rehabilitation must be the focus of our justice system. We need to give those in prison a sense of purpose, a method or means by which they can voice contrition and engage in behaviours that allow them to feel good about themselves, have a sense of useful purpose and ultimately contribute to society. In Scandinavia, prisons can't be filled because the anthropological perception or approach to criminal behaviour is first and foremost to rehabilitate. Of course, the Scandinavian anthropology and psychology is different from that prevailing among Irish people, which might go some way to explaining our resistance to rehabilitation for offenders. Irish people are more conscientious about presenting as good, doing the right thing (think of our football fans at Euro 2016, for example). We are a charitable nation, gregarious and social, we engage well with others and we always work hard. When others in our society don't present in the same way, we can be quite punitive and dismissive and belittle those who are unable to carry out the complex social tasks that we so much admire. Perhaps, then, we need to change as a culture, as a community, to improve the facilities of our prisons and to focus on giving people a second chance to feel like they can be useful participants in society.

It is clear to me that the justice system in Ireland has to change. Over the past two decades I have carried out hundreds of assessments, which have all featured specific, well-thought-out recommendations custom-built for the rehabilitation of that particular offender. It is very telling, and very frustrating, that less than 1% of my recommendations have been implemented.

Medical practice would never tolerate such a statistic with regard to treatment and follow-up for the patient. In reality, vocational training, review by the parole boards and psychotherapeutic intervention rarely ever take place for the juvenile or adult offenders that I have assessed, and this saddens me. We don't even have a process in our judicial system to follow up on offenders once released and to support them in their transition back into society. I feel there should be a method by which we review, study and carry out longitudinal research into how individuals develop, including those who have been part of the judicial system, those who have served a prison sentence, those who have been in residential care and those young people who have been in detention centres, monitoring how they reintegrate into the community after these experiences. We should follow this cohort in populations as part of our national census because knowing these trends is just as important as knowing the trends within the normal population.

I do find there is an increasing awareness of the value of psychologists, psychiatrists and mental health professionals in the prison system, but the problem is that the Prison Service doesn't have the resources to give supports to all prison officers or the facilities to keep all prisoners occupied on a daily basis. Idle hands often make for dangerous work among the prison population. I think the prison populations, as well as the police, the prison officers and supervisors, who are the ones who carry out the very important job of keeping the State safe and supervising our criminal population, need and deserve properly established support interventions by healthcare professionals. This need isn't being met, however, because the resources simply aren't there. I wish this situation could be improved. I am heartened, however, by the referendum results over recent years giving children a greater voice within the justice system. I also think that there are excellent social work authorities and healthcare professionals around the country who try to ensure the safety of children and adults. No matter what resources are put in place, children will always be vulnerable citizens, but those professionals I have worked with place a huge value on parental capacity assessments and psychological evaluation as well as intervention in order to keep children and babies safe. Although the shape of the family is changing in the twenty-first century, with blended families becoming the new norm, I have witnessed huge efforts on the part of social workers and healthcare professionals to maintain the family dynamic, against great odds, and this has been reflected in my core work. This has also heartened me throughout the years. I've seen a great improvement in the quality of care that is understood to be the right of children in our society, respect for the UN convention on children's rights is growing and this country, albeit with a lot of work still to do, is engaging in work and leadership both within the judicial systems and our social care teams that should make us proud.

If I could be omnipotent for a day, with unlimited ability to create real change, I would encourage everyone to engage in promoting and minding their psychology on a daily basis. I would ensure that people are assessed before they are sentenced or go to trial and that the recommendations in those assessment reports are implemented. I would put the resources in place in prisons to allow for rehabilitation and occupational therapy, and I would pay the police, the prison officers, the medical doctors, the psychologists, the social workers and other healthcare professions sufficiently so that their work was rewarded as the important, life-changing endeavour it is. I would also implement a method of following up and supporting prisoners as they re-enter the community, to decrease the likelihood of reoffending. I would have every prisoner gain some sort of employment or have a connection with the outside world that allows them to feel a sense of purpose and affirmation by others. I know that this growth in self-esteem and confidence would allow them to feel that they can make a valid contribution to a noble cause within society and become a valued member of a population cohort that contributes to the general positive development of themselves, their children, their families and the community at large.

I'm not omnipotent, so unfortunately I can't make these things happen, even though I can see such pressing need all around me. You might wonder why I do this work, given the limitations, the lowered bar of success for my clients and the difficulty of hearing stories that are disturbing and terribly sad and having few resources to effect real change. I can do it because I have a good reserve of patience (my family and friends might disagree!). The work of the psychologist is a long-term endeavour, changes don't occur quickly. To do this work you must be patient and must enjoy sticking with a complex task right to the end. The reward is in the feeling of achievement when the task is complete. Even though it is painstakingly slow at times, all psychology and practice of assessment and treatment is also exciting. Forensics is more interesting to me because it dovetails with the law and deals sometimes with very challenging personalities that you wouldn't see in primary care, which makes it continually stimulating for the practitioner. I think it is important, though, that forensic psychologists, all other types of psychologists, psychiatrists and healthcare professionals really understand the value of their contribution to society and, more importantly, actively take care of themselves so they can continue to do this work. For myself, I feel that the forensic populations I have dealt with have affected my development, sometimes for the better, sometimes for the worse. As I've said throughout this book, I think knowing, assessing, reflecting and thinking about others' motivations to engage in certain behaviours can be exciting, but also exhausting. If the healthcare professional is not careful, this work can lead to cynicism and universality about badness in people. This is why it is so essential that all of us involved in this complicated and demanding work be mindful of our mental health and receive psychological supervision on a regular basis.

I think anyone engaged in the sort of work I do is there because they want to make a positive difference. We want to redraw the line for these people, creating a new sense of perspective and self-understanding and encouraging them to quit the shadows and live in the light, where the benefits to mental health and personal development are their own reward. That is the guiding principle of our work. We see damaged, aggressive humans who are lost in their own emotions and behaviours, and we want to try to help them be better people. I thoroughly feel at home immersed in psychology and medicine. Being a healthcare professional is a privilege and is truly exciting and I encourage anyone who is thinking of such a career to go forward and really embrace it. I am a scientist and therefore don't have much faith or belief in reincarnation, but I believe how we engage in our behaviour is important in the now. Yes, it may have greater ramifications for or effects on society in general, but I always believe the value of your personality is how you behave on a daily basis. I'm not pious, I've made my own mistakes, but in my career as a healthcare professional I have always wanted to take care of others, understand their needs and facilitate their better and greater development while respecting their human psychology. This is at the core of the work I do and always will be, until the day I can't practise anymore.

THANK YOU

I have always had the utmost interest in people's stories and how the mind works and contributes to those stories as well as the development of others. This has been an interest and fascination of mine since I can remember. I think that 'nosiness' and wanting to know information about everything due to an insatiable appetite for many perspectives is a very good thing. Curiosity should be fostered and encouraged. In my own life, this is something that I enjoy and that has helped me be interested in attaining an education, but sometimes it can be a difficult burden. Having the knowledge that you're never going to get to the end of acquiring more information or understanding others is definitely a challenge to my job as a psychologist and a doctor. Ongoing frustration is present, coupled with impatience at times!

My interests, education and development to date have been fuelled by the help of many, mainly my family; my mum and dad kept me on the bright side of the line even though I've gone to darker places in life on occasion during my work as a forensic psychologist and engaging in the understanding of others who exhibit deviant asocial or difficult behaviour. Even being challenged by cases within the community has led me sometimes to a lot of soul-searching, frustrated by a limited intellect. But thank you, Mum and Dad, and my siblings, Andrew and Ronan, for also always providing a strong, affectionate but adequately critical disposition to help me overcome some of my own personal challenges and continue to engage in a career and a learning curve that would not have been possible without a brilliant childhood and upbringing. My brothers have provided many laughs, and our sense of humour is great emotional nourishment when we are together or texting across the globe.

Thank you to Conor Nagle, the commissioning editor who had the belief and insight, as well as encouragement, to help me write this book. Conor, Catherine Gough and all the team at Gill Books deserve every credit for the imprint that's placed upon the pages, which we all hope the readers thoroughly enjoy and, more importantly, will make them think. I'm so appreciative of the publisher's generosity and the opportunities given to me.

Thank you Sue Leonard, who started the writing journey and provided the platform to evolve the book – our conversations will always provide me with important memories.

Thank you Rachel Pierce, who heard me and wrote with a ferocious zealousness and truly impressive insight. Your skill is astounding and it's my fault entirely if the message isn't clear!

I want to make sure that my own children, Ruby and Sebastian, have every opportunity to explore their own intellectual depth and keep on the bright side of the line. Examining the line as well as personal psychology, as you'll understand from reading the text, is vital to maintain a robust, happy, contented and intellectually stimulated life. This is no small task, but rather a very complicated adventure that I hope to always share with you both. Your health and happiness is at the fore of my mind, always.

Thank you to their mum, Carrie, who continues to provide outstanding leadership for the children and friendship for me, and I hope we will continue to have that partnership throughout our future. Thank you for the encouragement.

I am continually trying to do new things and engage in different behaviours. For those around me it can be frustrating, and when I become bored it can become exasperating. Despite this, the patience of my team in Imagine Health, including other doctors and my esteemed and important stay-at-home, fight-the-fire team of Aisling and her assistants, Sam and Sherwyn, have made writing this book possible, not only in facilitating the logistics and times but giving me the mind space to indulge in a project I've always wished to fulfil.

I hope everyone understands my sincere thanks for all their help, but most of all, and not at the bottom of this page because it's last but solely because it's the most significant and appreciative thanks of all, my thanks to the patients and clients that I have worked with for many years. I always wanted to work in healthcare. I always wanted to support others to learn more about human personality and their physical as well as emotional well-being. Those patients who've come to me in search of help have enabled me to take a journey with them, which hopefully created a new evolutionary path and a bright future for their development. Those patients have exhibited courage, tenacity, a creative mindset and intellectual fortitude to engage with psychology and medicine throughout my work with them. Without them, every aspect of my training would have been a waste of time. The training, in fact, continues to evolve, change and improve with the help of those patients. I can only express my sincere and undoubting respect for every patient who has given me the privilege to contribute to their lives.

I hope that I still have a long career ahead of me and I hope to meet many more interesting people, patients and peers as well as colleagues. But I think we all need to recognise that everyone has challenges. Every one of us has the potential to be a patient and client. Communication, speaking our mind and growing our smarts in a way that isn't just reciting text from a book is fundamental to human evolution and the plasticity of our brains, and the paradigm shifts that we know about as humankind will continue to forge in amazing ways long after this text and the other work I've done is forgotten.

I hope you enjoy the book and very much look forward to meeting some of you in the future.

Many thanks,
Ian